SKI LODGE
Millers Idlewild Inn

Adventures in Snow Business

Virginia Miller Cornell

Manifest Publications
Carpinteria, California
1993

SKI LODGE
Millers Idlewild Inn
Adventures in Snow Business

Published by:
    Manifest Publications
    Post Office Box 429
    Carpinteria, CA 93014-0429

All rights reserved. No part of this book may be reproduced or transmitted in any form or by any means, electronic or mechanical, including photocopying, recording or by any information storage or retrieval system without written permission from the author, except for the inclusion of brief quotations in a review.

Copyright ©1993 by Virginia Miller Cornell

Printed in the United States of America

Publisher's Cataloging in Publication
Cornell, Virginia Miller, 1936-
    Ski Lodge Millers Idlewild Inn : adventures in snow business / Virginia Miller Cornell.—
      p. cm.
ISBN 0-9627896-6-6 (hardcover)
ISBN 0-9627896-7-4 (pbk.)

    1. Cornell, Virginia, 1936- 2. Hotelkeepers—Colorado—Winter Park—Biography. 3. Winter Park (Colo.)—History. I. Title.
TX910.5.C67C67 1993   647.94788'65'092
                                  QBI93-1045

CONTENTS

Introduction ix

Spring, 1973

Chapter 1 – Moon Over Millers 1
Chapter 2 – Mama's Broken Heart 4
Chapter 3 – Coming Home 13
Chapter 4 – Father's Last Hurrah 21
Chapter 5 – What's Wrong With Room 5? 33
Chapter 6 – By The Balls 40
Chapter 7 – Queen of the Police Ball 49

Summer, 1973

Chapter 8 – Where's Tonto? 54
Chapter 9 – Life Among the Maidens 62
Chapter 10 – The Close Shave 70
Chapter 11 – The George Armstrong Massacree 75
Chapter 12 – They're No Angels 91
Chapter 13 – Staff Re-shuffle 97

Autumn, 1973

Chapter 14 – The Great Peach Massacree	104
Chapter 15 – On Top of It All	114
Chapter 16 – When White is Black	123

Winter, 1973-1974

Chapter 17 – White Christmas	135
Chapter 18 – There's Always More	150
Chapter 19 – And Yet More	161
Chapter 20 – Heather on the Hill	167
Chapter 21 – Double Trouble	181
Chapter 22 – Another Year Older	189
Chapter 23 – Bad Chapter	202
Chapter 24 – Walter's Pigeon	214
Chapter 25 – Body of Evidence	221
Chapter 26 – The Making of a Mellow Fellow	226
Chapter 27 – This Means Business	234
Chapter 28 – One Last Big Splash	241

Postscript   249

*To my brothers —
Woodie and Dwight Miller*

*And to everybody else who has stories
to tell about Millers Idlewild Inn*

Introduction

My husband and I were on a cruise, somewhere southeast of the Panama Canal where the water was warm, the sun tropical, the breezes balmy. At dinner one evening a perky lady named Betty Brossman from Bryan, Texas, asked, "What was the name of that ski lodge you told me you managed out in Colorado?"

"Millers Idlewild Inn," I replied casually, shoveling in another delicious morsel of *gnocci*. Even though it was January, my adventures in snow business seemed long ago and far away.

Across the table, Dr. Charles Gebetsberger and his wife Maurine from Sepulpa, Oklahoma, simultaneously dropped their forks onto their plates. The resultant clanks were loud enough to be heard over chattering passengers and pulsing engine vibrations. My statement had torpedoed them dead in the water. "We stayed there many times," explained Charles. "It was our favorite ski lodge."

More *gnocci* was out of the question because I couldn't swallow. My throat was constricted as I choked back tears. These people were *not* guests during the five years I managed the Inn for my family. They had come later, after we sold the business to Teverbaugh-Heaton Enterprises. Nevertheless, the

Gebetsbergers had fallen under the unique spell the old place radiated. Almost fifteen years after I had ceased being manager of Millers Idlewild Inn, I had no idea a coincidence could affect me so deeply. We shared an attachment for a rustic old building — my family home, really.

The funky handmade ski lodge was built in Winter Park, Colorado, by my family in 1946. In the succeeding years my father, my brothers — even my mother ran it before I arrived to take over in 1973. I was the last Miller to hold the position of manager. Over that bite of *gnocci*, I knew I had to go back to my home in California and write about the incredible things that happened to me at Millers Idlewild Inn.

My first book, *Doc Susie: The True Story of a Country Physician in the Colorado Rockies,* was my effort to make a noble woman's life live forever in people's minds. This book is offered in an attempt to rebuild, with words, a colorful piece of my family history, and my own life. I fervently hope it will find many friends, former guests and employees, people who remember with affection their good times at our lodge. But I also hope that any skier who ever put two feet close to a roaring fire to warm them, who ate a delicious meal after a cold day on the slopes, who sank into a comfortable bed after a strenuous day in the out-of-doors — or anybody who ever wanted to — will enjoy the story of the time I spent managing Millers Idlewild Inn.

Names have not been changed unless specified by the initials NRN (Not Real Name). Some of my friends from those days asked that their names be changed, their mature successes having far outdistanced their youthful excesses. When I could locate people who played an extensive role in the book, I gave them the option of a pseudonym. In some cases, my recall has failed to span the twenty intervening years. Although faces and foibles are etched into my memory, names have been erased from my memory tapes. I must admit that I occasionally took advange of faulty recollection to build composite characters. For example, the hippie-ish employee Sandy became a receptacle for the frailties of several employees; Brad is similarly an aggregate of aggravation. If some of these events didn't actually happen that first year, I assure you they did later. I was too busy to keep a diary.

My brothers, Elwood "Woodie" and Dwight Miller, prompted my memory about specific details. If they ever choose to write their own books about Millers Idlewild Inn, their stories would be just as engrossing, but far different. My children, Keith and Gordon Cornell and Drew Cornell Korcal, shared their vivid memories. Had friends and former employees not been willing to prompt my memory, my narrative would indeed be sparse.

I would also like to thank members of my Santa Barbara writing group which we round up every two weeks and call "The Usual Suspects": Donna Humberd, Margaret Dear and Yvonne Kaleugher. Our mutual critique sessions supplied me with the pressure of deadlines and the benefits of helpful criticism. Thanks to Christine Nolt, computer wizard, who firmed up my floppy disk and made it into a book. I am grateful to proofreaders: Barbara Coster, Barbara Taylor, Donna Humberd, Charlie Petersen, Woody Miller, Mary Mock Miller and Jean Miller. Roger Roeck supplied many of the photos, including the one of the Inn on the front cover and the picture of my brothers and me on the back of the book. Robert Howard provided the attractive cover.

Once again, I am indebted to my friend, editor and "rent-a-mentor," Ted Berkman. He coached me out of the starting gate, gave advice on how to stay the course and was there to congratulate me when I finally crossed the finish line.

Spring, 1973

Chapter 1

Moon Over Millers

The first time I asked myself whether I was really cut out to be the manager of Millers Idlewild Inn was the day I arrived on the job, February 22, 1973.

"Take a heating pad to Fred Polenski in Room Number 3," ordered my father. "He hurt himself and came home early from skiing. You'll find it in the linen closet upstairs." I already knew that Fred (NRN)* was the leader of the Green Bay Ski Club, a group of fit, fun-loving, middle-aged skiers who came to Millers Idlewild Inn from Wisconsin every winter. Keeping Fred happy was important.

I was feeling a bit giddy; that morning I had been in Phoenix, Arizona, which was a comfortable 1,000 feet above sea level. I had flown to Denver, then taken a bus to Winter Park, Colorado — where the altitude was a breathtaking 9,000 feet. Yet I managed to bound up the two flights of stairs. At the top landing stood a full-length mirror. Back at me grinned my blue-eyed, freckled mug. People seemed surprised to learn that I had three young teen-agers. I fancied I didn't look the thirty-

---

* NRN means Not Real Name. I always wanted to write footnotes that were, if anything, more interesting than their book. While footnotes are not required reading, there's a lot of really good stuff in them.

seven years I would become in two days. I flipped my long, thick red braid from over my shoulder to down my back and jingled my new badge of office. Attached to a belt loop on my bell-bottom jeans were a dozen or so keys: master keys, Pepsi machine keys, padlock keys, storage room keys. I rattled them; they responded with a joyous little tinkle.

The stairway and the mirror were at the very heart of the old Inn's upstairs bedrooms. As I proceeded down the hallway I stepped across several patterns of mismatched carpeting; each signaled the end of one of my father's remodeling jobs and the beginning of the next.

I unlocked a padlock, threw back the hasp and opened a pine door, inhaling the fragrance of Cashmere Bouquet soap. The flowery perfume of individually wrapped bars permeated stacks of sheets, pillow cases and towels, and for a very good reason: it was the cheapest soap available.

By the light of a dim, bare bulb I groped along the closet shelves. Where was that heating pad? Ninety percent of innkeeping was going to be figuring out where everything was kept. Back at my former job, teaching English at Arizona State University, the only place I had to rummage through was my desk. How would I ever keep track of thousands of essentials needed to keep eighty guests comfortable?

Where would Mother keep heating pads? As though reading my way across stacked books in a library, I scanned the shelves.

Sure enough, inside an old wooden box labeled "Washington Dried Apples" I spotted a jumble of heating pad cords, ice packs and hot water bottles. Soon I would learn that skiers were forever banging, spraining, bruising and concussing themselves. As I pulled out a flannel-covered heating pad I noted that its dusty-rose cover was freshly laundered. Mother probably washed it between each usage. What a lot of details there were going to be to this job.

I hastened to deliver the pad.

"Fred, it's Virginia. I have your heating pad," I exclaimed loudly as I knocked on the rough pine door to Room Number 3.

"Door's unlocked," replied a male voice.

I pressed my thumb to lift the old doorlatch, pushed the door ajar and extended my arm to hand him the heating pad — its corded tail dangling like thick string from a heavy kite.

"Come in, come in," the voice insisted.

Room 3 was one of the smallest bedrooms at Millers Idlewild Inn. "Close the door behind you," Fred insisted. He had been resting in his bed, but threw back the covers and got up as I entered. Before me stood a pajama-clad, mild-mannered, balding insurance executive.

I was acutely uncomfortable; I had not yet become casual about breezing in and out of other people's bedrooms. "I'm sorry you got hurt. You all right?"

Fred looked at me thoughtfully for just a second, as though sizing me up. Then an impish expression crossed his face as though he had a naughty secret he wanted to share. He asked, "Want to see something awful?"

Had there been time enough, I probably would have been able to back my way out of the door. But before I could reply he hooked his thumb into the waistband of his pajama pants; with one swift motion he turned around, dropped his pants and asked in a loud voice, "Did you ever see anything like that?"

I gulped until I realized that he was referring to a very large bruise that was purpling its way across his fanny.

"That's a big one," I conceded. "Really big!"

That was only a preview, a glimpse of coming attractions that lurked along the road to becoming the manager of a ski lodge.

Chapter 2

Mama's Broken Heart

I became an innkeeper by accident. Well on my way to becoming a college professor, I was nearing the end of my goal: a Ph.D. in Renaissance English Literature. Just two weeks before the day I found myself surveying Fred's purple fanny I was asleep in my bed, in my snug little tract house on Oregon Street in Phoenix, Arizona.

The phone rang.

Floors are cold in Arizona winters. My Baby Ben read 11:30. I lightswitched my way into the kitchen, where my only phone rang and rang. Only drunks and disasters call in the middle of the night.

"Zidzy?" It seemed that everybody had a different nickname for me, but my father was the only person who ever called me Zidzy — my baby name.

"Trudy got sick." The constriction in his voice forced me wide awake. "The doctor says I must get your mother out of the mountains, take her somewhere lower, warmer. Soon. It's her heart. I knew she didn't feel good — shouldn't have let her stay up here so long. She didn't want you to know — waited to call until after she went to bed." Normally, Father phrased his words carefully. This time they just tumbled out.

I took several breaths, deep ones. For some time, my father had ignored Mother's obvious discomfort, as though her pain would go away if he didn't acknowledge it. "Dad, I'm really sorry. This is a real blow." Mother had trained her daughter too well, trained me that angry words never fix anything. So I didn't let loose the string of invective that was poised on the tip of my tongue. I wanted to scream, "Well, what did you expect?" But that wouldn't help Mother. The very best organ my mother possessed — her good heart — was giving out.

I had an idea: "Dad, you can send Mom here to me, in Phoenix. I'll look after her."

"No, that's my job. We've been married over fifty years; I won't desert her now." Good, at last Dad realized Mother was more important than the Inn — his lifelong obsession.

"Who will manage the Inn?"

"Your brothers can't do it. Dwight says he's in the middle of something to do with his road business. Woodie is under contract at Michigan State."

"You talked to them already." Maybe my father claimed he had raised me to be the equal of my brothers, but I was always the last to be consulted. Was it because I was the youngest? Or the girl?

"What about a professional manager? Is there anybody on the staff you would trust?"

"I don't know, I don't know." My father's voice was filled with despair.

Icy little fingers of fear clenched around my own heart. Mother was the family armature; we all clung to her. Whenever I had trouble — and because of my unhappy marriage and divorce I had seen plenty — there was always Mother. Her soothing voice, her oft-repeated words of support, were guaranteed to make me feel better.

My indignation swelled. How dared Dad keep my ailing mother so high in the Colorado mountains for so long? So scarce was oxygen that even young, healthy people frequently paused to catch their breath. She managed food service, supervised housekeeping and served as an eternally gracious hostess — strenuous duties.

Just the summer before I remembered watching Mother climb two short flights of stairs, then wrap her arms around the pine pole at its top as she panted for breath. "I know I should get out of here," she told me. "But what would your father do?"

As I listened to Father relate the medical details of mother's angina, I gradually became aware that he had not called just to impart disturbing information. No, he was worried about the other love of his life: Millers Idlewild Inn. He starting building it in 1946, just after World War II; it had continued as his fixation ever since. Gradually, I realized that I was his only hope, even though I had other plans. I had been single for three years. Determined to make something of my life, I had taken classes, studied, taught, with the goal of becoming a college teacher. That spring semester of 1973 I had taken time off from teaching to write my dissertation for a Ph.D. Soon I would be looking for a job.

"Dad, let me come out and run the Inn — at least until the season is over. You and Mom can come to Arizona, live in my house, look after my children until April."

"I can't let you do that, Zidzy," he said. "I'm afraid you'll never finish your degree. You've worked very hard. Your mother and I are so proud of you."

"Dad, I'm just proposing to put my degree on hold for a little while . . ."

"Virginia, you're a scholar. You have no idea how much work this job is. It is punishing, cruel. Look what it's done to your mother . . ."

"But I'm not sixty-nine years old, Dad. I'm only thirty-seven."

"I never raised you to go into business. I raised you to be a teacher. There's a lot you don't know about the economics of running a hotel."

"Now Dad, I've been around the Inn most of my life." That was true; I was only ten years old when my father and brothers started building the Inn. I reminded him, "Remember, I ran it by myself for those two summers so you and Mom could go to Europe and Alaska." That was true, too. But I knew that renting a few cabins in the summer was just house-sitting compared to winter business. During the ski season a staff of fifteen employees at the Inn fed, slept, transported and entertained from sixty to a hundred guests every week.

To this day, I am astounded that I came out of a sound sleep, survived the shock of learning about my mother's illness, then volunteered to take on a job about as different from academic life as warm library stacks are to standing under a cold shower.

"You'd better think about this some more. We'll talk tomorrow. I'll see what your mother says." When I cradled the receiver my hand shook, my shoulders shivered, my bare feet felt like two chunks of ice.

There would be no more sleep that night. I instinctively headed for my thinking place, the bath tub, and turned on the tap.

As I sank into the soothing hot tub, I swirled the water with my knees, riffling through possibilities and perils as quickly as I had been sorting three-by-five cards before I went to bed. Leave Arizona State University? Interrupt a career toward which I had been working for many years?

Those were difficult times at universities. Ever since Kent State in May of 1970, when four Viet Nam protesters were shot and killed by National Guardsmen, my draft-age students were unruly. I had become very interested in the budding women's movement. Hey, women were set to take on the world! No longer would women be relegated to traditional roles like that of — my mother.

My mother. Always there for her family. My brothers would agree that the very worst thing that could happen to us would be to lose Mother. And our reasons were selfish. Mother was the only person who could handle our frenetically energetic father. When Father didn't have enough to do, he frequently turned his attention to meddling in the lives of his children. But Mother could distract him, a task she undertook with devotion and finesse.

Towering over all considerations was the big old Inn itself. Warm, welcoming, our family home. Parting with its old pine walls would be like parting with — Mother. I couldn't bear to think of life without it. I wanted my children to spend as much time as possible amid the same mountain forests where I grew up. I wanted them to eat hundreds of hearty meals beneath the low log beams of the dining room. I wanted them to climb mountains, to fish, to ski.

As the water sloshed around my thighs I wondered. Did I have what it took to be an innkeeper? How tough could it be, managing a ski lodge? Until then, my idea of a hard task was learning enough German to pass an exam. Besides, maybe I could prove something to my brothers, who suspected that their much younger sister was rather a spoiled dilettante.

And what about moving my children to a new environment, away from familiar teachers and friends? Good kids, my three busy blonds were as well behaved in public as they were contentious at home. Because they were so close together in age — Keith was fourteen, Gordon thirteen, their sister Drew twelve — I held no illusions about remarriage. Any man who wanted to marry a woman with three untamed teen-agers would be crazy! I wouldn't want a guy like that. Besides, my track record with men was abysmal. So determined was I not to remarry that I usually referred to my children's father as "my *last* husband."

Such considerations flowed through my brain as I agitated my knees, swirling hot water over my belly button. The idea of leaving the books behind and dealing with real stuff — menus, bed linen, interesting people — beckoned. Finally, the effects of the hot water and late hour took their toll. I stood up, emptied the tub and dried myself off, then sank into bed for the second time that night.

It seemed but seconds until I heard the familiar clamor made by three kids as they bobbed around the house hunting for socks, hitting me up for lunch money, toasting Pop-tarts.

"Heard the phone ring last night," said Keith, the oldest, as well as the snoopiest.

"Granddad Miller called. Your grandmother is sick. She'll probably have to leave the mountains."

"What about the Inn?" asked Keith, a stricken look on his face.

"We'll see, we'll see."

❊ ❊ ❊ ❊ ❊

It seemed prudent to spend that day seeking opinions. I called Woodie, my brother eleven years older, who was on the faculty of Michigan State. Woodie called me 'Sis'.

I leveled with him: "For some time I've doubted that the university life is for me. I'm not sure I want to write dull papers nobody will ever read."

"Sis, maybe you have Ph.D. burn-out."

"Could be. Do you know what they will carve on my tombstone? 'She once created a perfect footnote!' How's that for a life-achievement award?"

Woodie chuckled. "However, I agree we should do everything possible to keep the Inn from being sold, Sis. My biggest concern is — what will we do with Dad? He'll go crazy in some retirement home."

"Either that, or drive us crazy."

Our father's boundless energy was a mixed blessing. He accomplished a lot but never learned to relax and take it easy.

Next I called Dwight, eight years my senior. Dwight called me 'Ginger.' He owned his own heavy construction and road maintenance business. "What do you know about managing a ski lodge? Don't do it, Ginger. It's brutal." Dwight spoke from experience. He had managed the Inn, then owned a separate lodge for a number of years. "We should sell the Inn."

"Sell our family home? We can't do that."

"Suit yourself, but the main thing I'm worried about is what Dad will do with his time. He'll try to run our lives."

I dialed up my professor in the English department. "Go into business? Business?" His voice trailed off as though business were both an unfathomable mystery and a tawdry means of supporting oneself. "If you leave, you'll never finish your dissertation," he warned. "Nobody ever does."

"Is that a threat?" I asked, anxious not to jeopardize my chances of completing my degree.

"No," he replied jovially. "Just a fact."

That day I drank eight cups of coffee. My brain whizzed along like a streamliner barreling down the main track.

I talked to my ex-husband, who lived nearby. He called me 'Gin'. His voice was sad. "I would really miss the children."

"That's why God invented airplanes."

I called my best friend, Bridget Collins (NRN). I loved Bridge, although normally I would be inclined to be jealous of someone elegantly six feet tall, slender, eleven years younger than I. Her wavy red hair flowed in sinuous billows down her ramrod straight back. Her skin was as creamy as peach ice cream. How good a friend was she? Once, a man asked me out on a date — a rare occurrence. Bridge volunteered to shepherd my sons to a Cub Scout Pack meeting so I could go to the symphony!

"Bridge, do you honestly think I could handle it?"

"Virginia, ever since I met you I knew you could do anything you really put your mind to. Go for it!"

When the kids came home, packing homework and the day's ragged school papers, I met them at the door. Normally, they paused only long enough to hit the refrigerator, then scatter in three directions to play with their friends.

"Sit down for a minute," I ordered. Expecting a lecture, they grumbled their little fannies onto the couch. "I have an important announcement. Next week Keith and I are going to Colorado to run the Inn for the rest of the season. Your grandparents will move here to look after Gordon and Drew, through April. If it works out OK, maybe we'll all move to Colorado!"

"To ski?" asked Keith.

"You bet," I answered. For once, I had their complete attention.

My youngest, pixie-cut Drew, looked earnest as she asked, "And Grandpa's going to come here and make pancakes for us? Soon?"

"Cool, Mom," said curly-headed Gordon. "We'll help Granddad look after Grandmom." They ran out the door to spread the word.

Finally, I called my father. "I want to run the Inn for you, Dad. The consensus is it would be a good idea. If it works out, I'll stay there for a year or two. But I have one big, important question."

"What's that?"

"If you leave the Inn, what will you do with your time?"

"I'll write a book!"

A grin crossed my face and I ceased to fret. I knew that when my father promised he would do something he always did it.

Chapter 3

Coming Home

Keith and I flew into Denver, then rode the airport bus from Stapleton Airport to the Winter Park Ski Area. As it labored up Clear Creek Canyon, the bus was about half loaded with skiers, who were also half loaded and talking Texan. Back in the seventies, bus drivers garnered tidy tips by welcoming visitors with a can of Coors because it was brewed in nearby Golden with "pure Rocky Mountain spring water" and was unavailable in other parts of the country until much later.

My son fidgeted in his seat, tugging at the cowlick that stuck out sideways from the rest of his blond thatch. I knew he was nearly as anxious as I was to get to Winter Park. Although he had skied just a few times, already he was better at it than I was.

"Look, Keith." I pointed up at frosted pine trees lining the walls of Clear Creek Canyon; they looked solid as wax Christmas candles. "And see how the water bubbles up between patches of ice."

When we neared the old mining town of Idaho Springs, I told him to turn his head. "You'll want to see the waterfall." Sure enough, a frozen waterfall was poised like a gigantic, threatening icicle above the village.

The other passengers were in an expectant, pre-holiday mood. Keith listened with interest as they compared their ski equipment — a topic that provided an opportunity to show off their knowledge and to brag about how much money they spent. "I usta have Heads, but I swear by my Dynastars. Honeycomb cores, you know."

"Nothing compares to Rossignols. They're the Cadillac of skis."

"How do you like your Scott boots?"

"Better'n I did my Hansens. Not sure about my Spademan bindings, though."

We wondered if any of them were going to Millers Idlewild Inn but decided to keep quiet and enjoy the ride as we switchbacked our way up Berthoud Pass. I wanted to think about the enormous responsibility I would shoulder at the end of this bus trip.

One of the Texans, clad in an SMU sweatshirt, was passing a pint. "This stuff'll cure rattlesnake bites and take the curves out of mountain roads."

It wasn't necessary to be from Dallas to feel queasy when looking down the two thousand-foot plunge to the valley below. Yet in some places snowbanks along the side of the road were as high as oncoming cars.

"Mom," said Keith, "if Gordon and Drew were here they'd want to stop the bus and make a snowman" — as though he were too mature to suggest that he'd like to scream for the bus to halt so he could leap into the nearest snowbank. My oldest child, Keith frequently tried to prove he was capable.

As we crept down the other side of the divide, the bus passed the base of the Winter Park Ski Area. The arriving guests, a little giddy from the combined euphoria of high altitude and high alcoholitude, cheered when the double chair lifts came into view. Skiers — suspended from cables, tenuous as spiders on a web — were being whisked up the side of the mountain.

"Oh Mom, can I go skiing this afternoon? Please?"

"Can you get your own gear together? If you find everything yourself, I don't mind."

Two miles farther down the road the bus ride ended at the town of Hideaway Park — as it was known before it changed its name to Winter Park to conform with the ski area — the village where most of the guests would stay in a handful of small lodges.

My father was there to meet us, standing beside his new red Ford van. He wore an outsized, plaid, red wool flannel jacket. Large ears protruded from either side of the red hard hat that protected his bald head from getting skinned up. His gray eyes squinted from behind plastic-framed spectacles. He gathered us up, Keith under one wing and me under the other, "Jumpin' Jeehosaphat, it's good to see you." I wanted to ask him so much, about Mother, about our plans — but guests always came first.

He immediately turned to assist a young couple who were putting their skis into the rack on the back of the van. "Hello, I'm C.D. Miller. You should be glad you met me because I'm worth knowing," he proclaimed with the impudence of a banty rooster. The guests were momentarily startled by his blatant immodesty, but I grinned because I knew he was right. They had just met someone they would never forget.*

"I'm Dr. Allison, Dr. Wayne Allison, and this is my wife Marsha." (NRNs) The plump doctor beamed at his skinny

---

* My father's energy became legendary. Perhaps it was best summed up by my uncle, Morgan Webster, who remembered my father when he was an energetic young schoolteacher in Kansas. Uncle Morgan once commented, "It's a good thing C.D. Miller wasn't born a sex fiend, or there'd be three times as many people in Western Kansas!"

young wife. She smiled back, forcing her lips into an arc. Father introduced us.

"On your honeymoon, I'm told," said Dad. "My wife and I have been married for fifty-three years. You will be, too," he assured them. "Are you a physician?"

"No, I'm a dentist." I would learn that people who made reservations in the name of doctor so-and-so were generally dentists. Medical doctors tried to conceal their profession so they wouldn't be pestered with symptoms over dinner; Ph.D. doctors got tired of explaining why they weren't "real" doctors.

Dad lifted his hard hat to scratch his shiny head. Clifford Dwight Miller, known to almost everybody as C.D., never grew to be taller than five-feet-seven inches tall. Any fat Father might have gained from consuming enormous portions of our cook's apple pies, he ran off in pursuit of his hordes of chores. Yet my father expanded to fill any room he entered, quickly becoming the center of attention. It was 1973 so Dad was seventy-three because he was born in 1900. My brothers say they can remember a time when his head had hair on it; I take their word for it because a fringe was all I ever saw.

He turned to his new guests. "Now when we get to the Inn I want you to act as if you owned the place or else act like you don't care who owns it."

That was something I had heard Dad say many, many times. But I wasn't in the mood for jocularity just then; I was anxious to get to the Inn and to see Mother.

"How's Mom?" I slid the van door shut to secure Keith and our new guests, then climbed into the front passenger seat.

"About the same," said Dad as he jammed the van into gear. "She's anxious to leave. The Green Bay group is here, you know."

"Is it far?" asked the dentist.

"No," chirped in Keith. "Just up the road."

In a couple of minutes the old Inn came into view. "Look at all those pretty flags," said the new Mrs. Allison when she saw the banners displayed along the log fence out front.

"Millers Idlewild Inn, Since 1946," read her husband.

The old Inn stretched out before us, the equivalent of half a city block. At first sight, guests might think the Inn was a log building. In reality, frame construction was faced with log slabs. The main lodge and its outbuildings were all painted mahogany rez, reddish-brown. Sunshine was causing snow to slide in uneven slabs off the shiny aluminum roof.

"I thought the brochure said there was a creek," said Dr. Allison as he helped Father unload several suitcases.

"There is, in back of the Inn by the cabins. But you don't see much of it this time of year. It's frozen over," explained Father. Behind the Inn were five cabins.

Marsha Allison did not offer to carry luggage. The tiny woman was practically swallowed by her huge, fake-fur coat. Maybe she was feeling ill from the effects of altitude. Many people did. But she looked up and read a sign aloud in a thin voice, "'Let me live in a house by the side of the road and be a friend to man, Sam Walter Foss.' That's nice."

In fact, the young couple read their way right into the Inn. Inside the outer front door was a sign: "How beautiful it is to do nothing and then afterward to rest," in both English and Spanish.

Just inside the lobby was a portrait my dad had commissioned of the hero of a novel he admired, *Scaramouche*. Dr. Allison read the legend, "'He was born with a gift of laughter and a sense that the world was mad, Rafael Sabatini.' I like that."

"Welcome to Millers," said Anita Bernbeck, my dad's secretary. "You'll be in Room 5." She dandled a key attached by a length of chain to a small log. New guests were always surprised by the thick logs. Purposely chunky, they prevented people from taking their keys to the slopes where they frequently lost them. Keith grabbed their luggage and headed up the stairs.

"'No Ski Boots Upstairs,' that's a good one," commented Wayne Allison.

Marsha Allison looked up the two flights of stairs as though she could never possibly make it to the top. I was afraid she might break into tears when she said to her husband, "You were right about one thing. This certainly is no Holiday Inn." I did not take the comparison to be complimentary.

"My, my, just smell that bread baking," declared her husband; I could see he was trying to cheer her up.

"We bake all of our own bread," I explained. "We even have a flour mill where we grind our own organic flour: wheat, corn and rye."

"Is that why they call this place Millers? And are you the Millers' daughter?" I'll bet he was a regular Novocaine riot around the office.

I glanced at Marsha Allison. Behind her rouged cheeks, the color had all drained from her face. "Are you all right?" I asked.

"Yes," she sniffed. "I'm just fine."

Keith reappeared. "Mom, Mom, can I go skiing now?"

"Yes. Get on with you. But run up and say hello to your grandmother first; get our suitcases from the van and find your things. The shuttle bus should come by soon." He was off in a flash.

As the couple disappeared up the stairs I greeted Anita. Dad encouraged his employees to think of themselves as members of the family. Both Mother and Dad thought highly of the slender, quiet, dark-haired Anita: of her skills, her attention to detail. "Talk to you later, I want to see Mother," I told her.

The TV was turned on in my parents' apartment, indicating that Mother's favorite soap opera had just concluded. Mother had two families; the one on *As The World Turns* had become more interesting than her own. Certainly she saw more of them.

Everybody called her Trudy; she hated her given name, Gertrude. Mom grinned up at me from her rocker. In the six months since I had seen her she had lost weight. The flesh around her brown eyes sagged. Her face was ashen.

I knew when I saw her that I had not come a moment too soon. Tears welled in my eyes, because at that moment, I suffered a great loss. I could never again use my mother as a pillar to lean on. Now I was the mother. I was for leaning on. And I didn't like it one bit.

Her eyes sparkled up at me from beneath those tired lids. "So you're finally here," she said, reaching her hand toward me. I bent down to hug her.

Then I stood back and lied, "You're lookin' good, Mom."

"You might have said I was good lookin'." Her sassy remark reassured me. "Glad you've come. Barely left this apartment since my attack. Tired of sitting like a lump. Clifford won't let me do anything." It was as though the breath necessary for uttering complete sentences was not available.

"You can leave day after tomorrow, Mom. Are you sure my kids won't be too much for you when you get to Phoenix?"

"Yes, I know I'll feel better when I get to a lower altitude. They are good children. Your father will help." Her square face, with its high cheekbones, was framed by thick salt and pepper hair. No matter which beauty operator cut it, it always styled itself into exactly the same classic waves.

It had surprised me a couple of times to overhear men comment that my mom was one of the sexiest women they had ever met. It couldn't have been because she flirted; perhaps, I thought, they admired her full Rubens figure. But eventually I realized that her sympathetic ear attracted men who were starved for warmth.

Just then my father came into the room. He gave my mother's hand a quick little squeeze, saying, "Your mother is a most remarkable woman." He said that — often. But he meant it every time. Sometimes the closeness between my parents was nearly unbearable for me to watch. All marriages are supposed to be like theirs. They held hands every time they sat on a couch together. I knew that they still made love at night. As much as my father loved his old Inn, when it came to a choice he loved my mother ten times more. I could see that he lived in terror that she might die apart from him.

"Were the Allisons on the bus?" Mom asked. She always studied the chart of arrivals, made it her business to know every guest's name in advance.

"Yes, but Mrs. Allison, her name is Marsha, looked kind of droopy. Too bad, they're on their honeymoon," I said.

Mom leaned back into her rocking chair. "Anita said her mother has called twice already, wanting to talk to her before she even got here. It generally takes a bride a few days to get over a wedding — not all they're cracked up to be." She leaned forward and said in a low voice, "I always did say that weddings and funerals bring out the worst in people."

Chapter 4

Father's Last Hurrah

"Come on folks, let's get goin'. It's alarm clock time, and everyone's in their prime." When I heard my father's wake-up chant I groaned as I rolled over in my bunk.

I hadn't slept very well. Members of the Green Bay group had indulged in a late-night sauna; the women's sauna was just beneath my bedroom.* Very few guests summoned the courage to roll in the snow as part of their sauna ritual. Most settled for a cold shower. But those hardy Wisconsonites — most of them well into their fifties — dashed out in the middle of the night and hurled their naked bodies into a convenient snowbank. Every time their hot flesh hit the snow, a top-of-the-lungs scream pierced the silence.

* We had two saunas, one for men and one for women. The rules were simple. Before dinner, men used the sauna in the Balcony House, which was kept very hot, about 200 degrees. Women were to use the one in the main lodge, which was fired to a cooler 160 degrees. After dinner, guests were free to use either sauna as they pleased. My father, euphemistically, referred to those hours as "family time." Dressing room doors could be locked from the inside. Clothing was declared optional. Sometimes the staff would hold a "Wesson Oil Party," for the purpose of communal backrubs. Hot tubs, or Jacuzzis, were not yet in fashion.

Promptly at seven every morning Father went into the office, warmed up an amplifier, turned on a microphone, then droned that inane alarm clock rhyme through a public address system to awaken our guests. Father was tone-deaf, so by the time he bellowed out "everyone's in their prime," his voice trailed off, flat as the Kansas prairie from whence he came. But people listened because his reveille was followed by a weather forecast, really just a guess. Nobody could predict storms very accurately in that mountainous area. Weather was of great interest to people who wanted to spend their entire day at the mercy of it. One thing Father did know was the correct temperature. If his thermometer read below ten degrees, guests knew they should add an extra layer of longjohns.

You could hear feet hitting the floor all over the Inn those mornings when he sang out, "Nine inches of fresh powder!"

It never occurred to Father that some suffering, hungover guest might like to sleep late and should be allowed to do so. Not many people complained. Occasionally we would find speaker wires clipped outside somebody's bedroom door, so evidently I wasn't the only one who objected to the wake-up call. Of course, the midnight clipper might also have preferred music other than father's perennial favorites, *Oklahoma* and *South Pacific*. The jury-rigged wiring between speakers caused the crackle of static to accumulate as Mary Martin belted, "I'm as corny as Kansas in August," toward the cabins across the creek.

I resolved that the wake-up call would be history when I took over.

That wake-up call was Father's last hurrah as sovereign of Millers Idlewild Inn. I have to admit that I was growing restless because he had been hurrahing his way through his last twenty-four hours in residence. I was anxious to take over, to get Mother out of there, to try my hand — for better or for worse — at management.

Father's third-to-last hurrah had been a lengthy valediction given at dinner the night before — between the pork roast and the homemade peppermint ice cream. "I'll bet you'd like to know how I lived to be so old — " he queried.

"How?" came back a cheerful shout from one of the Green Bay skiers who was still feeling his cocktail hour.

"Because the devil's in no hurry to take them he's sure of." Dad then proceeded to philosophize for about twenty minutes about the meaning of life — surely an unanticipated dividend for guests who thought their entire vacation would be devoted to skiing. The poor ski bums who waited the tables moved restlessly from one foot to the other, their eyeballs rolling from the floor to the ceiling. It was clear that they wished Dad would finish his speech so they could serve the ice cream, which was threatening to melt. After a day spent working and skiing, the young people wanted to finish clearing the tables and doing dishes.

Father's second-to-last hurrah was delivered in front of the lounge fireplace later that same evening. Some guests settled themselves on the couches and chairs in front of the fireplace, arranged to encourage conversation. Above them swung an old oxen yoke, wired as a light fixture.

I noted that Dr. Allison sat on a couch, hanging onto Father's every word. Marsha was nowhere to be seen. Nor had she appeared for dinner. We sent up a tray to her room, but she just picked at her food. Dr. Allison said his wife wasn't ill — just exhausted. Still, I couldn't figure out why honeymooners would want to spend an evening apart.

My father was a skilled storyteller; he mimicked accents, imitated characters that ranged from young girls to old men. He knew how to elevate suspense, wring pathos. For some reason he chose to relate Tennyson's story of *Enoch Arden*. By the time luckless old Enoch languished on his deathbed, there wasn't a dry eye in the room — except, of course, for those lids which had long since thickened and shut. So successful was the effect that Father quoted, from memory, of course, all five verses of "Let me Live in a House by the Side of the Road and be a Friend to Man."

❄ ❄ ❄ ❄ ❄

The next morning, in blinding bright sunshine, Anita, Myrtle the cook, Neil the maintenance man, the entire staff walked Father and Mother out to Amity, their homemade camper. They were leaving for Arizona. As our feet crunched through the packed snow Father kept up a nonstop litany: "And don't forget," "You should phone the snowplower," "Don't forget to light the tiki torches every night."

"Be sure to . . . to . . . to . . ."

"Yes, Dad, sure, Dad, I'll get right on it, Dad . . ."

Mother had already climbed into the passenger's side of the truck. I could see that these long goodbyes were tiring her. "Enough, Clifford," my mother finally interrupted. "You didn't raise and educate a dummy!"

I wasn't really paying close attention to his last-minute instructions because I could hardly wait for that camper to back down the driveway. I wanted to be on my own, even though I was terrified the whole place would go to pieces the moment they left.

Employees were hanging onto my parents' hands through the pickup windows. My father's eyes were full of tears; my mother was trying not to cough because the cold air choked her. Father finally gunned the accelerator — several times as usual — rammed the truck into gear and lurched toward the highway. One of the ski bums called, "Three cheers for C.D. and Trudy!"

"Hip Hip Hurrah! Hip Hip Hurrah! Hip Hip . . . !" We watched until the rattling metal camper disappeared around a bend in the road.

"Let's get to work," I ordered. Everyone scurried off to wash the dishes, make the beds, sweep the floors, shovel the snow, drive the buses, carry the wood, type the letters, mix the bread, oil the hinges, clean the bathrooms. The ski bums sprang to; the faster they finished their chores the sooner they could hit the slopes. And it promised to be a gorgeous day.

As we headed up the boardwalk, our cook, Myrtle Ashton, appeared at my elbow. "Could I have a few words with you?" Of course she could. I already knew that although theoretically guests come first, as a practical matter keeping the cook happy ranked way above keeping anybody else happy. The most terrifying words known to a hotel manager are: "The cook quit!"

A sign over the kitchen door pretty much said it all: "Keep Out — Mad Cook and Tired Dishwasher."

My mother once commented that cooks come in two sizes: very thin and extra large. "Stay away from the thin ones. They drink," advised Mother. Myrtle Ashton was a reassuringly good advertisement for her meals. She completely filled the space between the prep table and the range. It was difficult to believe that a soft-spoken, generally pleasant person like Myrtle could frighten anybody. Soon I would learn that the quieter she got, the more closely I ought to listen. Another "member of the family," she had cooked at the Inn for several winters; her food was as delicious as the servings were generous.

When I went to the kitchen, Myrtle was stirring a gigantic vat of fragrant, steaming turkey broth that would accrue vegetables and noodles to become soup by dinner time. She wiped her hands on her white apron. "I noticed you didn't eat much breakfast. Here, have a bun."

She put a sticky cinnamon roll — soft, fluffy, with a lot of pecans and very few raisins — onto a saucer. I really wasn't hungry, but I sensed that it would be good politics to eat it. When I sat at the dining room table Myrtle drew a cup of coffee from the urn and joined me, told me how pleased she was that Mother would get a chance to feel better.

"I didn't want to bother your mother and dad about this, but you need to know that I'm going on Social Security. I want to work fewer days next winter." At that time, she worked a five-day week.

"But you will come back next winter?"

Myrtle sighed the sigh of a not-very-well-off elderly woman who would much rather put her feet up and crochet than dish meals from a hot, muggy kitchen. I was terrified at the thought that she might not want to return the next winter.

"I'll certainly try to work out something," I promised.

❄ ❄ ❄ ❄ ❄

I had already made my first big management decision: the manager of a ski lodge should know how to ski. Neither my mother nor my father ever took up the sport. They didn't move fulltime to the mountains until after my father retired from his job with the Wichita school system; perhaps they thought themselves too old.

Many things had changed since my first skiing ventures when I was a teen-ager. Although clothes were lighter, brighter and tighter than the old war-surplus parkas and khakis we used to wear, they still had to be donned with ritual care. The most boring aspect of skiing is getting dressed. Like a samurai preparing for battle, each garment must be anticipated. Any neglected step could provoke discomfort, if not disaster, later in the day.

Long underwear was a given, but should I don one turtleneck sweater or two? Would I be too cold with just one? Which socks would be best? The cotton ones might make my feet sweaty — a situation that could lead to cold feet later in the day. Woolen ones "wicked" the perspiration away, but scratched my ankles. Should I take goggles? And was the parka I borrowed from my mother waterproof?

When I finally shoved my feet into my stiff, heavy ski boots, I felt more like a rigid mummy than a samurai armed for battle. I clunked by the office to tell Anita I was on my way out.

"Virginia, I didn't want to bother your parents with this, but I think you should know that I'm giving notice for the end of ski season." Anita certainly came right to the point.

"You mean, you won't be coming back next year?"

"Yes, I've found a year-round job."

Although losing a secretary isn't as serious as losing a cook, it was another complication I hadn't anticipated. I had hoped that all of the key employees would be willing to return next season. But I couldn't blame Anita. Seasonal employment is hard on employers and employees.

"I'll be happy to help you train my replacement."

"Thanks, Anita. I know you have to do what you have to do."

One good thing about wearing ski boots. You can stomp your feet and nobody knows when you're having a tantrum. The euphoria I felt at my parents' departure was quickly grounded.

Neil Brubaker drove me the two miles to the ski area. Although only twenty, Neil assumed the responsibility for the Inn's maintenance. Tall, slender, he sported a mane of wavy red hair, a robust beard, thick glasses and a perpetual grin. Father had recommended him with his ultimate compliment, "Neil has spitherinctum." If a person had *spitherinctum* Father meant he was energetic, resourceful and ambitious. A person lacking those essential character traits he dismissed as a "neversweat."

Although he had been there just a few months, Neil had mastered the tricky systems that governed the old Inn's heating, electrical and plumbing circuits. I was surprised someone only twenty years old would eagerly assume so much responsibility. Whenever he was asked to go do something he would say, "Got it," do a funny little dippy-do motion with his shoulders and be on his way to get the job done. One of his chores was to chauffeur guests to and from the ski area. He joked with the guests; all the girls were crazy about him.

Neil had a bedroom to himself, right next to the lobby, so he could greet late check-ins or tend to emergencies at night. It was so small that he built his bed on top of his dresser. He had to climb into it at night, but it saved space.

I decided I might as well brace myself for whatever might come. "Neil, will you be back next winter?"

"Far as I know, far as I know. Your brother asked me to drive dozers and road maintainers next summer for him. Pay's pretty good, too."

"Would you be able to do maintenance around the Inn, too?"

"Nope. Better if you get someone full time. I could help him learn the ropes. I need to make more money — want to buy a motorcycle. Could I keep my room at the Inn through the summer, then come back to work maintenance in the fall?"

"Of course. It'd be great to have you around in case something comes up. I'll just have to find someone else to do summer maintenance."

I lapsed into a brooding silence. Needing advice, I decided that before hitting the slopes I would stop by Carolyn Taylor's office at the ski area for a chat. Carolyn was a friend to my family and a friend to me. Although she was too young to be known as an "old family retainer," Carolyn had suffered through many years of employment with the Millers. Tiny and pretty, she was about my age; I envied her perfect size three figure. She had come west from Cleveland to work as secretary for my brother Dwight at his ski lodge. Later, when

Dwight sold his lodge, she came to the Inn. I'm sure that neither Dwight nor my dad quite understood how much they owed to her meticulous records, her diplomatic treatment of guests, her bookkeeping skills and her discretion. She left us for the same reason most employees did, she took a year-round job as a bookkeeper at the ski area.

She smiled when I appeared at her office door. "How's it going? Did C.D. and Trudy leave?"

"Finally, yes. I thought Dad never would get Mom out of here. Looks like everybody waited until they left to give me bad news." I flopped down on a chair by her desk. "Anita is quitting, Myrtle wants to work fewer days, and Neil says he's going to work for Dwight next summer."

"Not to worry," promised Carolyn. "I'll help you learn Anita's front desk job. Come fall, we'll hire someone and train them. Somebody will turn up to do maintenance. And we'll figure out how to fill in for Myrtle."

If Carolyn dreaded tutoring one more Miller, she never showed it. To Carolyn fell the chore of making a business woman out of me. I often wondered why Carolyn, so capable she could find employment anywhere she wanted it, chose to work so long for the Millers. Maybe we became the close family she didn't have. Or maybe she just liked the excitement of being around a ski lodge.

"Go on out and ski. It'll clear your mind and do you good."

As I clunked through the warming house, I noted that Marsha Allison was sitting — alone — in a corner. She looked up; her eyes were rheumy. I hoped that she was suffering from faulty contact lenses, not from disappointment in her marriage. I said, "What, not skiing on such a beautiful day?"

She looked down at her lap, which was covered with envelopes. "I have to write my thank you notes for wedding gifts." Marsha had been on the pay phone to her mother every single evening. "Mummy says they can't wait."

"Wouldn't you rather ski?"

"No. I don't think so," she sniffed.

She looked so forlorn there by herself. I wondered if I should sit down to chat for awhile, but I was reluctant to pry. Soon enough, I would learn that part of an innkeeper's job is serving as mother confessor. But I had problems of my own just then.

❄ ❄ ❄ ❄ ❄

"Single!" I yelled. Skiing by one's self has its benefits. A lone skier can usually find a partner at the head of the lift line, saving a long wait.

The day was a real freckle-popper. The air was cold, yet the sun's direct, high altitude rays warmed my back as I rode up the lift. With the passing of every lift tower, I felt better. Pillows of fresh snow sat lightly on the branches of tall pines. Small puffs of a breeze sent sparkling diamonds flying through the sunshine. Fortunately, my fellow "single" was not a talker.

As I slid from the chairlift, the snow was soft and creamy beneath my skis. Scanning a sign map, I picked out a green square which pointed to the safety of a bunny slope named Jack Kendrick. Standing at the top of the run, I felt like I was gazing down the sides of a frosted birthday cake — an appropriate thought, because it really was my birthday. All white, perfect, inviting. Never mind that as I poled myself forward my skis slipped out from under me, hurling me headlong down the slope. I got up again, fell again. About the third time, I fell with such force that I practically dug through the icing to the chocolate base beneath. I scooped out several sitzmarks, the skier's equivalent of divots. I had never been, and never would become, an accomplished skier. But that hardly mattered. A few more bumptuous falls drove home to me the one prime principle of skiing: always keep your weight on the downhill ski.

The sport has certain imperatives. One is that the eyes stay in direct communication with the feet. In this world of wheels, very few people stop to think about where their feet are — unless they stub a toe. Once on the slopes it was impossible to think about a cook or a secretary giving notice. My only concern was where my feet would be in the next second, fifteen seconds, minute or half hour. Nothing else was important, because any breakdown in communication between my brain and my feet caused another rarely thought-of part of my body — my fanny — to come in sudden contact with cold, hard reality.

Ski apparel had changed; so had ski equipment. Gone were the long wooden shafts that required their owner to execute clumsy "snowplow" turns. Little short skis just whisked me down the slope. About all I had to do to cause them to turn was to shift my weight, slightly. I resolved to take some lessons.

I had chosen an easy slope like Jack Kendrick in the hope that I would not be seen by guests, the staff or my son Keith; I didn't want anyone to know what a turkey skier I really was. But as I painstakingly tried to carve some turns, someone called, "Hey, there's Virginia!"

Standing along one side of the hill, lined up as though they were taking a group lesson, were members of the Green Bay Ski Club. Mother had joked that they liked to ski because all of their names ended in -ski: Baronskis, Jarowskis, all on their real -skis. I made a mental note to refrain from telling Polack jokes, which were all the rage.

"Hey Virginia, have a nip!"

I skied toward them. Several mittened hands offered to share a sip from a bota bag or flask.

"My, my, what do we have here?" I asked.

"Brandy!" I took a very large swig from a leather-sheathed flask.

"Virginia, we're so glad you will be running the Inn. We've been so worried about C.D. and Trudy. Promise us you'll be here when we come back next year."

"I think I will, if I can ever get the hang of this skiing thing."

"Have another sip! It will loosen you up."

I did. It did.

Chapter 5

What's Wrong with Room 5?

Arvid Ray Calhoun (NRN) was my first Bubba. All Bubbas are from the South, tall, a little overweight, loud, friendly as pups, eager to please, deferential to women and equipped with two first names. Fun-loving party animals, their entire lives revolve around whether they spent their formative years as Gators, Cougars, Tigers, Bears, Mustangs, Razorbacks or Longhorns.

Arvid Ray was an Aggie. His family, which consisted of a cheerleader-pretty wife and two no-necked sons, had stayed at the Inn before. Arvid Ray — I was corrected when I called him Arvid — loved the old place and was anxious that every guest feel exactly the same way he did. I'm sure Arvid Ray fancied himself an unofficial host. "Y'all having a good time here?" was how he opened a conversation.

In the dining room, guests ate family-style at long tables set for eight. Because they were forced to talk to each other, people got acquainted; often they ended up skiing together.

As I was pouring coffee refills at breakfast one morning, I

overheard a casual remark Arvid Ray made to Wayne Allison. Dr. A, as usual, ate alone while his bride remained upstairs in their room. Poor Wayne, he spent his evenings wandering about the lounge, eagerly proffering medical advice to skiers who had crashed and burned on the slope that day. "I'm a dentist, but of course I know all about medicine," he assured them.

The night before he had offered to take a look at another guest's wrist, unaware his would-be patient was a surgeon from Enid, Oklahoma. The incognito doctor turned him down, of course, with a look of benign amusement. Other guests were whispering about the groom whose bride kept to her room. I was grateful to Arvid Ray for taking the lonesome dentist under his wing. Wayne Allison needed a friend.

Inside Arvid Ray's square jaw, a piece of bacon was in mid-chew when he turned to Wayne and asked, "What room they got you in, Wayne?"

"Room 5," answered the dentist.

Arvid Ray hesitated a moment, guffawed hugely, then pummeled Wayne on the back with the kind of vigor that can produce a sudden clog in the windpipe if a person is caught while swallowing, "Don't worry. If they like you, they'll give you a better one next time."

I didn't want to let on I was eavesdropping, but I was genuinely distressed. What was wrong with Room 5? I tried to pour my way back toward their conversation, with my ears pricked for more information. Alas, just then my pot ran dry so I was forced to return to the urn. I hated to think the Inn would make anyone unhappy; I resolved to confront Arvid Ray. But when I looked up my Bubba was out the door — eager to catch the first bus for the ski area. Wayne Allison picked up the tray Myrtle had prepared for him to take up to Marsha. The man was as obedient as a whipped whelp.

After the Allisons boarded Neil's last shuttle to the slopes,

I resolved to launch an investigation into the enigma of Room 5, to try to figure out what the problem was. Perhaps it could be remedied. And while I was at it, maybe there would be a clue as to what ailed Marsha.

What could be wrong with Room Number 5, or at least, what was wronger with it than other rooms? At first I thought maybe the problem was noise; it was located at the head of the stairs where people, especially teen-agers, frequently gathered to chat. I had already asked Anita if they complained about the noise. They hadn't.

I knocked on the door to assure myself its occupants weren't there, wondering at the same time what on earth I was going to say if someone called, "Come in." Nobody answered so I slipped my master key into the lock and entered.

Unmade rooms always look a sight, but this one wasn't too bad. Both beds had been slept in. Not a good honeymoon sign. Or else a good sign if both had been really rumpled. Although the room wasn't large, there was space to walk around its two double beds and still have room for a dresser and a chair. Marsha Allison's remark about Millers Idlewild Inn not being a "Holiday Inn" came to mind. By Holiday Inn standards, Room 5 was indeed small — but we had smaller. Over one of the beds a dormer window showed a lovely view toward James Peak. The sloping roofline might have imposed a bit of a stoop on the dentist, but not on his smaller wife.

Did the pitch in the roof, which lowered the headroom, prevent some of the livelier postures associated with lovemaking? Mentally, I tried to position the bridal couple in action. No, the slope in the roof wasn't *that* severe.

I thought about those low ceilings because although my short father never said a word against tall men, his resentment came out in subtler ways. I noted men over six feet tall could often be seen standing in doorways, passing their hands between the top of their heads and the lintels, estimating the odds of bashing their noggins. The Inn was built on a small scale. Ceilings were low, halls were narrow, windows were tiny. Father had a horror of wasting anything; headspace was no exception.

    I searched for a light switch. Sure enough, I located it behind the door — hard to find and installed upside down. Father, like me, was left-handed. He got even with the world by treating it with as much logic as it treated him. When you're left-handed it seems that everything is backwards. Maybe that's why guests often found that hot and cold water came out of the wrong taps. Still, the accumulation of these minor details didn't seem enough to make a guest angry.

    The Allisons' personal effects were stowed in tidy fashion. I opened their closet and took a peek. All in order. I even looked under their beds. Often people stow liquor under the beds, certain that maids searching for a short snort will never think to look there. No booze below. The bathroom in Number 5 was a bit bigger than some other bathrooms. Maybe Arvid Ray made his derogatory comment because the unit didn't have a shower. The slope of the roof made it impractical to install a showerhead. But then none of the showerheads were higher than Father thought they ought to be. One tall guest said they were great showers — if you didn't want to rinse anything above your navel.

    Room 5's tub was full-length and comfortable. Compared to Room 10 down the hall, this bathroom was huge. One woman who stayed in Number 10 claimed she could sit on the john, wash her feet in the bathtub and brush her teeth at the same time! I speculated that in his youth my father must have admired the arrangement of a sleeping compartment on a train where plumbing fixtures actually folded into the wall. The arrangement appealed to his sense of thrift. Tiny bathrooms saved both pipes and floorspace. From then on he was always trying to figure out how many fixtures he could engineer into the smallest area.*

Did Room 5 smell bad because it was next to the closet where dirty linen awaited the laundry man? I didn't think so; the room had good ventilation. Besides, the forced-air heat kept that part of the building cozy. I liked the look of the room; afternoon sunlight streaming through the windowpanes of the dormer played interesting patterns onto the bedspreads.

So why did Arvid Ray make such a big deal of it? Marsha Allison's obvious distress was becoming my problem, too. The medicine cabinet held no medications to indicate she was ill or taking sedatives. As long as I had sunk this low, I thought I might as well check the contents of the bathroom wastebasket, too. But at that moment I heard the cleaning girls trundling their vacuum cleaners down the hall. Ashamed at stooping to such tactics, I left. I had no better clue to the problem of Room 5 and its unhappy occupants than when I entered it.

Each time I tried to get Arvid Ray aside to ask what was wrong, he was busy detailing the specifics of some memorable football game. Bubbas can give you a play-by-play rerun of every football game their team ever played from the date they enrolled as freshmen. Before granting degrees, Southern colleges must require students to fill blue books with football strategy. Certainly a knowledge of football seems a prerequisite to doing business in that part of the world.

That night I didn't sleep very well, trying to figure out why Room 5 was ruining Wayne and Marsha Allison's honeymoon.

* Sometimes I was asked if the Inn had a ghost. Yes, there was one. In one corner of the main lounge was an ugly set of pipes, which, for some reason, my father had left exposed. Mother planted a pot of ivy in an attempt to disguise them with greenery. In that set of pipes which we referred to as "the family tree," and in the bathroom just above them dwelt a real ghost. I have no idea what made our plumbing spook mad, but no matter how often we did repairs, those pipes leaked.

Fortunately, the next morning the bride finally came down to breakfast. She didn't say much, but I was encouraged when she ate two helpings of pancakes and four links of sausage.

The Allisons and Arvid Ray were scheduled to depart on the same day. Wayne Allison paid his bill first. Mother had advised me to make a habit of saying goodbye to departing guests, of giving them a friendly send-off. Once again, Marsha looked like a tiny mouse inside her huge coat. "We had a wonderful time," said Wayne Allison in a firm voice.

"You have a really nice place," sniffed Marsha as she extended a very limp hand. "I'm so glad *something* went right," whereupon she burst into tears as she fled out the front door.

Now it was imperative I learn what the problem was with Room 5.

Half an hour later, Arvid Ray and his family lugged their bags to the front desk. After a few days of informality at the Inn, nobody asked for help with suitcases. Arvid Ray, as usual, was expansive. "I just don't know how y'all do it. Every year things get better around here." My father said the word-of-mouth recommendation from a guy like Arvid Ray was more valuable than buying $1,000 worth of advertising in a Houston newspaper.

When he signed over the last of his traveler's checks and Anita had counted out his change, I looked Arvid Ray in the eye. Texans insist on being looked right in the eye. I think a Texan prefers a right-in-the-eye lie to a shiftily delivered truth.

"Arvid Ray, I know I shouldn't have been eavesdropping but I heard you tell Dr. Allison that if we liked him, we wouldn't make him stay in Room Number 5 again. I've been trying and trying to figure out — what's wrong with Room Number 5?"

Arvid Ray turned as red as a Texas sunset and looked down at his city shoes. Then he wrapped his big arm around my shoulders. "Now honey, don't you worry a bit about Number 5. It's a very nice room."

"No, I really want to know what's wrong. Maybe I can fix it."

"Not unless you raise the roof, you can't."

"The roof?"

Arvid Ray still looked uneasy, but he glanced at his wife, who nodded for him to tell me.

"Well, you being a little lady and all, you probably wouldn't have noticed."

Ever alert to being patronized on account of my sex I began to bristle.

"Honey, a man can't stand up to take a leak in that room because the slanted roof makes him bend over backwards!"

Chapter 6

By the Balls

"Things are off to a great start," I lamented. "Anita is quitting, Myrtle wants to cook four instead of five days next year and Neil is going to work for you."

My brother Dwight nodded his head sympathetically, "'Bout par for the course, I'd say. Employees come and go."

When Dwight was a kid, his hair was scarlet. But it took more than frost on the pumpkin to diminish the puckishness of my brother's disposition. Forever freckled, he started most conversations with the latest bawdy joke from his vast repertory. Dwight didn't live very far away, just six miles down the road in a villagette called Tabernash. Although he made it clear I was on my own when it came to the management of Millers Idlewild Inn, he also made it a habit to show up occasionally to share a cup of coffee or down a "pop," his term for a shot of bourbon. Because he had nearly twenty years' experience in the ski lodge business, he knew the territory. I am grateful that throughout the next year Dwight would exhibit an uncanny knack for appearing just when I was desperate to talk with someone — confidentially.

That day, he was maddeningly calm in the face of what I perceived to be an employee crisis. "I know Father always tried to turn everybody he hired into a member of the family. He had the notion if he hired somebody they were going to stay forever. But Ginger, it just doesn't work that way.

"Let me tell you the most important thing about this business. *Never let the cook get you by the balls.*" He clenched his fingers behind one knee that was crossed over the other and pulled up on it, just to emphasize his point.

I must have looked a little puzzled at his baldly stated warning until I realized he was referring to my metaphorical balls.

He hastened to explain, "Never let an employee think he or she is so important you can't do without them — or you've had it. Ginger, you're going to have to learn how every single thing works around here, learn it so well you can step into anybody's job and do it until you can hire someone else. Gotta know enough to train the next person you hire. If any employee convinces you that you can't run your business without him, he's got you by the balls and he'll take terrible advantage. But above all, be sure you can step into the kitchen for four or five days and do the cooking if you have to. I'm not saying a word against Myrtle but if she gets sick or quits . . ."

That would be the best management advice I ever received. The very heart of the ski lodge business is the kitchen; he was right to emphasize it. I immediately resolved to learn everything I could about food service.

But I was more than a little apprehensive about invading Myrtle's territory; the kitchen, I knew, had been the site of terrible frays between Myrtle and the ski bums who worked for her.

Within her domain, Myrtle headed her own pecking order. She generally got along well with whoever she chose to be cook's helper; that assistant held a place of honor and helped dish out meals from the cook's side of the steam table. Myrtle's size required ample turning room; there wasn't space for two assistants. Less fortunate were the waiters and waitresses who hastened the steaming plates to the tables. The lowest untouchable was the dishwasher. Myrtle almost never got along with the dishwasher.

"Can't you ever stack those soup bowls the way I tell you to?"

"You are the sloppiest boy who ever worked in my kitchen. Don't blame me if someone slips and falls on that wet floor and breaks their neck."

"Your mother must not have had any sense, because she sure didn't raise you to have any either."

At first I thought there would be an easy remedy to this problem. I would simply transfer the hapless employee from dishwashing to housekeeping, then rotate someone new to the dishwashing job. It took me a while to realize Myrtle needed a sacrificial scapegoat; the chances were very good she would make the next kid as miserable as the last. One time the curly-headed teenager who was her current goat barged into the office under a full head of steam: "Either that woman goes," he proclaimed, gesturing in the direction of the kitchen, "or I go!" He must have been watching a lot of TV.

"Start packing," I advised.

He didn't.

Myrtle wasn't all bad; she set out a plateful of cookies for her ski bums when they came home from skiing. But harmony in the kitchen was fleeting.

Most kids came straight from college or from the bosoms of their families; often they had been former guests. From the guests' point of view, working at a ski lodge was a glamorous occupation. But in truth, the work was grueling.

Employees arose early in the morning, tried to complete their chores by noon so they could ski, then returned to serve dinner and do the dishes. Their preoccupation with the triple delights of skiing, beer and sex left little incentive to focus on the finer points of their chores. Back in their homes, most young people had been allowed to argue with their mothers; spoiled youngsters quickly learned Myrtle wasn't Mother.

Generally soft-spoken, she controlled the kitchen through a delicate pattern of sighs. Anyone who wanted to get along with her learned to interpret them.

There was the sigh of fatigue, which she uttered just before she finally sat down to eat — generally a large bowl of mashed potatoes and gravy.

A slightly higher-pitched sigh served as warning that her patience was wearing thin. An alert ski bum would read it, quit gossiping, and hasten to get the dishes stacked and into the huge dishwasher.

The sudden repetition of exhalations could serve as warning Myrtle was mad enough to hurl a bowl of hot scrambled eggs in the face of the next kid who vexed her.

Eventually I came to appreciate her point of view. A cook at mealtime is like the captain of a ship in the midst of a storm. Don't ask questions. The cook has her reasons. She's under a lot of pressure and she knows what she's doing because she's been doing it for many years.

But most of all, if Myrtle raised her voice and called out, "HOT STUFF!" she meant, "Get out of the way I'm coming through with a heavy pot of steaming food! If you don't get out of my way you're going to get hurt."

If I asked for guidance, would Myrtle think I was interfering on her turf? I summoned my courage. "Myrtle, I would really like to learn more about how the kitchen is run. Would you mind if I come into the kitchen, serve as an unofficial assistant?"

For just a moment she stared at me. Then, in a very kind voice she said, "I'd be very pleased to show you what I do."

To my relief, Myrtle seemed flattered at my interest in her doughs, crusts, broths and sauces. "Where do you want to start?"

"You make the best fried chicken in the world," I replied, because everybody else said so, too. "Might as well teach me how you do it."

Together, Myrtle and I dragged a heavy case of chickens out of the walk-in refrigerator and scooted it along the floor toward the maple table. When I removed the lid I gazed down at the pile of dead pink bodies without much enthusiasm. "Can't you just buy these things already cut up, like at the supermarket?"

Myrtle chuckled. "If you want to pay almost double." She seemed quite impressed with the lot. "Yes, these are very nice. You have to watch your supplier. These came from Nobel Mercantile and they're just about right. See how fresh they look? There's still ice on the top." As she spoke, she held a carcass in one hand and patted it lovingly with the other. She sniffed it. She pinched it. She looked up its butt.

"But best of all, they're the right size. Portion control is quite important. Most people put two pieces of chicken on their plate to start with. If the chickens are too big, you lose money because people can't eat all they take. If they're too small, they take three pieces. A three-pounder divides up just right."

Wonder what my Chaucer professor would say if he could see me gazing up a chicken where the sun don't shine?

I rinsed the birds while Myrtle explained. I mixed a little hot water in with the cold because mountain water comes out of the tap so frigid that if you sink your hands in it for long, your arms get numb up to the elbows.

"Now I'll teach you how to cut them." Myrtle slapped two weapons on the thick table top: a hefty butcher knife and a freshly sharpened meat cleaver. "Breast down, grasp the neck, cut along the backbone," she ordered. Reluctantly, I reached inside the chicken's neckhole. The sharp knife severed the bones with surprising ease. She splayed open the corpse, indicating where to cut next. Using the knife, I sliced through all of the proper joints until we got to the breast. With utter authority, Myrtle lifted her cleaver and whacked the breast into four neat pieces, "Whack 'em hard." Soon I found myself clobbering away as though I'd been doing it all my life. "Good thing to do when you're mad at somebody," advised Myrtle. After my first few cases of chickens I always glanced at the clock. Tried to break my personal best time for whacking them up. Finally got so I could do a sixty-pound case in twenty-three minutes — pretty good.

Myrtle taught me the proportions of flour to mix with seasonings, how to gauge the heat in the deep fryer, how to stack pieces into the steam table so they wouldn't get soggy. There's no easy way to fry chicken. By the end of the process, fatigue squeezed the base of my neck; my eyeglasses were filmed with grease; the kitchen felt hotter than the sauna. And if I wasn't careful, I got painful little burns up my arms from hot, spattering oil. Cooking for a lot of people is arduous, dangerous work.

"Where do you keep your soup recipes so I can learn how to make them?" I asked.

Myrtle snorted. "You don't make soup, you build it. Go in the walk-in and tell me what's there."

I stood in the walk-in as long as I could stand the cold, looking up and down the shelves: "There's a platter of turkey bones, a whole bunch of left-over mashed potatoes and a lot of celery that came back from the relish plates last night."

"Sounds like potato soup to me. Now bust up the turkey bones and put them in this biggest pot with a couple of onions and some of the celery tops. Later today you can dice the rest of the celery along with some onions and brown them all in some oleo. Fish out the bones, add a little soup base for flavor and throw in the mashed potatoes."

She taught me to think of leftovers as possibilities, not problems. We wasted very little food. A ham bone became a treasure trove of potential in my eyes.

Sometimes I was surprised to hear myself quote Macbeth's witches as I stirred the pot: "Double, double, toil and trouble, Fire burn and cauldron bubble." Literature mattered so little in that line of work.

Fortunately, ravenously hungry skiers bolted their soup, rarely questioning it. "This is delicious, what do you call it?"

"Walk-In Soup," I would reply. "Exact contents unknown. Enjoy it. It will not pass this way again."

My next lesson was bread baking. Father had already taught me how to grind grain through our stone mill, an hourglass-shaped affair about the size of a refrigerator. Myrtle would ask me to grind her a bushel of corn, wheat, buckwheat or rye.

"The most important thing is to get the temperature right for the yeast," she cautioned. "If your milk or water is too hot it kills the leavening. Too cool and it takes too long to rise. Just leave the mixer running while you throw in the rest of the ingredients." Everything was dumped into the enormous steel bowl of our Hobart mixer where a dough hook the size of my arm rotated forcefully. Eventually the dough clung to the hook; when it had been slapped against the side of the bowl for a few minutes, we removed the hook and left the dough to rise.

Bread dough is magic. I used to sneak into the kitchen to lift the towel, reassuring myself yeast was alive and pumping. It's a pretty sight to see a dome of elastic dough expanding over the rim of a mixing bowl.

"Each loaf should have about a pound of dough. You'd better weigh it until you get the feel of it." Myrtle taught me to shape dough into neat little pillows before popping them into greased pans. When the dough doubled in bulk again, we shoved loaves into our two spacious convection ovens, where they baked very quickly because fans recirculated hot air. In the process they blasted divine fragrance all over the Inn. Skiers returning from the slopes found themselves salivating the moment they opened the front door. Brave ones would hazard the "Mad Cook and Tired Dishwasher" sign above the kitchen door to humbly beg a slice of fresh bread. Myrtle could be formidable; however, a silver-tongued guest who applied the emolument of flattery was generally rewarded with a slice of warm bread and butter.

The evening menu rotation was fairly predictable: pork roast with apples and sauerkraut, fried chicken, roast baron of beef, roast turkey (always on Thursday), trout or some other kind of fish, ham, spaghetti, meatloaf. Myrtle's food was simple, nourishing and above all, plentiful. The only time people complained was when we ran out of it.

Skiers, like armies, travel on their bellies. I am told a person skiing on a cold day consumes about the same number of calories as a workman operating a jack hammer. Food was quite literally the meat of our business. The seventies were wonderful times in which to feed and be fed. I can't recall a single guest who demanded special consideration because of a "life-style preference." Cholesterol hadn't been invented yet. If vegetarians existed, they didn't ski. De-caf? We kept some packets of the instant stuff on hand but nobody under age sixty-five ever asked for it. Very few people claimed allergies. "Does this food have preservatives in it?" was about the only question asked.

Myrtle rarely talked about herself, yet in the course of our time together I discovered that her life had been very difficult. Her husband abandoned her with several children to raise, returning home only when he was so sick and broke that he needed Myrtle to nurse him through his final illness. A couple of her brood had died violently. Others had been injured in terrible accidents. Home was a cramped mobile home, some forty miles distant, where pipes remained frozen all winter. But she never spoke of those things unless asked, keeping her heartache to herself.

Myrtle's lessons served me well, time and time again. Eventually emergencies did arise, forcing me to step into the kitchen and produce a few meals. I will always be grateful to Myrtle. When I look back at my years at the Inn, my fondest memories are of people sitting around tables, enjoying the wonderful meals we fixed. It never occurred to me to resent the fact that in a few hours everybody would need to be fed again.

Chapter 7

Queen of the Police Ball

Meanwhile, Father was a little bored down in Arizona, so he occupied himself thinking up chores for me to accomplish in my "free" time. Almost daily he phoned to see how things were going, to remind me of some impending tax payment or publicity deadline. I came to dread the moment when he said, "While you're at it," because I knew some very big assignment was about to follow that innocent prelude. One day he said, "While you're at it, you'd better get out the invitations for the policemen's banquet."

"Pardon?" This was the first I had heard of such a thing.

"Every spring we invite all the county policemen for dinner. Shows them we appreciate them. Myrtle knows all about it."

"How many policemen?"

"'Bout forty, fifty. Tell you what, I'll send a note over to the courthouse in Hot Sulphur Springs for you. I'll take care of everything." As I hung up I thought to myself, "Sure you'll take care of everything. From Arizona you'll bake the bread and wash the dishes."

As always, I approached the kitchen with caution. Myrtle usually scowled when I informed her we had drop-ins or unexpected guests and I announced: "Six more for dinner." God knows how she would react to the idea of preparing one more large meal — so close to the end of the ski season.

Myrtle didn't seem fazed. "I was wondering if we would do that again. No, I don't mind."

"How many people usually come?" I asked.

"Their families are invited, of course. Last year we had about sixty. Don't worry about the menu. I'll take care of everything."

Relieved, I resolved to get in a little more skiing before the end of the season. One of the enduring mysteries of the ski business is why, just when skiing is at its very best in April, guests quit coming. I suspect the greening of golf courses down in the flatlands poisons people's minds against snow. On a beautiful spring day you can ski in blue jeans with your shirtsleeves rolled up. Zinc oxide on noses, to prevent sunburn, makes skiers look like clowns. And indeed, everybody acted a little goofy.

I bought myself a nifty pair of Dynastar skis and some Scott boots. At last, I was skiing well enough to actually make it from the top of the mountain to the bottom without falling. Not very fast, mind you, but my enjoyment of the sport increased with every successful run. Sometimes my son Keith stayed with me for a run or two — literally skiing circles around his uncoordinated mother. It is a wonderful thing, at age fourteen, to make your mother look silly.

By the evening of the policemen's dinner, we had only a handful of guests; the ski area would close down in a couple of days. Many of the ski bums had already left; we were very short-handed, although Keith had been pressed into service to wait tables and wash dishes. Nevertheless, Myrtle was in a remarkably good mood. She hummed a little as she baked and cooked what I perceived to be an extraordinary amount of food. "Just cleaning out the deep-freezes at the end of the season," she explained.

"How many places should we set at the tables?" Keith asked Myrtle.

"Better set them all." I was a bit apprehensive. Sixty places? Sounded like a lot of people to me. Would Myrtle have enough food? And if she fixed too much, what would we do with leftovers? As I doled out the knives and forks I tried to talk myself into a better mood. Perhaps my attitude was held hostage to my years at the university. Words like "pig" and "narc" came readily to mind.

People began arriving even before the announced dinner time of 6:30. One of the first was Sheriff Huck Henderson. I did a double-take when he and his wife walked through the door because the stocky fellow was instantly recognizable as a rural law enforcement official. He was the spittin' image of the tough-talking "Dodge Sheriff" in a TV commercial. Irreverent, outspoken, witty — Henderson couldn't have been much over thirty. On the surface, he seemed jolly and relaxed. But I sensed his lap dog good humor could turn to a Doberman snarl the instant he smelled danger.

He introduced me to his men and their families as they arrived. Henderson was amused when I confused patrolmen, deputies, marshals and such. Like most people, I didn't realize the sheriff enforces law for the county while the state highway patrol is in charge of the roads that run through it.

"All my deputies are Viet Nam vets," Henderson boasted. "No long-haired, dope-smokin' hippies on my force. Most people don't appreciate veterans, but I do." Then he added glowingly, "I just love war."

And indeed the appearance of the young men stood light-years away from my shaggy students back at the university. The fellows looked every inch the Marines they had so recently been. As I recall, every single one of them wore a little black moustache. To this day, when I meet a neatly barbered fellow with a trim black moustache I immediately suspect I am talking to a policeman.

Highway patrolmen, on the other hand, are uniformly tall. I wondered if they had to be at least six-foot-two in order to apply for the job — must be so they can pat the top of your car roof when they stop you.

Even though most of the young men were out of uniform, for the early seventies they presented a remarkably kempt group. At that time there were no women in local law enforcement and there wouldn't be until Sheriff Henderson finally got around to elevating a female dogcatcher to the position of deputy several years later.

Almost as soon as the officers arrived, Myrtle started to serve. People were polite, appreciative and hungry. I was beginning to relax in their company. But every time I got into a conversation the front door swung open and another group turned up — ready to be greeted and fed.

Before long the tables were full, so I asked the next arrivals to wait in the lounge.

"Uh, Sheriff Henderson, how many deputies do you have?" I inquired.

"Regulars or the voluntary reserves?"

"I didn't see my father's invitation. What did it say?"

"Said everybody was invited. We're spelling the jailor; he'll be late."

Suddenly I panicked. Father probably hadn't realized that in addition to the professional police, he was inviting twenty or so volunteer deputies, plus their families. More people kept coming and I was dead certain we would run out of food. What would we do? It would be embarrassing to turn people away. I swallowed hard, then headed to the kitchen to break the news to Myrtle. "Uh, Myrtle, I think there might be a few more people than we had counted on. I just don't think I can give you an exact number."

I expected a blimp-sized sigh of anger, but she didn't look particularly perturbed. "That's all right. I'll just pop a few more things in the oven."

Miraculously, as more and more people arrived, Myrtle produced more and more food. "I imagine some of them won't be able to make it until they get off their shift at the mill," she commented. Some thirty-five miles distant, an alloy called molybdenum was mined. Their shift didn't end until eight!

Relieved at her good humor, I returned to our guests. "Gosh, Sheriff," I inquired, "Who's minding the store? Who's looking after Grand County?" U.S. Highway 40 stretched nearly a hundred miles from the Inn to the top of Rabbit Ears Pass.

"We're rotating shifts so everyone can make it," he replied cheerfully. "This is a great chance to get together, catch up on gossip." I was pleased to note that every single person stopped by the kitchen to thank Myrtle.

I finally realized why Myrtle took this occasion in stride. Many of these people were friends; she knew most of the rest, or their families. It was as though she, personally, had asked a lot of her neighbors over for a nice dinner. Cooking for strangers is OK, but it made a nice change of pace to see her food disappear down the gullets of her friends — especially when someone else was footing the bill.

That night, Myrtle was queen of the policemen's ball.

Summer, 1973

Chapter 8

Where's Tonto?

In mid-April I returned to Phoenix. Throughout the process of selling my house, holding my carport sale, packing, cleaning out ten years of household grunge and bidding goodbye to friends, my spirits remained high. By early June it was getting hot in Phoenix, but even that didn't bother me.

Fortunately, Carolyn — my friend who had worked for the family for so many years — volunteered to fly to Phoenix and drive back with me. With my two younger children, Drew and Gordon — plus our little black and tan half-dachshund, Pepper — we drove along. We played tourist, stopping to take a look at the Grand Canyon, Monument Valley and Arches National Monument. I was glad for adult company; besides, all along those eight hundred miles Carolyn tutored me about the ins and outs of innkeeping. There were so many obscure corners of management whose existence I surmised, without really grasping. Later I suspected she planned the whole trip as a training exercise. She knew what I did not: the life of an innkeeper means constantly being interrupted. Into my temporarily undivided attention she poured useful information.

She would say: "I'll teach you a good way to balance the Inn's checkbook."

"Inquiries, whether written or telephoned, must be answered the same day."

"Be sure to alter the reservation chart the minute you take or cancel a booking. Otherwise, you'll never remember to do it."

"Above all, don't forget to deposit your IRS payroll deductions on the fifteenth of every month. The tax people have no sense of humor."

We were towing a U-Haul trailer behind my little green Ford Maverick. All went well with my overloaded vehicle until we were climbing the steep west slope of Gore Pass, just an hour from home. Suddenly a red light on the dashboard flickered on and off, warning that my engine was overheating. The car slowed to twenty, fifteen, ten miles an hour, even though my foot was floorboarded to the accelerator.

It didn't help when, from the back seat, the children chanted: "I think I can, I think I can . . ."

We were within a hundred yards of the summit — a spit of snow was falling — when four dainty deer stepped out of the woods, paused in front of my car and stared at us for a moment. I was so surprised I lifted my foot from the accelerator, causing my little car to lose every erg of its momentum. The deer, of course, wandered off. But my Ford refused to climb another inch.

"You'd better get out and walk," I sighed to Carolyn and the kids.

"OK, race you to the top!" Drew challenged Gordon. They were mighty tired of sitting anyhow. The dog yapped happily at their heels. Our load lightened by a couple of hundred pounds, the car slowly pulled itself to the top; perspiration soaked my armpits. Later, I would blame those deer for the expensive new valve job my car required.

As I pulled into the Inn I was totally exhausted; I promised myself a few days of relaxation before I started getting cabins ready for summer rentals.

The sight that greeted me, when I once again threw open the big pine front door, took away what little breath I had left.

The lobby carpet looked as if an army with muddy boots had tracked in and out. Stacked in the living room were mattresses, boxes of toilet paper, clean laundry in plastic bags — anything someone didn't know what else to do with. Unanswered mail was piled so high on the office desk it had fallen over, spilling catalogs and brochures onto the floor. The inside of the Inn was as frigid as a meat-packing plant; there was no reason to keep the big building warm during the off season.

In the kitchen, dirty dishes were abandoned in the sink and across every drain board, prep table and flat surface. I lifted the lid to one deep-freeze in search of something to cook for dinner; before me stretched bag upon plastic bag of what appeared to be chunks of ice. On closer examination I realized Myrtle had left her winter's accumulation of chicken necks and giblets.

In the rest of the world it was summer; shirt-sleeved people worked and played in balmy warmth. But high in the mountains spring had barely arrived. On the north side of the Inn three-foot snowbanks had yet to melt. Willows along the creek would not leaf out for another week. Dozens of unopened beer cans emerged from the melting snow. All winter long, guests had set them on their window ledges to cool. Sometimes they forgot about them; the cans slipped and fell to the ground below — disappearing into the soft snow. Beer, once frozen, is useless: watery, tasteless, flat.

I would always be astonished at how quickly, when the Inn stood untended for a few days, chaos reasserted itself. There was no use blaming Neil. He worked days; his only charge was to sleep in the chilly Inn at nights, to be sure the buildings were secure. All by himself the Inn must have been a big, cold, lonesome place. At this moment, he was off at work somewhere.

Gone were the warmth, the happy guests, the efficient staff. It began to dawn on me that a mountain lodge must be reinvented every season. As I sat, feeling a little giddy from altitude and surveying the mess, I thought back with regret toward the bridges I had left flaming behind me. My tacky little tract home on Oregon Street hadn't been so bad. I had a sudden urge to set up my typewriter. Maybe if I worked really hard I could finish my dissertation, tuck my tail between my legs, slink back to the university and plead with them to give me back my teaching job.

But my academic reverie lasted only a minute. My dad's genes or maybe his training kicked in. If C.D. Miller said he would do a thing he did it. So would I. And I said I would run the Inn. What a glorious fire you could make, if you could burn chips off the old block in the fireplace along with those bridges.

Hands thrust into my pockets for warmth, it didn't take very long to get bored with feeling sorry for myself. Suddenly I remembered. My dad would be here in two days! What would he say if he could see this mess?

The slump of my shoulders and the frown on my brow telegraphed my state of mind to Carolyn. "It's not so bad," she said cheerily. "I've actually seen it a lot worse." Cold comfort, offered in a helpful tone. She quickly riffled through the office mail, pointing out which items were likely to be important and relegating the rest to a "get-around-to" pile.

The kids were so excited about seeing snow they barely paused to bolt down a peanut butter sandwich. When I looked out my office window, I watched them frolicking in a dirty snowbank. Well, I had to start someplace so I found some clean rags, window cleaner and got to work.

"What are you doing?" asked Carolyn, when she saw me.

"Washing windows," I replied — a little miffed she should ask the obvious.

"You don't wash windows, especially now," she exclaimed.

"Why not? They're dirty."

"You delegate. You get someone else to wash the windows. You are the manager. And besides, you've got to learn to prioritize your chores. That window is far less important than answering this mail."

Delegate and Prioritize. Dumb, simple, those would become my two biggest management challenges.

Certainly the windows could wait until next week, when my new maintenance man — the very first employee I hired on my own — would arrive.

❅ ❅ ❅ ❅ ❅

Back at ASU, we called Maynard Jacob vanToon by the name of Jake (NRN). Fans of *Saturday Night Live* thought Jake looked like the madcap John Belushi, a comparison Jake encouraged. But football enthusiasts were just as certain he resembled defensive back Lyle Alzado. His Dutch-Mexican ancestry bestowed earthy, girthy virility. His curly black hair grew down into his sideburns and a Fu Manchu moustache was in progress. He liked to pull at its corners when pausing to think something through.

Jake — nobody called him Maynard or Jacob — asked me for a summer job, explaining he was ready for a change. After many years of effort, and more than a few false starts, he had finally completed his bachelor's degree at ASU. One of Jake's revolving majors had been engineering; he knew his way around a tool kit, was clever about fixing things. I thought his good sense of humor might make him a logical choice for maintenance man; the Inn's wacky systems needed to be tended by someone who could take a joke.

There was only one problem. Jake had been dating my buddy, Bridget. However, it was she who suggested that Jake might help me out. When I pleaded with her to come along, she was reluctant to leave her job in Arizona. Until that summer I was certainly closer to the statuesque, golden-headed Bridget than I had been to Jake. Evidently I was more uneasy about their separation than they were. They assured me they were mutually agreed that a summer apart would be a good idea. "Jake wants to get out of Phoenix, do something different, 'drop out' for a while," Bridge assured me. "Besides, we have an open relationship."

That summer I was to have a vacation from mothering. In a few days my sons were to fly to England with their father; my daughter was headed for Kansas City to visit her paternal grandmother. Before me stretched several weeks free from piles of dirty clothes, from carping at kids who had not completed their chores. There would be no blood feuds between siblings, no necessity to set a good example. Time cracked open for a couple of months, allowing me to indulge in the youth I almost missed.

While we awaited Jake's arrival, Father came up for a few days to help me plan the summer's projects; he left Mother with my brother Woodie and his family in Boulder.

One morning, as Father pushed a wheelbarrow loaded with two bags of dry cement toward the concrete mixer, he asked, "When's your sidekick supposed to arrive?"

"Monday, Dad," I answered.

"What did you say his name was?"

"Maynard Jacob vanToon. We call him Jake."

Later that same week, Dad asked again, "When is your new man coming?"

"Monday, Dad." Jake had called me the evening before, saying he was ready to leave Phoenix in the 1956 MG-A he had overhauled for the trip. Because the trip from Phoenix could be easily accomplished in two days, there shouldn't be any problem with a Monday arrival.

Several times, as he added yet another chore to my lengthening list, Father said, "Remind me to tell your new sidekick about..."

Or my father would say, "This is pretty complicated. I don't know if your sidekick can handle it." For a fact, I was worried that Jake might not live up to my father's expectations — few people ever did. I assured Dad we would go over everything on Monday.

When that Monday in June finally rolled around — Maynard Jacob vanToon did not. My father snorted in disgust.

I was a bit miffed Jake had not appeared, too. But I covered for my friend by explaining he was driving an old car and had probably run into some trouble.

Finally, about noon on Tuesday I heard the unmistakable roar of a sports car, its engine hiccuping just a little, as it pulled into the Inn driveway. A sunburned Jake apologized; his car had been acting up. So he had dallied along the way, exploring a dry gulch here, a mining town there, babying his rebuilt engine as it chugged across deserts and up mountains.

"Dad, he's here! This is Jake vanToon — the guy you call my sidekick."

My father barely looked up from the lamp he was rewiring, "Well hello, Tonto!" he exclaimed as he touched the rim of his hard hat, then lifted it like the Lone Ranger in greeting.

Tonto. The name stuck. To this day anybody asking for Maynard or Jacob or Jake or even Mr. vanToon is usually greeted by a blank stare because everybody calls him Tonto.

Fortunately, my father was pleased with the quick way Tonto learned the systems. As he examined a fuse box, Jake said, "My, that certainly is interesting, how you've worked out this breaker series. If the dining room lights go out you have to run all the way outside to the garage to flip the breaker." The enthusiasm in his voice belied the glint of irony in his eyes. For the next three days, as Tonto went over the Inn's peculiarities with my father, he repeated over and over, "Virginia, I am just *amazed*!" He explained that Father's systems were ingenious — Rube Goldberg couldn't have done better.

Father's heart was completely won over by Tonto's manic response to our mechanical wood splitter — an inspired device my father had personally imported after seeing one at work in Finland. At one end of a shaft a gigantic saw blade cut logs into lengths to fit the fireplaces. At the other end of the shaft, the operator could shove the side of the log into a screw, which grabbed the wood and pulled it toward two iron wedges, where it was instantly split apart. It was a mechanical wonder and labor saver — especially to anybody faced with supplying fourteen fireplaces and two wood-burning saunas. Tonto was delighted. He started splitting wood with the élan of John Belushi delivering a samurai thrust, accompanied by the power of Lyle Alzado sacking a quarterback.

"He'll do," said Father. "Tonto has *spitherinctum*."

Chapter 9

Life Among the Maidens

All of us were a little in love with Tonto that summer. Tonto really did like the Inn. He liked being in the mountains, he liked the crazy old buildings he was charged with tending; he liked me. And I liked him, more than a woman should like her best friend's boyfriend.

We had been friends for a couple of years back in Arizona. He knew me well — knew about the difficulties of my divorce, knew I had been virtually celibate since that time. Now, watching me nurse subterranean worries about my new job, where I was walking a mental and emotional tightrope, he had concluded that I was far too up-tight. He had taken it as a personal challenge to see to it that I loosen up and "get with it."

One evening, while we were listening to an LP record on my stereo, Tonto noticed I was rotating my shoulders, stretching my neck muscles the way women do when they suffer from a stiff neck. "I'm an expert at neck massage," he declared. "Let me loosen that knot."

There was truth in his advertisement. He began gently, rubbing the sore spot. Then he branched out the methodical finger pressure toward the muscles running along my shoulder blades. It was magical the way tension diminished at his hypnotic touch.

"Thanks a lot, that was great," I said after a while, pulling away.

"Shhh, it's nowhere near loose enough," he countered as my stereo emitted strains of the Moody Blues. "Stretch out on the floor and put your arms up at the side." He inserted a pillow under one shoulder.

I made a couple of half-hearted attempts to protest but the backrub just kept feeling better and better as it moved wider and wider, lower and lower.

It was crazy to become involved with someone ten years my junior, but maybe I was attracted because he was so utterly unsuitable. Any question of a long-term romance was impossible, especially because Tonto frequently stated his dislike of children. Maybe it was easier to venture a little fling, knowing that when my family came together again in the fall the affair would be all flung out. Besides, it had been so long since anybody had flirted with me, or shown me any affection, I was the proverbial sitting duck; to be truthful I didn't even try to fly from Tonto's clutches.

❄ ❄ ❄ ❄ ❄

But Tonto wasn't my only employee that summer. One by one, the girls I came to refer to as my Four Lovely Maidens began to arrive. Why four? To be truthful, I had yet to learn that almost everybody wanted a job in the mountains — or more precisely everybody wanted to be in the mountains. "Dropping out" was fashionable just then, even with people so young they had no notion what they were dropping out of. In those early days I had a hard time saying no to applicants. Consequently, I hired four teen-agers who had just graduated from their respective high schools in Arizona, Nebraska and Colorado. But I would have no problem keeping them busy because nearly every wall in the Inn could use a fresh coat of paint.

Norma (NRN) was the first to arrive. She was an energetic girl who belonged to my daughter's track club back in Phoenix. Norma was thoroughly sensible, resistant to peer pressure, and proved to be an efficient worker. I wouldn't exactly call her square, but soon we began to use Norma as a yardstick for measuring our attitudes and actions. We nicknamed her Norma Normal. I, for one, was grateful to have a resident reality-check because the summer promised to be far from average.

There was only one thing about Norma that wasn't Normal. Every morning she arose early and donned her track shoes to jog and sprint about ten miles along forest roads. Norma intended to use her spare time to train in the altitude. Barely anybody ran marathons in those days — let alone teenage girls.

At breakfast, while the rest of us ate in sleepy silence, Norma would exclaim, "And I rounded the corner, and there was a doe with two fawns. That was near the place that I saw the bear yesterday. Those pretty bluebells are beginning to bloom up along the Water Board road." In retrospect, Norma wasn't Normal at all.

Flossie Jean and Sally Sawyer (NRNs) hailed from Lincoln, Nebraska. To say that the Sawyer sisters were ebullient would be to downplay the nature of bubbles. Flossie had many charms, but the two largest were guaranteed to halt male admirers in their tracks. I admit I was envious of Flossie's round figure. "High I.Q., small bust-line," was but one of the derisive comments which had been directed toward *my* measurements in the past. Floss seemed to exude that certain smugness that comes with a well-rounded figure. She cheerfully ignored fellows when they ogled, leered or whistled — preferring to discuss her tennis stroke.

By contrast, her sister Sally's compact body was wiry, athletic tough. The challenge of the Sawyer sisters was to bring cheer to others, all the time, whether they wanted it or not. They fired off giggles in volleys, salvos, fusillades. Few could resist their infectious attitude. Their laughter was an epidemic that would infect the community for many years to come. When the two sisters got the giggles — which happened several times a day — rafters, floors and window panes rattled all over the Inn.

"Go for it!" yelled my niece Cheryl when she arrived from Boulder. The Millionth VW van chugged to a halt, the motor stopped, then it coughed and belched a couple of times for good measure.*

Cheryl had fitted out her van as a camper; its interior decor was somewhere between army surplus and harem boudoir. Blonde, zaftig, Cheryl generally wore peasant blouses tucked into her jeans. Although her giggle carried less volume than

* For seven years, the Millionth Volkswagen had belonged to the Inn. Indeed, it still had the Inn's logo painted to its sides. On the back quarterpanels were two small brass plaques my father affixed to it: "Millionth Volkswagen for Export. Honoring the Miller Family at Hanover, Germany, 1966." That year, my brother Woodie had decided to take his wife Barbara and their four children to Europe for the summer. When he told my dad that they planned to camp, the proverbial lightbulb went off in Father's brain.

"Why not stop by the Volkswagen factory in West Germany and pick up a van? You can drive it around Europe, then we can ship it back and use it at the Inn to haul skiers."

When the Elwood Miller family arrived in Hanover, they were very surprised to be greeted with great ceremony by Volkswagen management. They informed Woodie that his father had purchased the 1,000,000th VW for export. Volkswagen was very generous. At several cities along their route Woodie's family was housed in elegant hotels; local newspapers printed feature stories about the millionth van, which was hauling a typical American family across the continent, and then would become a ski bus. Eventually it was shipped back to the U.S. to become part of the Inn's modest "fleet." When Father finally decided to replace it with a new Ford, Cheryl pleaded to own it.

the Sawyer sisters', she wasn't a bit stingy with it. Her job was to man, or more properly woman, the office that summer.

Ultimately, the girlish shenanigans of the maidens would wear my patience. But for a neophyte innkeeper overburdened with present duties and future uncertainties, they provided welcome diversion.

Most of the time they were good workers, cheerfully followed suggestions and showed considerable resourcefulness about accomplishing their chores. Consequently, I made the fateful decision to work with them as peers, rather than from a position of authority. I wanted to be a "team leader" instead of a boss. When Tonto or my maidens urged, "Lighten up, Lady!" I did.

For some reason, the four maidens started calling me 'Lady'. I can't remember why, but it can't be because I was acting like one. Theoretically, I was old enough to be the mother of this gaggle of seething hormones — but I had taught freshman English to too many giddy students to want to assume the chore of parent-in-residence. Besides, the moment I shipped my kids off I left mothering behind for the summer.

Flossie worked with me in the kitchen, helping to feed a ravenous group that included Neil, who paid for his room and board. Cheryl's brother Andy was in and out. Floss could be pretty creative and loved playing with food. When packing a lunch for Neil or Andy, she liked to tuck silly notes between the cheese and baloney in their sandwiches; Neil had learned to approach his lunch bucket with caution. On one occasion Floss was folding up a note accordion style, trying to figure out how to insert it into a banana. She turned to Norma. "Do you think this is normal?"

"No, Flossie, I don't," Norma replied honestly.*

---

* One of Flossie's jobs was to brew sugar and red water for the hummingbirds. We had at least seven hummingbird feeders appended

Floss was relieved. She wanted nothing to do with being normal.

Besides Tonto, Neil was the only other man living at the Inn — red-headed, red-bearded, bespectacled Neil. The girls were certainly interested in the tall, well-muscled fellow, but he didn't have much time to play. Days he worked for my brother Dwight driving a road maintainer. Evenings he devoted to his new volunteer position as a fireman; he was very serious about it. Many evenings he attended drills or studied his smoke manuals.

In Neil's honor, we tried to attend all of the fires. A little town sponsors very few social events; fires were an opportunity to greet and meet. The first time they heard the siren, my four maidens were startled when I yelled, "Grab a six-pack, we're going to the fire!"

They soon learned why I chased fire engines. If we stayed at home, the next day someone at the post office was sure to say, in a stern tone of disapproval, as though a formal, engraved invitation had been ignored, "We missed you at the fire."

It was inevitable that the girls became intrigued with Tonto. To them he was the personification of the waning sixties — akin to the ragtag hippies their parents hated so fervently. Tonto had read everything Carlos Castenada had written. Tonto proclaimed, "I have no intention of living beyond the age of forty. It won't be worth it." As though to underline this vow, Tonto proceeded to taste, swallow, inhale, explore, drink, feel and experience anything or anybody within reach. If he

outside various windows around the Inn and the cabins. It seemed like everytime we got very busy in the kitchen some guest's kid would be at the door saying, "We need more hummingbird juice." So slothful and gluttonous were those birds, it's a wonder they didn't get too fat to fly. After I left the Inn I refused to ever hang another feeder for hummingbirds. Let the little pests fend for themselves.

had a goal that summer, it might have been the perfection of hedonism. After working hours, of course.

It was like living in Shangri-La, there in that mountain valley. We rarely read a newspaper or listened to the radio; reception was just awful. We were so far removed we were able to ignore the unfolding Watergate scandal in Washington.

Tonto was only too happy to play first fiddle in an all-girl orchestra. He declared he was glad to be out of Arizona, out of school and "out-of-sight!" The maidens and I gossiped about whether "out-of-Bridget" was part of the bargain. Tonto made no secret of the fact that he and Bridge wrote back and forth regularly, and talked on the phone. But both of them declared they were just friends, for now. My current position, as one side of a triangle, wasn't very comfortable.

My work rules were few. Number One was that no matter how hard or how long we played at night, everybody should be fit to put in a good day's work the next morning.

Most of the fun was innocent enough. Frequently we fired up one of the saunas. I can't recall now which of the maidens enjoyed being nudely co-ed and which pleaded modesty and joined us wrapped in a towel. I don't think we pressured anyone to shed clothing. After an evening sauna, we often formed ourselves into a circle in the pillow lounge for a "cluster massage." Each person was rubbing some portion of the next person's anatomy. I tried to keep an eye on who Tonto was rubbing where, knowing all too well where a little expert pressure could lead. I was pretty sure that the maidens knew what Tonto and I were up to. But in the absence of my acknowledgement of our affair, there was no reason for them not to consider him fair game.

The pinching, flirting, innuendo and teasing that punctuated mealtimes led inevitably to practical jokes. Stupid efforts like the shorting of Norma's sheets escalated into cramming Cheryl's van full of crumpled newspaper. That called for retaliation: transferring the crumpled newspaper to pack Sally's bathroom to the ceiling.

Sally's birthday was July 23. That day, Sally's assignment was to clean cabins. Cheryl and Flossie were determined to decorate the dining room for a surprise party, but they had to figure a way to keep Sally busy and out of their hair. I don't remember which girl came up with the idea, but they slipped into the rooms Sally was to clean, scattered cracker crumbs and ground them into the carpets so her vacuuming chore would be twice as difficult.

When she finally finished Sally charged toward the kitchen, full fume ahead. "You'll never believe what slobs people can be!" she uttered as she burst through the door — the guest at her own surprise party.

Another evening Floss and Sally crowded into the phone booth beneath the stairway to call their mom and dad back in Nebraska. Cheryl got the bright idea to squirt a dollop of whipped cream from an aerosol can into a letter envelope. She quickly opened the phone booth door, slipped the envelope along the door jamb and slammed it shut — thus causing whipped cream to shower the sisters. It's a wonder their parents' eardrums at the other end of the wire survived the resulting screams and laughter.

Flossie lived in perpetual fear that her pets, her cat Muffin and her little bird, would fall victims to pranksters.

Aside from predictable differences of opinion about music — Floss loved The Doors; her roommate Cheryl loved John Denver but hated The Doors — everybody got along well.

But I doubt any of us could have predicted just how far our hijinks would escalate.

Chapter 10

The Close Shave

"Lady, guess who asked Tonto to pop her cherry?" One of the maidens scurried toward me, breathless with the news that another of the maidens had requested Tonto to relieve her of the burden of her virginity. To be fair, it wasn't the sort of invitation many men would turn down.

Looking back, it would be nice to say that the inspiration for what ensued sprang from my solemn duty to protect the young woman's chastity. However, it's far more likely that my motive was the same as that of the other participants — pure green-eyed devilment. The quest for Tonto's favors had become a game. Each player worked hard to exclude the others from her objective — Tonto. However, in such emergencies, it was necessary to give up the solo strategy and band together.

Our first problem was to isolate the location of the tryst, a monumental chore considering that an empty lodge offers a literal hotbed of opportunity. The defloration could be taking place behind any one of about fifty different doors. In summer we never locked any of the rooms or cabins because keeping track of keys was just too much trouble. Obviously, we must search the Inn for the one locked door.

"Let's try Tonto's room, first," I suggested. He bunked in a little room that opened on the back side of the Balcony House, under the sod roof with the rabbit on top. Sometimes I wished that rabbit could tell me about the comings and goings to Tonto's room, but the bunny just sat up there doing his job: munching grass and clover so we didn't have to mow the roof.

Of course nobody was in Tonto's room, but there on his bureau stood two brand new aerosol cans of Mennen Shave Cream — menthol. "The perfect weapon!" exclaimed one of the maidens. We grasped the cans, yanked the tops off with our teeth like macho soldiers pulling the pin from a grenade, and brandished them as we rushed to resume the search.

Down halls, corridors, and along pathways we quietly padded, checking rooms and door latches as we went. I rounded a corner to spy one of the maidens standing at the end of a corridor, her finger pressed tightly against her lips in warning as she pointed to a room where spare mattresses were stored. She tried the doorknob, then nodded that the room was locked. Pressing my ear to the door rewarded me with the sound of moans and heavy breathing.

My keys were on my belt; I fingered the correct one. Who knows what we would find on the other side of the rough, old door? As I carefully inserted my master key into the lock, turned the knob gently, it's a wonder the couple on the other side weren't warned by the pounding of my heart. I knew very well that the hinges would probably squeak so I traded stealth for a frontal attack. I flung the door open and we burst through, yelling: "Found You!"

Our ambush was a complete surprise. Two pairs of eyes shot open in disbelief. The maiden's blouse was unbuttoned; Tonto's belt was loosened and his pants unzipped. But otherwise it appeared our cavalry charge arrived in the nick of time.

"Oh damn!" screamed the maiden.
"Oh shit!" cursed Tonto.

The rescuers leapt onto the mattresses like tag-team wrestlers springing into the ring. Having the advantage of surprise, we inserted the nozzles of the aerosol cans into her blouse and his Levis. It took but a moment for Tonto to wrench the shaving cream from my hands, pull apart the waistband of my jeans and return fire. No holds barred, this was as close to both love and war I had ever been.

Immediately, the mattresses were slathered with foam. Indeed the sparring, disheveled Tonto was sliding back and forth across the mattress like a 747 skidding along a foam-lined runway. The slick foam made it difficult to grab and hold onto any specific limb or piece of clothing.

If you have never experienced the sensation caused when a squirted wad of menthol shaving cream finds its way to a sensitive membrane, I invite you to imagine the fresh, yea acute, tingle of Mennen Menthol. If a "little dab'll do ya," envision the blast produced when a large foamy gob envelops a private part!

Tonto — smarting with pain — bellowed, sprang from the mattresses, fled down the hall and lurched out-of-doors. Zipping his pants as he ran, he looked like a Bacchus leading a troop of screaming *maenads*. Not even the sharp stones on the driveway slowed his bare and flying feet. In his attempt to escape he climbed into the van. However, in the few crucial seconds it took to fire up the lumbering red beast, the rest of us had time to slide the back door open and pile in behind the driver. By now the un-deflowered maiden had joined in the fray and was squirting shaving cream down Tonto's neck as he tried to drive. She then turned her nozzle on us. Soon the van ceiling, windows and seats were covered with a white coat of foam.

Carolyn Taylor's house was only a quarter of a mile away. Why Tonto chose to point the van in that direction soon became apparent.

As I recall, Carolyn was happily munching her dinner salad when we invaded her tiny house. We tried to explain — but our giggling, chortling, snickering, sobbing voices were too excited and choked to produce a coherent story. Our eyes were streaming menthol-induced tears.

"Carolyn, may I please use your bathroom?"

"Why certainly, Tonto," she replied to so reasonable a request. Whereupon Tonto calmly walked into her bathroom, locked the door behind him and turned on the shower. He stayed there for a long, long time. We could hear moans of pleasure as he rinsed shave cream from his — body.

When he emerged, a towel wrapped around his middle, he resembled one of those little brass buddha incense burners, or maybe a sumo wrestler. "Don't even *think* of following me into Carolyn's shower. She has no more hot water."

The time lapse had not lessened the sting of the menthol. By then the shave cream was refreshing our ears, noses, eyes, and worse — orifices never intended for the insertion of shaving cream. I, for one, was nearly dancing in pain. Consequently, when Tonto suggested we return to the Inn it was a quieter — if still fidgety crew — that piled into the van to head for the ample hot water supply at home. Tonto tossed his pungent clothes over his shoulder, toward the back seats.

I remember that as we passed one small cabin, bright lights shone from its window. Through it I saw the elderly couple who lived there — friends of my parents. She was knitting, he was reading *National Geographic*. I was enormously grateful when they didn't look out their cabin window to notice us that chilly evening. How to explain our towel-wrapped driver, his writhing passengers, a van full of foam?

❄ ❄ ❄ ❄ ❄

I was grateful a few hours too soon. The couple in the cabin, a retired high school football coach and his petite wife, took a little exercise every morning by walking to the post office. As a rule, Tonto just waved to them as he drove by, en route to and from picking up the mail.

But on the morning after our melee the husband stepped toward the van as Tonto returned to the Inn and signaled him to stop. "My wife is feeling a little dizzy. Could we ride with you?"

What could Tonto say? He could hardly reply, "No, because C.D. Miller's van is full of menthol shaving cream." Tonto hastily rolled down the window on his driver's side of the car in a vain attempt to refresh the van with odorless mountain air. Alas, the minty scent of menthol does not die so easily.

No sooner had the pair climbed into the van than Tonto became acutely aware that wispy little stalactites of shave cream were suspended from the headliner. The car's windows looked as though they had been smeared by a Halloween soap prankster. At the feet of his dignified passengers, a messy pile of men's underwear exuded the bracing aroma of menthol.

"My, my, what happened here?" asked the wife.

Tonto started to turn to them, fighting madly for a plausible explanation, but for once found himself unable to say anything. Although the rest of the short trip was made in silence, Tonto reported that through the rear-view mirror he could see the elderly couple's eyes rolling left, right, up, down — taking in remnants of the evening that came to be remembered as The Shaving Cream Mass-a-cree.

Chapter 11

The George Armstrong Massacree

It was raining on the fateful day when George Armstrong (NRN) stormed into our lives. Flossie, Tonto and I were piecing carpet scraps together on the floor of the Rec Room, bent on creating a gigantic sunburst which we intended to glue to the ceiling of my apartment. I wanted my space to be a cozy, comforting cocoon I could crawl into after a hard day's work; walls, ceiling, furniture and even the floors would be covered with carpeting. In those days of Peter Max billboards and black-lit psychedelic posters, it didn't seem that a carpeted cell made of fuzzy remnants was such a goofy idea. Besides, I could hardly wait to see people's faces when I invited them to visit my "pad."

Floss and Tonto had their heads together, planning the palette for the rays of the fuzzy mural. It seemed that we had more green scraps than any other color, a problem when it comes to sunbursts.

"But sunrises aren't green!" objected Norma Normal.

"Well, they can be," countered Tonto. "I've seen them lots of times." Nobody wanted to know under what circumstances.

Summer was almost over. Fortunately, demand for cabins as weekly rentals was high. I could truthfully tell my father that business was good.

Tonto was hurrying to finish my redecorating project before two impending arrivals: those of my children, rejoining me after their summer vacations, and of Bridget. I could sense my life was about to change — a lot. I was a little surprised to realize I could hardly wait to see the children again. Bridget was something else.

A few days earlier Tonto had broken the news to me, as gently as such news can be broken. "Bridge has decided she wants to join me for the winter. She'll be here right after Labor Day."

"Is that what you want, too?"

"Yes, it is." I couldn't fault his honesty.

"What are we going to tell Bridget?"

"Nothing. She knows all about us."

"Oh, thanks a whole lot. Who else have you told? When you decide to let it all hang out, I'm hanging out there, too. Can't some things stay private?"

"You'll see," he tried to assure me. "We'll all be friends again."

The prospect seemed about as likely as an end to the Viet Nam War.

I stared at the fuzzy sunburst, intended to cheer up my space. But as I watched Tonto piecing the carpeting together I felt like the sun was going down, not up. Always, I knew Tonto was a passing fancy in my life. Why had I allowed myself to get into this mess? I wasn't sure which was worse, to lose Tonto or to give up my friendship with Bridget. Bridge and I had been such good friends. So what did I do? Helped myself to *her sidekick*, Tonto. Sharing has its limits. My intention that summer had been to get things in order at the Inn. The

Inn was slowly shaping up, but my life seemed more disordered in August than it did in June.

"Lay in some of that orange stuff next to the green," advised Flossie over her shoulder, busily trying to keep up with two projects. Every few minutes she disappeared into the adjacent kitchen to stir a kettle of spaghetti sauce; this was the day of our annual spaghetti potluck dinner. We didn't make spaghetti, we declared it: "Come for potluck spaghetti. Just drop by sometime during the day and throw something into the pot," I explained when I invited friends and family.

When they asked what kind of ingredients, I replied: "Oh, just a can of tomatoes, a whole chicken, Italian sausage, meatballs, whatever you like to find in your spaghetti." The pot simmered on the back of the stove all afternoon, its tangy aroma promising an especially delicious dinner. One by one, donors arrived, added a link of sausage or some whole mushrooms, sampled and corrected the sauce to their own taste, then went on their way until six o'clock, when we would all gather to eat it. By some miracle, the sauce was always delicious.

The rain continued to pound away. When the outside door of the Rec Room swung open, the first thing we all saw was a black umbrella in the act of collapsing. It was followed by a shortish baldish fellow wearing a tan trenchcoat over a polyester suit. In those parts, a necktie forewarned of a flatland salesman — slick, probably. But this man looked vaguely familiar.

"Hello, Virginia. Surprised to see me? George Armstrong?" Indeed I was surprised to see George Armstrong, the mild-mannered accountant, husband of a professional woman I had first met at a women's lib meeting in Phoenix. "Got a room for the night?"

"Well, this is a hotel," I assured him. I didn't know the man well; we had exchanged pleasantries for a few minutes at a couple of parties.

"I had business in Denver. Thought I'd see what you're up to." His glance roved over the rear end of my blue jeans as if he were assessing a spread sheet. "I'd like to take you out to dinner."

Tonto smirked out of the side of his mouth George Armstrong couldn't see. I showed George to a room, told him it would cost him sixteen dollars for one night. "But I can't make it for dinner. We're having a spaghetti party tonight. You're welcome to join us, on the house. Besides, one of our guests, Hal Richardson, is giving a cocktail party down in his cabin. You would be welcome."

"This will be fine," George smiled warmly, as he looked around his room. "Quite a place you have here, really something. And it's great to see you again." He gave my arm a meaningful squeeze, as though we were the longest of lost buddies.

"You'll excuse me if I get back to our project." I hastily backed toward the door.

"I need to work over some figures" — he pointed to his briefcase — "then I'll come down and join you."

When I returned to the Rec Room I found Flossie and Tonto rolling all over my sunburst, wrestling and sharing fits of giggles. Tonto and Floss must have sensed my foul mood because they quickly cut the horseplay and got back to business.

"Remember me? George Armstrong?" mimicked Tonto.

"Honest, I barely know the man," I protested.

"Sure, Lady. Just how barely have you known him?" Floss and her sister Sally went into gales of laughter at Sally's bad pun.

"I can't figure what's going on," I said. "From what I know of his wife Ruth, she's the jealous type. She told me once that she'd scratch the eyes out of anybody who tried to take George away from her. And from the looks of her manicure, she could get the job done."

From time to time the other maidens dropped by to suggest artistic improvements — to Tonto. The maidens were miffed with me. They hadn't been invited to Hal's annual martini party, which had become something of a legend around the Inn. The girls suspected that I had told Hal not to invite them. And they were right. My patience with the maidens was growing very short.

Just before lunch that same day I had lost my temper. When the maidens started their chores each morning, they frequently shoved a tape into the PA system so their favorite cacophony could follow them around. Although I liked the Beatles and Rolling Stones well enough, an eight-track tape by somebody called the Amazing Rhythmaires was jarring my nerves. Those damned eight-tracks would run forever unless somebody pulled them out of their misery. The dissonant racket got to me; I yanked the Amazing Rhythmaires from the PA deck, hooked my finger through the tape, gleefully spooled it right out of its cassette and bit the tape in two. The maidens were outraged when they found me stomping the tangled tape on the gritty office floor. When I turned to them, nasaled my voice and whined out "Rocky Mountain High," they rescued their John Denver tapes and hastened to hide them.

But in that moment, I learned something. Although team leading had looked good on paper when I first learned about it back at the university, my unanticipated tantrum had earned me something akin to respect in the maidens' eyes. Suddenly I understood that an essential element of being a boss is the prudent administration of terror. I resolved to assert more authority when I hired my winter staff.

With the exception of Sally, who applied for work the following winter, the enthusiasm of the maidens for their chores had slackened precipitously as their thoughts turned back toward school. Maybe they had been my "training employees." But they weren't being trained. I was.

When George appeared later, having removed his necktie and pulled on a collegiate-looking woolen sweater, a bottle of wine was tucked under his arm. "Jaunty," I thought to myself. "This man is trying to look *jaunty*."

"This is a particularly nice wine that we discovered while we were touring Napa last summer," said George, reading the label to me.

"You and Ruth? How is Ruth? And do tell me all about the children."

He changed the subject back to wineries, as I led him down the slippery path to a cabin called the Alpine Fir, trying to dodge raindrops that still dripped from the pines.

"Come down to the Fir for some martini juice," was the way Hal Richardson usually issued his invitation. Each year, the Richardsons gave at least one martini party.

Inside the Alpine Fir, I introduced George to the Richardsons, emphasizing that his *wife* was a friend of mine.

"Glad you could make it, George." Hal, as usual, was expansive and welcoming. "Want some martini juice?"

Hal was an American History teacher in a Phoenix high school, but his real enthusiasms were military life and Western history. Hal was also a Colonel in the U.S. Army Reserve. About six feet tall and solidly built, he was rarely seen without a very large, reasonably smelly, cigar in his mouth. He would practice sucking in his gut and gruffing up his voice to Colonel volume before leaving for his two- or three- week stint at Leavenworth or some other army installation. While he was gone his wife and two children preferred to spend his absence with us in the mountains, certainly it was cooler than the oven they left behind in Phoenix.

"Har-old!" his wife Connie would entreat whenever Hal's barracks vocabulary threatened to outrun polite conversation. She served as a good governor on his spicy vocabulary. Petite, neat, Connie always wore make-up and looked properly turned out even when we went for a hike or worked in the garden.

Most people think of martinis as a sophisticated little cocktail, to be sipped from a chilled glass with a tall stem. Hal preferred the clunky restaurant glasses we furnished in the cabins. They didn't matter, because to Hal, a martini was something to be generously poured into a big glass full of ice. Vermouth? He'd give you some if you wanted but he never touched the stuff. He'd even issue you an olive if you asked for it. Hal himself was a purist. His martini was, quite simply, a tumbler full of gin.

George hesitated but accepted the glass. "I don't usually drink." We didn't pay any attention to his remark — at the time. George seated himself beside me on a couch, closer than I would have preferred.

Tonto was sitting near the creekside window; he looked at me curiously, then at George, as though trying to figure something out. Well, let him. It had never crossed my mind to try to make Tonto jealous, but at that moment it didn't seem like a bad idea.

My days were always strenuous and long, so I was happy just to be sitting down, relaxed. With gentle rain falling outside, it was pleasant chatting in front of the fireplace.

Hal's parties were the only time I ever drank martinis — a dangerous libation, in my opinion. As usual, Connie had a rum and coke. Three or four other guests, Carolyn and Tonto rounded out the group.

"Nice bolo," George commented to Hal, admiring his turquoise and bear-claw bolo tie.

"Got it on the reservation," said Hal.

The subject veered from Indian craftsmanship to Indian wars, Custers Last Stand and such.

I wasn't paying attention. My mind wandered from wondering if dinner was coming together in the kitchen, to speculation on what George Armstrong was doing here, to thinking about what would happen when Bridget arrived.

Every time one of the tumblers looked low, watchful Harold would tip in a bit more Beefeaters. George Armstrong seemed to be an agreeable fellow; he made some witty comments as he pulled on a pipe filled with one of those tobaccos so aromatic it smells like somebody torched a gunny sack full of vanilla beans.

I gazed out the window toward the creek, roiled with brown water from the storm. Why so many guests requested the Alpine Fir year after year astonished me. True, anyone who rented this cabin could sleep to the soothing gurgling of a mountain stream. But because the cabin's original foundation consisted of no more than railroad ties strewn across the boggy creekbank, it tilted ominously, as though creeping closer to the stream, preparing to jump into it. Every year the undulating floors slanted more precipitously. The last time I was in it I noted that the water level in a glass on the kitchen table was visibly askew. In fact, the floor's slope had come to resemble a ramp — you could teach beginners how to ski on a gentle slope like that.

Somehow the conversation got around to the subject of our saunas. George's eyelids flew open with interest. "Always wanted to try one of those things," he said.

"That's easy," I offered, not thinking of the possible consequences, "We'll build a fire and all have a sauna before bedtime."

An expression somewhere between a smirk and a leer crossed George's eyes. "I didn't bring a bathing suit."

"Oh nobody wears bathing suits," I assured him. "In fact, nobody wears anything."

"Keen!" George exclaimed.

"I think I'll just excuse myself to go check the sauna fire," said Tonto.

Before long, we went back into the Inn to eat spaghetti. My martinis had mellowed me; I thought to myself with relief, "So far, the evening has been pleasant enough." The maidens, Neil, my nephews Andy and James plus other friends and assorted relatives were already enjoying dinner. Wisely, Flossie had decided to go ahead and feed the younger crew; they could get mean when they were hungry. They were downing beers and laughing hugely at Neil's expense. He reported he had fallen out of bed the night before — and couldn't figure out how it happened.

"Thought you were Captain Kirk, did you? Did you try to step into the Transporter?" ribbed Andy.

The martini squad sat at a separate table. We drank the rest of George's wine, then opened a bottle of chianti. The communal spaghetti was very good. As I was downing a bite of sausage, I felt something bump against my shin. I wondered if my dog Pepper had broken the rules and ventured into the dining room. No, as usual the little fellow was napping with his nose on his paw just outside the entrance to the forbidden dining room. I suspected George was playing footsie under the table but couldn't be certain until the arrival of nudge number two. Tonto saw me flinch. He hastily wiped a napkin over his mustache to disguise a grin.

"Please stop that," I muttered under my breath.

George leaned toward my ear and said, "You know, Virginia, I came for more than just a nice chat."

I had been propositioned! Right there in my very own lodge, at my very own table, in front of my very own friends. And I didn't like it one bit. "Too bad, George, because that's all you're going to get," I replied as firmly as I could without raising my voice.

During the custard course, George's fingers definitely clenched themselves around my knee. I tried, not very successfully, to pass off my violent jerk as a harmless belch. But I rose, left the table and busied myself in the kitchen where the maidens were doing dishes. I offered to help clean up.

"We wouldn't dream of coming between you and your company," grinned Cheryl. "Hey, when you've got a little action lined up . . ." She gave me a studied wink. "We can handle everything. Can you?"

Were the maidens throwing me out of my very own kitchen? Denying me the right to hide out there? Yes, they were. At that moment dried-out tomato sauce bonded to dirty dishes looked far more attractive than an evening in the company of George.

When I returned to the table I took a deep breath and said, "I have a wonderful idea. There's a bit of daylight left. The rain has stopped. Let's all go for a walk!" If booze was George's problem, an invigorating walk would probably sober him up.

"Come over to my house for coffee," offered Carolyn.

"How about that sauna?" George reminded me. How could I have been so dumb as to plant that bit of information in his brain? I had been hoping nobody would mention the sauna, that its fire would go out if it wasn't stoked. That way, it would be too cool to use later in the evening.

"Oh, you can't get into a sauna on a full stomach," I told him, truthfully.

Tonto jumped up. "Tell you what, I'll stoke it so you can have a nice, soothing sauna before bedtime." Why did Tonto have to be so damned helpful?

"Then all of us can have a nice sauna together. Right?" I added.

"Wonderful, wonderful," agreed George. So Tonto, the Richardsons, Carolyn and I started out the door into the refreshing evening air. Tonto fed the fire, then caught up with us a few hundred yards up the road.

Why is it that short men always hang onto your arm in that possessive manner? My upper arm was numbed in the vise of George's fingers. Was it Hal's martinis? I didn't think so. The man hadn't had an abnormal amount to drink; he didn't stumble or slur his words.

Like Carolyn herself, her house was a perfect miniature. While the coffee perked, she set out mugs on the quaint old stove, a gift two friends had enameled it a bright coral shade as a housewarming gift. It served as a coffee table. We admired her lovely view, of the mountains in the waning light. I had tried to motion to Tonto that he should sit next to me on the couch, but before I could complete the signal George plunked himself down and pulled me next to him, edging closer until his pipe breath was right under my nose. But even as he stroked my fingers, I could see that George was looking past my shoulder, eyeing Carolyn's slender form as she bustled around her kitchen. George leaned over to me, turned his mouth so it was practically atop my nose and said, "Don't worry about Ruth. We have an open marriage, you know, an understanding."

"Whose understanding? Hers or yours?"

"You really turn me on, Virginia."

It was time to turn up an ace: "I'm sorry, but I am already romantically linked to someone else. Call it 'going steady,' if you like."

I expected an argument. Instead, George sprang to his feet and took the short distance across Carolyn's tiny living room in one leap. This time he leaned his face into hers. Almost immediately I heard Carolyn say in a voice as loud as she ever used, "I certainly would not."

It was as though a hummingbird had flown against her plateglass window; that suddenly the conversation died. George did not seem to notice; he turned his head to ogle Connie, who was as respectable and married as a woman can get. It was then that I finally grasped the fact that I had a real pest on my hands. Desperately, I tried to figure out what to do with this guy who seemed hell-bent to haul any female body within reach into bed. We couldn't leave him there with Carolyn, so I suggested, "Let's all walk down to the Swiss House of Fondue, have a beer and show George how lively night life is in Hideaway Park. Who knows? They might even have fixed the pinball machine."

Although it was getting very dark, we managed to sidestep puddles as the clean, damp air cooled our cheeks. George slouched along, his hands thrust deeply into his pockets.

The smoky pandemonium of the Swiss House — the liveliest local bar — seemed to revive George. On a Saturday night, the Swiss House was always crammed with litters of ski bunnies even in the summer. We ordered a pitcher of beer.

On the juke box, Jerry Lee Lewis was rocking out "Goodness, gracious, great balls of fire!" Even if we had been able to hear each other, it was plain that George was not very interested in keeping up his end of the conversation. He looked down the bar, sizing up every stool's worth of fanny. "Who's that?" he would inquire about every woman who came through the door.

Tonto had been to the Swiss House enough times to know that on a Saturday night, fights were just waiting to happen. He yelled admonitory briefings to George over the volume of the music: "Oh that's Big Hilda. She has a brown belt in karate," or "That's Tillie. Her husband is the butcher down at the market."

Seeing nothing that looked available, George returned his attentions to me and whined in my ear, "I came all of this way to see you — "

Suddenly I had what seemed at the time to be a brilliant idea. "Tell you what, George. Up at the Inn I have four beautiful maidens who work for me. Two of them have decided they don't want to be maidens."

He bounded to his feet, grabbed his jacket and ran out of the bar without uttering another word, abandoning his half-finished beer.

Tonto and I looked at the Richardsons, whose shoulders relaxed in visible relief. What a strange man!

Finally, Tonto began to squirm a little. "Maybe we'd better check on things at the Inn . . ."

We walked back under the watchful eyes of thousands of stars, stars that refuse to reveal themselves except in the mountains. The crunch of the gravel road beneath our feet was loud in the night.

As we rounded the corner, we saw that the Inn was lit up like an ocean liner. Someone had gone into every room, turned on every light switch. We drew nearer. I heard screams. Tonto and I broke into a trot.

As the old front door slammed behind me I heard squeals, wails and the banging of doors. Girlish heads began popping up from in back of couches, peeking out from behind draperies.

One of the maidens ran screaming down a corridor, long hair flying out behind her. George Armstrong charged around the corner in full pursuit. "Just a minute. Stop. Let me tell you how wonderful . . ."

I felt as though I had stumbled into an old Marx Brothers movie featuring a bimbo-chase by Harpo.

George's cornering maneuver failed; barely able to escape banging into a wall, he veered and set out after another maiden, Sally.

"Lady, he's after us!" wailed Sally, as she shot up the stairway.

I caught George by his arm. "George! What are you doing?"

"You said some of them didn't want to be maidens!"

"Ever hear of the word subtle?"

I looked to Tonto. "Is the sauna still hot?" It had been my experience that a hot sauna — far from arousing an ardent male to heights of ecstasy — more often took the starch right out of him.

"George, follow me and take off your clothes!" I ordered. George, who was looking up the stairway, contemplating pursuit, turned to me with revived interest, perked up and said, "Follow you anywhere."

"Come on, everybody. Let's have a nice sauna." I hoped the maidens and everyone else would join us. I wanted a big group, a big protective group in that hot room with George and me.

"Not us!" the girls shrieked and vanished. Tonto and Hal agreed to come along — probably out of fears for my safety. Connie and Carolyn had long since made polite excuses.

I showed George out the Rec Room door and across the driveway to the Balcony House, as far as the dressing room of the men's sauna — in the summer we declared it co-ed. I excused myself to pick up my bathrobe and a few toiletries. It was nearly midnight and I was exhausted. But suddenly, dollar signs on the electric bill flashed before my eyes so I had to trudge through the Inn and turn off all of those damned lights. George must have thrown open every door in search of the maidens.

As I finally sat down on a dressing room bench to take off my shoes and socks, I inhaled the sauna scent: hot, scorched wood mixed with steam.

When I opened the door to the hot room it was impenetrably steamy. George had thrown too much water onto the hot rocks atop the oven. I hated it when people steamed up the sauna before we had a chance to enjoy its dry, penetrating heat.

Through the fog I could barely make out George, who stood — naked, of course — with his feet far apart. Tonto and Hal were sitting on different levels of the stair-stepped benches. I laid out my towel and stretched out on my stomach, enjoying the sensation of being prone in the nice hot room. We tried to chat and relax, the way people should in a friendly sauna. But George kept pacing back and forth and babbling.

"Lay off the steam, George," ordered Hal in a military tone. "Keep your hands off that dipper."

I glanced through the steam and did a double-take. There was something different about George — something physically different.

Although he wasn't very tall, he was singularly well endowed. He had one outstanding physical characteristic — indeed one that reached his knees. Hal saw the expression on my face and nodded that he had noticed, too.

When George's back was turned I motioned to Tonto, spreading my hands apart as though I were telling a fish tale. Tonto's belly heaved with laughter.

The next time George's back was turned, Tonto made a motion like a gigantic clock pendulum, swinging slowly.

Life isn't fair. George couldn't show *it* off; he couldn't even bring *it* up in conversation.

Fortunately, George was finally winding down. The combined effects of altitude, alcohol and the sauna had taken their toll. Or maybe he was satisfied now that we knew about —

and presumably could appreciate — his big secret. In any case, he pulled on his pants, yawned and stumbled back to his room — rendered harmless at last.

❊ ❊ ❊ ❊ ❊

The next morning, I learned that all four of the maidens had slept in Tonto's room for protection. I approved, although normally that arrangement would have been equivalent to setting the fox to guard the chickens.

"Lady, how could you do that to us?" accused Flossie as I arrived for breakfast.

"Inspiration. Total inspiration," I responded. I wasn't a bit sorry that I'd sicked George on the maidens. "He must have been a whole lot drunker than we thought he was. Betcha he won't show for breakfast."

Floss shook her head. "Nothing around here would surprise me."

Just then, George Armstrong did indeed stroll in. He appeared, all things considered, to be in reasonably good shape. "What's for breakfast?" He looked bright, chipper and awake — until Floss plunked down hash browns and eggs in front of him that weren't just greasy — she had lubricated them.

Quickly, George looked away. "I really shouldn't drink," he commented.

"No, you shouldn't!" chorused Flossie, Tonto and myself.

George looked at his oozing eggs. "Guess I'm not very hungry after all."

Half an hour later, looking very pale, George paid his sixteen bucks plus tax, got into his rented car and drove away. "Say hi to Ruth," I called after him.

But I had learned something. It is a truth universally acknowledged that a single woman in possession of a nice ski lodge must be in want of a lover.

Chapter 12

They're No Angels

"L lady, come quick. There's a motorcycle gang coming up the road." Norma Normal came racing into the backyard where I lolled near the creek on a chaise lounge, reading the Sunday Denver Post. Although it was late August, the maidens were stretched out in their bikinis, trying to layer on one more coat of tan before school started.

"What if it's the Hell's Angels?" She looked genuinely terrified.

"Roger," I yelled, jumping to my feet and bolting down the driveway.

About a dozen noisy motorcycles — mostly Harley-Davidsons and BMW's — drove slowly, parading up the road past the Inn, then doubling back to our parking lot. Male riders dismounted, stomped down kick-stands, unzipped black leather jackets. Two men emerged from the pack, strolling toward me on long, lean legs as they unbuckled and doffed their helmets.

"Roger, Russ, 'bout time you got up to see me!" I immediately embraced Roger. Of medium height, he sported a neatly trimmed brown moustache and beard over his very young face. Six inches taller, two shades darker, maybe ten years older, was his roommate Russ Stratton — his hair thinning ever so slightly. Beneath their leather jackets both men wore western-style shirts with pearlized snaps in lieu of buttons.

Roger declared, "Our bike club was doing the circle drive up through Estes Park over Trail Ridge Road to Grand Lake. We couldn't go by without stopping." Even Norma could see that these trim, well-groomed young men were no Hell's Angels.

The maidens were aflutter at the sudden arrival of so many "cute dudes." And all on motorcycles! Although the bikes weren't elongated "choppers," I could see the girls had romantic visions of the popular movie *Easy Rider*.

My niece ran up to Roger. "Remember me? Cheryl?"

He gave her a brotherly hug. "I haven't seen you since you were practically a baby. How are your folks?"

Roger turned to his friends, waved for them to follow him. He assumed the role of tour guide, leading his buddies around and through the Inn, pointing out this and that.

Roger Roeck was one of Father's "family" of employees. Originally from Illinois, he first came to the Inn eight years earlier when he was in high school — as a guest. When Roger announced his plans to enroll in the School of Hotel and Restaurant Management at the University of Denver, Father persuaded him to do his "intern" stint at the Inn. Because my parents hadn't the foggiest notions about how hotels were managed by people who did it professionally, Roger — through his "book learning" — taught as much as he learned. My parents were very fond of the clean-cut, industrious young student.

My mother frequently quoted from Roger's font of useful information about institutional management. Household Hints from Roger included: "Roger says we should always wash the windows with newspapers instead of paper towels. They work better and they're lint free."

"Roger told us to get these walk-off mats from the linen service to protect the carpets from kitchen dirt and grease."

"Roger says we should keep exact records of kitchen expenses."

After he graduated, Roger worked for various restaurants in the Denver area. But he remained interested in the Inn, often providing expertise and labor on kitchen remodeling jobs.

Two summers earlier my father, his brow creased, his lips slightly pursed, had pulled me aside. "Sit down, I have something serious to tell you." From the tone of his voice, I figured one of my nephews had been busted for protesting the war or smoking pot.

"What's wrong?"

Because he could think of no gentle way to break the news, Father blurted, "Roger is a homo!"

I frowned for the moment it took a moment his announcement to register. "You mean homosexual?"

"Yes. Some workmen who were staying here overheard Roger talking to someone, I don't know what was said. But they told me they suspected Roger was a homo and told me about it. Your mother and I were shocked, but when we talked it over, we decided it must be true. Remember we told you about this girl named Judy who was working in the kitchen the year Roger interned? She was crazy about him but he wouldn't give her a tumble. He broke her heart. Now we understand why."

"That would account for it."

"And we thought it was strange when Roger's father sent him a subscription to *Playboy*. I never heard of a father doing that. Maybe he was trying to interest his son in girls."

The news about Roger's sexual preference *did* surprise me. I too had wondered why Roger never had a girlfriend, but it had never crossed my mind that he might be gay. The limp-wristed stereotype certainly did not fit Roger; macho came more readily to mind.

Perhaps I was less shocked than my father on first hearing the news because I knew several people who acknowledged their homosexuality — both men and women — at the university. In the roiling sixties gays were demanding liberation right along with women and blacks.

"So, did you talk to him about it?" I asked.

"Do you think we should have confronted him, told him we know he is a homo? Should we tell him we don't want to see him any more?" It was one of the few times I ever saw my father truly perplexed.

"Gay, Dad. They like to be called gay. Of course you shouldn't send him away."

My father could not tolerate bigotry toward any man — or woman. Raised on a dirt-poor Oklahoma sharecropper's cotton farm, he had somehow avoided becoming a redneck. He told me once that he couldn't stand to see how cruelly Indians were treated where he grew up. So he decided he would always respect anybody, as long as they deserved it. On many occasions, my father had extended himself on behalf of black teachers and students when he was with the Wichita school system. I treasured his attitude.

But when he learned about Roger's sexual preference Dad's broad-mindedness was put to a severe test. After all, how many years had my father taught Methodist Sunday School? Dad had never dealt with a homosexual face to face — or thought he hadn't. Only recently had gays dared to "come out of the closet." Roger's gayness was totally alien to my father — the man who claimed he and my mother were both virgins on their wedding night and had remained loving and faithful for over fifty years.

Father continued. "Your mother said, 'Well, Roger's no different today than he was last week. We liked him then, didn't we?' So Trudy and I decided it doesn't make any difference to us. But we're worried about what guests might think."

"Dad, as long as Roger doesn't make any big deal of it, I don't think you have a problem," I advised.

So Dad resisted the notion of discussing "things" with Roger; they remained friendly.

As for me, I liked Roger, was interested in him and his gay friends. Fun-loving and enthusiastic, they were a fascinating array of fellows.

While Roger and company explored the premises, Cheryl clued the other maidens into the facts of life about Roger and his friends. "No!" sighed Sally, whose eyes had clamped onto a dark, long-locked youth with devastating china-blue eyes.

Except for Cheryl, gayness was new to the maidens, too. If the girls thought of gays as mincing queens, they weren't prepared for these handsome fellows who looked like cigarette models on billboards.

"Neil here?" called Roger as his troop tromped back over the bridge planks, their motorcycle boots sounding like stomping trolls over the Billy Goats Gruff. "I think I've found a motorcycle for him."

"He's down at the firehouse. He'll be right back." Neil still intended to spend his summer wages on a motorcycle. Roger, who knew everything there was to know about motorcycles in Denver, was helping him locate one.

The bikers pulled sandwiches and beer from the panniers of their bikes, settling down along the creek for a picnic. I took advantage of Roger's unexpected visit to pick his brains. Russ pulled up one of our old folding metal chairs, sat on it backwards, resting his arms as he pulled on a long-neck beer. He lit another link in his day's chain of cigarettes.

"Myrtle wants to work fewer days next winter. Four, I guess. I'm trying to figure out what to do about the other three. Got any ideas?"

"Hire me." I could tell from Roger's astonished laugh that he had been thinking about asking me for a job.

"Are you available? What about your job?"

"Russ and I are going into business for ourselves, the leather business. A part-time job for me would help us swing it."

I was excited, and relieved, to think Roger might come to work for me. Although Myrtle was an excellent cook, Roger's catering ideas would provide an interesting counterpoint to Myrtle's humble fare. I could learn a lot from him.

"Are you going to make motorcycle clothes?" I asked Russ.

Russ smiled and thrust his tattooed arm forward. "See!" Around his wrist was buckled an impressive, brutally handsome cuff; multiple rows of formidable silver studs shone menacingly in the sunlight.

"But Roger, what about Russ? And your other — friends?" I gestured toward the bikers. "Won't you be lonely?"

"Not a problem. I'll be here part-time. There'll still be plenty of opportunity to party in Denver."

Soon Neil returned; he and Roger put their heads together to talk about dirt bikes. Norma looked anxiously toward Neil, then turned her wide questioning eyes to Cheryl, "Neil? Is he?"

Cheryl laughed and shook her head. "Definitely not."

Weather changes fast in the mountains. A breeze, a black cloud, a sprinkle of rain sent the men racing toward their bikes to fasten snaps, straps, zippers and buckles. In pairs they mounted their bikes and rumbled down the road toward Denver.

Sally turned to Cheryl and sighed. "What a waste."

Chapter 13

Staff Re-shuffle

"Virginia. Got a proposition for you," declared Tonto.
I was sitting in the office, typing a response to a request for brochures. Cheryl would leave soon; she planned a trip to Europe. I was handling a lot of the correspondence myself. As September approached our post office box was stuffed with letters asking for brochures, prices, but especially Christmas reservations. It seemed I spent more and more of my time in the office.

When I looked up I noticed Tonto was not dressed in his grungiest pants, the out-at-the-knees jeans he wore to change oil in the bus or crawl beneath the drain of a sink. His hair was parted; he had attempted to comb his wiry buffalo curls into subjection.

"Little late for propositions, don't you think?"

"No, no, not that. I want to apply for the job of secretary."

"Secretary?" I was stunned. Male phone operators were just beginning to make themselves heard at the other end of the line. I'm not sure I had ever witnessed a male secretary in action.

"I'm not kidding. I was talking to Carolyn. I can type, I can spell, I can add. I'm pretty well organized."

I had assumed that at the end of summer Tonto would want to find a job somewhere else. I also figured my life would be a lot simpler if I weren't reminded, daily, of happier times.

"So far, you've been able to keep the reservations in order yourself. You won't be able to do that now that people are calling, asking about winter. As soon as Dwight finishes that road — and I understand there are only a couple of weeks' work left — Neil will want his maintenance job back."

It was clear Tonto had thought this thing through because he argued his case cogently: "What about your dissertation? Did you know that it's important to me, and to Bridget, that you finish it?"

"Tonto, I appreciate your suggestion. But after what's been between us — I just don't know whether that would work out."

"You need me. I mean to protect you from all the distractions around here, to look after your business so well that people won't bother you. You can set up your typewriter, away from the telephone, and get to work.

"Virginia," Tonto took my hand and put his arm around me in a protective manner. "Can you think of any reason in the whole world why we can't be friends and work together? We had a wonderful summer. We'll always remember it that way. Your children are coming back and I know you'll be very glad to see them. You know how I feel about kids."

"But what about Bridget?"

"Talk to her. The biggest thing she's worried about is how you feel about her. She really wants you to be her friend again."

"We'll see," I promised.

At first I wasn't in a mood to "see," at all. What a silly idea, to have a male secretary! But as I sat fingering a large stack of mail that needed answering, I wondered, could I be accused of discrimination? Against a man? Then slowly a smile forced my lips outward, upward, pushing up my cheeks. A male secretary. A Big Male Secretary! The role reversal was deliciously irresistible, even in the face of complications to my private life.

The inevitable round of "What do you think?" phone calls ensued: to Father and Mother, to our former secretary Anita, to Carolyn. Of course none of them knew of my personal reasons for feeling awkward. Perhaps I hoped someone else would veto Tonto's scheme because the idea of a male secretary was so — untraditional.

To my surprise, everybody thought it was a *good* idea. "Doesn't hurt a man to have experience like that," said my father, delivering the clinching vote. "Tonto makes a good impression over the phone."

Immediately, Tonto set about learning the office chores. I enjoyed referring to him as "my lovely male secretary." In acknowledgement, he would pull up a pant leg and wiggle his ankle in imitation of an effeminate gesture.

He quickly set himself to the job of penciling reservations on the chart, replying to correspondence, filling out bank deposits. He was pretty good at it, too.

"I must be getting weird," said Neil at breakfast one morning. "I think I fell out of bed again. When I woke up, there I was in the middle of the floor."

"Did you drink much beer last night?" I asked, knowing he had been to a meeting of the volunteer firemen — occasions when the first item of business was the passing of the six-pack. "Maybe you'd better put your bed back on the floor."

"Anybody else fall out with you?" teased Tonto, as he glanced suggestively toward the maidens.

Neil shrugged. "Probably I was just sleepwalking or something. I'm catching a ride to Denver, gonna pick up my motorcycle today."

When he brought it back, Neil was bursting with pride as — one by one — he loaded the maidens behind him for a spin down the road. Flossie honored his new machine with her favorite accolade: "Spiff." When Neil parked his new motorcycle next to his battered old Jeep, it looked slick and beautiful. He would stand there, admiring it, tweaking it occasionally with a wrench.

Of course he rode it through the brisk August mornings to his construction job — about twenty miles distant.

At the Inn, we were already working on the enormous job of getting the place ready for winter. Roger had suggested that we inventory the stock on hand in the kitchen. Floss and Cheryl started counting cans, jotting numbers on a clipboard. A little radio provided their requisite background racket.

"Disco," snorted Flossie. "I hate disco. Disco is ruining rock and roll."

I was supervising the arrangement of jam and jelly on the shelves when Tonto appeared in the kitchen — summoning me to the phone. "Dwight wants to talk to you. He says it's important and he didn't tell any jokes. I get the idea that something's happened to Neil."

Any time Dwight didn't take time to preface a conversation with a story, it had to be serious. When I grabbed the receiver Dwight's voice was grimly matter-of-fact. "Virginia, Neil has had an accident." Immediately my thoughts flew to the new bike. But I was wrong. "He drove my Caterpillar scraper off the side of the mountain."

The scraper was used to adjust fills and cuts in the road, to smooth it out. It would be difficult to imagine somebody losing control of one. "How could he do that?"

"I don't know. I can't understand it myself. I thought maybe the bank caved in, but it didn't. Nobody saw it happen. He might have tried to jump clear when it went over or else he was thrown free. He landed next to a log which evidently took most of the blow when the scraper rolled over him. If it had landed on top of him — it would have been tap city, you know, all-she-wrote."

"How is he?"

"He's alive, but he's pretty bad."

"When did it happen?"

"This morning, about ten. The county ambulance took him to Granby. They called a helicopter from Denver and flew him to St. Anthony's. The Doc at the clinic doesn't think he'll make it. He's in a coma."

"Not make it?"

By now, the maidens had gathered on the lobby side of the registration desk. Somewhere far in the distance Donna Summer wailed.

Dwight gave me hospital details, where to call.

"What about his family?"

"I called his father. They said they'd call the hospital. They may fly out. Sure hope they make it in time."

By the time I hung up, the maidens were standing at the office counter, looking as though someone had slapped each one down the line, in turn, across the face.

"Neil, oh no, not Neil," said Sally — as the color beneath her tan drained from her cheeks. Flossie inhaled her sobs; Cheryl ran outside to seek the comfort of her van. Norma and Sally put their arms around each other.

"Let's not jump to conclusions," I offered lamely. "Maybe he'll make it."

Everything fell silent, as though someone had put a big lid on the Inn. At dinner we poked at our food, regarding it listlessly through thickened eyelids. No giggles from the Sawyer sisters pealed through the kitchen. Each time the phone rang we glanced at each other with dread. Tonto hastened to answer, but it was always someone asking about Neil. The news spread through Neil's friends at the volunteer fire department as quickly as if the rural area still had party phone lines. But the incessant rings never brought further word.

The next morning we called Roger, who was generally a good source of information, and asked if he could find out anything. "Of course," said Roger. "One of my motorcycle club members works in the emergency room."

At about eleven Roger called back. "He's still critical — but stable. They said he's fully conscious now. It looks like he'll make it; he's not paralyzed. They don't think he has any broken bones."

Good news!

A couple of days later, Flossie, Sally and Cheryl decided they could no longer rely on second-hand information. Early one morning they struck out for Denver in the Sawyer sisters' little yellow Vega to see for themselves how Neil was faring.

We were stunned when, before lunch, they returned with Neil himself in tow. Tonto, Carolyn, Norma and I suppressed our natural urge to leap forward to embrace him. He was a shocking sight — gaunt, his chin immobilized in a neck brace. Beneath his mane of crimson hair his face was lacerated, bruised; he had two black eyes. The color had vanished from his fair cheeks; his eyeballs raged scarlet from broken blood vessels. He was so sore he could hardly walk. "Don't know how I'm going to get up in that bed of mine," he said. "Just couldn't hang around that hospital any longer." Neil winced when he tried to make his habitual little dippy-doo gesture; his body language signaled the conversation was ended and he was going on to do something else.

The fellow was young and strong. Miraculously, in just a few days, he was out in the garage, sandblasting paint off the hood of his old Jeep.

"Neil, how'd you manage to roll that scraper? Do you remember the accident at all?" I asked.

"I don't know what happened," he said. "I guess I blacked out. But they ran all kinds of tests on my head. Couldn't find anything wrong with it. Sure would like to get back on the job."

Dwight offered to let him work in his shop, but didn't want him to drive his machines. "Ginger. It's not easy to drive a scraper off the shoulder of a road. Something's wrong with the guy. I just can't have him operating my equipment. He's a talented mechanic, though."

Neil decided not to go back to work for Dwight.

"Take a few days, Neil," I advised. "You can start your maintenance duties here when you feel better."

Neil's father and mother arrived from Arizona, expecting to find him still in the hospital in Denver, happy to learn he was out of the hospital so soon. His folks were nice people — modest, unassuming types. But then that didn't surprise me. His father was solid, capable, with the kind of assurance that comes from being respected and respectful. His mother was friendly, interested in how the Inn was run. A shy sparkle in her eye reminded me of her son's flashing grin. The family was originally from Wyoming, so they decided to drive up to Rock Springs to visit Neil's uncles and aunts while he was recuperating.

I was enormously relieved when Neil recovered, apparently fully. The young man was so pleasant, so able, so tuned in to my father's strangely engineered equipment systems. I remember hoping that my own sons would turn out as well.

One evening over dinner, Neil told us the worst part of his ordeal came when he was being airlifted in the helicopter. Half-conscious, unable to speak, he heard the medics and nurses agree: "Doesn't look like this one's gonna make it."

Autumn, 1973

Chapter 14

The Great Peach Massacree

Stars spangled across the sky as we sat in front of a roaring campfire, gazing up through spires of swaying pines that moaned softly to the tune of a gentle treetop breeze. We were camped high in the mountains, maybe 10,000 feet.

I glanced from face to face in the light of the campfire. These not-very-happy campers clutched their bellies and belched audibly, competitively. Everybody was suffering — and it was all my fault.

We huddled closer to the fire. "Probably freeze before dawn," commented Neil. "But if anybody gets cold, I'll come over and breathe on you. That'll warm you up." From beneath his red moustache he exhaled a fair imitation of a dragon, the steam of his breath issuing into the frosty night air.

The cold boulder I sat on offered no padding; my fanny was numbed like a foot that "goes to sleep." My own stomach churned. And I dreaded tomorrow, when Bridget would arrive from Arizona. To top it off, everybody was having a huge joke at my expense.

"While you're at it . . ." my father had remarked two weeks earlier, "Go over to Grand Junction and get a van full of peaches for the deep freeze." Every fall, my parents drove to Grand Junction, about 200 miles west of the Inn, to buy delicious peaches that grow along the Colorado River. Mother would freeze them; all winter long my dad made fresh peach ice cream for the delight of his guests, then regaled them with the story of how he personally had fetched the fruit.

"Hey, anybody want to go to Grand Junction and get peaches? We can go camping," I yelled when I hung up the phone. The departure of the maidens had left the Inn's atmosphere deadly quiet, dull. The suggestion was met with great enthusiasm and was quickly dubbed "The Peach Massacree."

Neil, apparently recovered, was eager to go. Tonto was up for it. I figured a trip would help me get my mind off Bridget's impending arrival — which I anticipated as enthusiastically as I would a migraine.

My children had just returned from summer with their father; I wanted to treat them to a little trip, have some fun with them before school started. Tonto was right. I was happy to see those three towheaded scamps; summer's vacation from motherhood had made me realize, even though they frequently infuriated me, they were my buddies. From time to time I would glance at their freckled faces, as pleased as if they had been returned to me from Never, Never Land.

Roger and Russ, hearing of the expedition, scrambled to join us. On the phone I said, "Rog, I'll make some of my famous Mexican turkey *mole*. It's yummy — the sauce has chili, peanut butter and chocolate in it. You'll love it." I welcomed an opportunity to prove to Roger that I was a pretty fair cook myself. I would prepare the food ahead of time so all we had to do in camp was heat up the stew.

"We'll meet you at the swimming pool in Glenwood Springs," promised Roger. The enormous outdoor swimming pool would make a logical rendezvous, as well as a pleasant stop along the way.

It was a treat to swim in the naturally hot water, which bubbles right out of the mountain. We romped for a couple of hours, bobbing and ducking in the huge swimming pool. My kids practically jumped the diving board limp while I relaxed in the scalding therapy pool.

It was late in the afternoon when we left the pool to find a place to camp. "I think I know where there's a Forest Service campground," said Roger. We followed Rog and Russ in their VW beetle up a gravel road. They must have been mistaken, because as the sun sank lower, I abandoned hopes of setting up a camp where wooden tables and outdoor privies would be available.

"Mom, I'm hungry," complained Gordon.

Rog signaled a stop, jumped out of his V-dub and ran back to us. "Don't think my memory served me right. Maybe we'd better make camp the first good place we come to." In about a quarter of a mile we spotted a grassy glen.

Neil rigged up a table so I could heat up the dinner. "I'll take you camping anywhere," I commented. He responded with his little dippy-doo of assent and went on about the business of making himself useful.

In the gathering darkness, aromatic fumes from my *mole* sauce boiling on the Coleman stove permeated the night air. The kids hung over the hissing burner, inhaling spicy vapors; they missed the Mexican food they loved so much back in Phoenix. Everybody bustled to set up tents, roll out sleeping bags and tidy up gear before daylight was completely extinguished. Ravenously hungry after their swim, they pestered me, "Is dinner about ready? It smells fantastic."

Finally, as the turkey simmered in thick, maroon sauce, I spooned it over rice, sprinkling a few toasted sesame seeds on top. It looked really good; I reflected this was as gracious as living could get in a primitive campground.

My first inkling anything was wrong was when long, skinny Russ bellowed, sprang to his feet, jumped in the air and leapt a trajectory clear over the campfire as he dove for a plastic jug. "WATER!" he screamed. He chugged six huge swallows, wiped his mouth with his sleeve and roared, "Virginia, what the hell did you do to this stuff?"

When I looked to the others, I saw tears squirting from their eyes; I saw fingers clutching throats; I saw tongues hanging out.

"Mom," said Drew pitifully, "I can't eat this stuff."

Indeed the only firmly loyal person was my son Gordon, who always bragged no food would ever be hot enough to melt his iron pipes. He declared he loved it and helped himself again. In fact, Gordon and Neil launched an obnoxious contest to see who could stomach the most fire. Quietly, Keith and Drew poked through my camp gear in search of peanut butter for a sandwich.

My mother once joked, "In the innkeeping business, you eat your mistakes." One taste of that *mole* and I, too, sneezed, choked, coughed and gagged. The roof of my mouth was afire. But my pride forced me to wear a brave face, so I gulped as much of the lava as I could bear.

Had we been anywhere near civilization, I'm sure we would have buried the stuff and gone to McDonalds. Ever the food analyst, Roger began to grill me. "Where'd you get the chili powder."

"I couldn't find any *mole* mix, the kind I bought in Phoenix, so I concocted it with the chili powder at the Inn. The stuff in the two-pound can."

"Virginia, I know for a fact that can has been on the shelf at least ten years. Maybe more. Myrtle never uses it. How much did you put in?"

"Oh, I just guessed. Ordinary chili powder is usually so mild. I added extra, because I know this gang likes spicy food."

Roger frowned. "Probably the chili underwent some kind of chemical reaction — call it spontaneous combustion if you like."

"Spontaneous combustion. I'll have to make a note of it in my fireman's manual," chimed in Neil. "Might prevent future disasters."

Russ said, "Maybe you should package the stuff. If you can guarantee something will get stronger as it gets older, you can sell it."

About the only person who didn't put in a dig was Tonto. He was uncharacteristically quiet, perhaps uncomfortable for the same reason I was — Bridget's impending arrival.

This was not a crowd to politely ignore such a blunder. While they ate, sluicing the turkey down with all the water, beer, milk and soda pop in camp, they serenaded me with a chorus of jibes: "Lady, where'd you learn to cook — in an iron foundry?"

"Anybody want to take some chili to bed with you? To keep your feet warm?"

Had I cooked a perfect meal, it would long ago have been forgotten. I didn't, so it became the stuff of legend — gurgling, belching legend. With every retelling, the chili got hotter.

In a perverse way, the blisters on the roof of my mouth comforted me. Tangible pain took my mind from dreading tomorrow — when Bridget would re-enter our lives.

❈ ❈ ❈ ❈ ❈

The next afternoon when Tonto backed the van into the Inn driveway it smelled like a jam factory. I've never eaten a fresh Georgia peach, but it couldn't be more luscious than one from Western Colorado. The fragrant, juicy, ripe, sweet, tangy fruit irritated chili blisters lingering in our throats. But they tasted so good we ate greedily; by the time we got home the chili and peaches were brawling along the darkened tunnels of our digestive tracts. Add the curves of mountain roads, and we wore bilious green faces as we stared from the windows of the Inn's red bus.

No sooner had Tonto killed the motor than Bridget's blue and white van, her beloved Volkswagen, pulled right up to our van — nose to nose. My heart sank. It was face-the-music time.

"Great timing!" she yelled when she saw us, waving enthusiastically. She unfolded her long, shapely legs and slid to the ground. I couldn't have been more aware I was thirty-seven years old, disheveled, smelly from camping; whereas she was twenty-four — tall, slim, gorgeous and fresh as a mountain spring.

Tonto jumped into her embrace. "Have a nice trip?" he asked. It hurt to see the delight in his face.

"Great, no problems at all." Her strawberry blond curls billowed as she ran toward me, tickling my cheek when she stooped to give me a hug which I didn't return.

She held me at arm's length, by both of my shoulders, "Hey, you still my pal?"

"Sure, sure," I squeezed the words past the lump in my throat. "'Scuse me, Bridge, Drew isn't feeling too well. All those peaches, you know." I wanted to be somewhere else. Anywhere else. "See you later, I know you two have a lot to talk about," I called as I fled up the back stairs toward my quarters.

Children have their uses, when it comes to excuses.

From an upstairs window I watched as Tonto took the wheel of Bridget's van, driving them to the apartment he had rented half a block down the road.

Mercifully, Tonto took Bridge out to dinner so the children and I had the evening to ourselves. I dreaded the confrontation I knew was in the offing.

The next morning I started to "put up" the peaches. The ripest ones would become jam. The rest I would freeze. In the walk-in refrigerator twelve bushels of peaches awaited me. Good to keep busy, I thought to myself.*

I was blanching peaches when I heard Tonto's voice; he was showing Bridge around the Inn, pointing out the projects he had accomplished that summer. My urge was to flee, to hide in the walk-in. But it was full of peaches.

They strolled into the kitchen. "Hi, need some help?" volunteered Bridget.

"No, I'll make out just fine."

"But I want to help."

Tonto slipped away, leaving us alone. Damn his eyes.

I sighed. "You really don't have to do this. You must have a lot to do, getting your apartment fixed up and all."

"Please, I want to help." She was firm. Next she would be stubborn. When Bridge went from firm to stubborn her mind was made up. I don't remember a single instance when she ever changed it.

"Very well." I handed her a colander and a clean dish towel so she could pat the peach fuzz dry.

Silence. More silence. I searched long and hard for a neutral topic, finally asked, "Do you like your apartment?"

---

* It isn't very difficult to freeze peaches for later use. All you have to do is wash them, drain them, arrange them on a cookie sheet, then put them into the freezer for a couple of hours. When they are hard they won't freeze to each other when you drop them into plastic bags. Then, when you are ready to use them, take as many as you need from the freezer, allow them to thaw part way. The skins will slip right off. They can be sliced and eaten with a little sugar or diced into small pieces to flavor ice cream.

"I really do. It's very nice." She laid out peaches on the cookie tins in precise rows. A librarian by trade, she was precise about everything. "Virginia, we're still friends, aren't we?"

"Sure, why not?"

"Jake . . ." it sounded so strange to hear somebody call him that, "OK, I forgot to call him by his new name. Tonto thinks you're worried I'll be upset about your summer together. He thinks you blame yourself for what happened."

"Well, shouldn't I? I mean I have two perfectly good friends and I get right in the middle of it."

She came closer to me, smiling firmly. "Did you have any fun?"

I glanced up at her, looked her in the eye for the first time. "Yea. Yes, it *was* a lot of fun. Probably more fun than I've had — maybe ever. Could be why I'm reluctant to give it up."

"Well, it doesn't have to end if you don't want it to."

The peach I was peeling slipped from between my fingers, dropped to the floor and slimed its way under the stove. "You mean — you want to *share* Tonto?" I pointed a finger toward the front office where I heard him pecking away at the typewriter.

"If that would make you feel better."

Not sure I was hearing what I was hearing, I dropped to the floor, took my time fishing the peach from beneath the stove with a long-handled spoon. Finally it squirted back out — covered with black-speckled stove grime.

As I slowly got to my feet I blinked at Bridge. I was astonished to see she was perfectly serious. "I don't think I could handle that, Bridge. But gee, you sure are a sport to offer." I started to laugh. I couldn't help it; the thought of us as a *ménage à trois* was — preposterous.

And I kept on laughing. I laughed until tears ran down my cheeks. I laughed until I had to squeeze my thighs together to control my bladder.

Bridget laughed too. She braced her long back against the jamb of the dining room door and chuckled. "Just thought I'd offer."

Tonto sauntered to the kitchen, unsure whether he should be anxious or relieved at the sound of our raucous laughter. "What's so funny?"

Bridget put her finger to her mouth to shush me.

"You'll never know."

The air had cleared. Puzzled, Tonto shrugged and went back to work.

"Brid-get," I snuffled, "I don't think I'm quite that liberated."

"No?"

"Maybe I'm a fifties person who just can't get used to sixties notions here in the seventies. Let's just say — that's *way* more than I can handle."

We peached the day away. We gossiped; I told her about the Shaving Cream Massacre and the George Armstrong Massacree. She brought me up to speed on friends back in Arizona, winked as she confided her summer had been eventful, too. We peached and patted and tasted and froze.

I was vastly relieved. "I'll get over it. I knew all along what I was doing was just a lark. But it smarts all the same. My mind will be occupied, getting this place up and running by Thanksgiving." I waved my hand to indicate the mess around me.

"From the looks of things you could use help from somebody who's organized. Why don't you hire me as your head housekeeper?"

"I can't pay you librarian's wages."

"Didn't expect you to. My coming here is an adventure, just like Tonto's."

Now I had a head housekeeper, too. Why was it members of my future staff had a way of finding me, instead of the other way around?

Toward the end of the afternoon Bridge put her arm around me. "You want to know what's the most important thing to me?"

"What, Bridge?"

"That we stay friends. We were such good friends. Sure, I decided to come out because Tonto wanted me to. It sounded like everybody was having so much fun. But the real reason I came was because I wanted to be with both of you."

"I'll try to keep that in mind."

Chapter 15

On Top of It All

"How's that dissertation coming?" asked Father, phoning from deep in the heart of Texas. In late August my parents had driven their camper south to McAllen, where they planned to spend the winter. Before I could reply he plunged into what was really on his mind.

"While you're at it . . . " Oh dear, here it came again. What would be my next assignment?

"Put a new cold roof over the room."

"A cold roof? What the heck is a cold roof?"

"Just build a new roof over the old one, leaving air space in between. Cold air will keep the snow from thawing and freezing so the roof won't leak all the time. Those gigantic icicles won't build up and you shouldn't have to shovel it again, ever."

I had to admit the roof was a problem. Every spring the roof over the dining room — and the bedrooms above it — leaked, causing disgusting little black puddles to trickle onto a guest's bed or into a suitcase. I had already been annoyed the previous April when an inebriated guest, complaining about a wet spot on his mattress, woke me up at midnight, insisting I change his bedding.

Addition by addition, Father had simply widened the expanse of roof, lengthened it, patched it and unfurled another roll of roofing felt. Snow piled up on the nearly flat surface. Then heat from the building thawed it; water ran into little cracks, froze, expanded, thawed again. Eventually rivulets soaked into the wood, rafters, insulation and sheetrock. Water puddled through the paint in search of a pristine bedspread and sometimes made it all the way down to the dining room below — adding extra flavor to the soup.

On the outside of the building icicles as big around as a man dangled — menacingly — from the eaves.

Although the problem was undeniable, the thought of such a huge project was daunting.

"Can't it wait a season, Dad? There's so much to do around here. Besides, I thought *I* was supposed to be running this place."

There, I'd finally said it.

But he hadn't heard me. "You've got both Tonto and Neil. Those fellows can take care of it."

"Have you forgotten, Dad? Tonto is supposed to be a secretary."

"Not enough for him to do, yet. Send him up on the roof half days."

"Dad, I'm not sure I want to send Neil up on the roof. What if he has another spell, or whatever he had?"

"Has he fainted or anything?"

"No."

"Do him good. Help him get his confidence back." I could just see my little father sweating away in ninety-five-degree Texas heat, "engineering" the Inn's cold roof via long distance.

"Dad," I wasn't going to agree so easily. "Maybe we need a roof, but I have three kids starting a new school, I'm trying to write a dissertation, I need to hire a staff for winter. And we're out of money. Besides, I don't know anything about cold roofs. Dad, I have enough to do."

"I'm just trying to help," he said in his hurt-tone voice. I knew that tone, knew he would see to it that I was the one who would end up feeling guilty if I didn't give in to him.

There was no stopping him. "Nothing to it, nothing to it. Just go to the lumberyard in Denver and buy two-by-fours and four-by-eight plywood. Neil and Tonto can take care of the whole thing. You stay on top of it, go up there and see they're keeping busy, but they can handle it. I'll drop a set of plans in the mail to you this afternoon. You aren't afraid of heights, are you?"

"Of course not," I lied.

"We'll get a cashflow loan from the bank. Do it every fall. I'll get back to you about that."

"What about *your* book, Dad? Shouldn't you be spending your time on that?"

"It's coming fine, I've written four chapters so far." I sighed as I hung up. Would my dad's reservoir of energy never drain?

As if rebuilding the roof didn't offer enough complication, in his next call Father ordered: "And while you're at it, re-do the waterfall in the dining room. Go next door and see Bill Cullen. He'll fix it up." Bill Cullen was our neighbor — a mellow neighbor, very unlike the TV game-show host of the same name. Our Bill couldn't be bothered with annoyances like telephones. Occasionally someone would phone for him at the Inn and we had to run next door to fetch him. I don't recall that we minded. Tall, thin, good-looking, he sported a dense sandy beard. His income came from several rental properties he had acquired and remodeled. More artist than carpenter, he was what my father called "an independent cuss," who avoided working for other people. But occasionally, if a project interested him, he'd agree to do it.

On a camper trip cross-country, my father got the bright idea of having a waterfall in the dining room. He and Mother were having a romantic dinner one evening at a Howard Johnson's restaurant when his eye fell on a small waterfall splashing in one corner of the room. Enchanted with this bit of indoor plumbing, Father resolved to build one in his lodge. He hastened home to lay up his own waterfall.

That first fountain was not one of Father's "engineering" successes. Unfortunately, the water poured straight down, like in a shower stall with no curtain. When Dad turned on the circulating pump during dinner, guests within three tables fled like picnickers before a lawn sprinkler; the adjacent maroon carpet was perpetually soggy.

Resigned, I trooped across the driveway to ask Bill Cullen if he would consider remodeling the waterfall. Bill pondered a minute, then said, "I've been thinking about building a concrete boat. This will give me a chance to practice."

"Sure, Bill, a concrete boat. Sure." When he noted my puzzlement, he reached a skinny, freckled arm toward a shelf, taking down a book. He showed me a couple of pictures of boats. He proposed to build our waterfall just like a boat's hull — only concave instead of convex. Somehow the idea of building the hull of a boat upside down in one corner of our dining room, then sluicing water over it, didn't seem too outlandish.

While the roof was being hammered above him, Bill knocked out the old waterfall. Then he and his girlfriend Candy (NRN) started laying up new rocks. Strong, blond, *Playboy*-centerfold-stunning, Candy manned the cement mixer and was the best-looking hod carrier any of the fellows had ever seen. While the weather was still warm enough, Candy wore her standard work uniform, a bikini. Neil and Tonto — up on the roof — took frequent scenery breaks; they reported the view from above was magnificent.

Bill would sight by his upheld thumb, move rocks, study which way the water would trickle, call to Candy for a palette of cement, then scoop the "mud" onto a trowel and spike it into place with the élan of a sculptor.

He expanded the pond at its base, then angled an interesting, weathered tree trunk in front of the rock work. The effect looked promising, as though a little mountain creek were skipping over a fallen log. Bill pointed out where potted ferns could be positioned.

I kept a close eye on Bill's progress but postponed going up on the roof to check on Neil and Tonto.

From the advantage of far-away Texas, Father said, "And while you're at it, go down to the Bank of Winter Park and see that new banker. Name's Lightfoot. Get a cashflow loan." He made it sound as simple as though he were sending me to the hardware store for a pair of hinges.

"What should I say?"

"I'll give you some numbers. Write this down." I jotted some figures as Dad rattled them off.

The idea of asking for a loan was nearly as intimidating as going up on the roof. Somewhere in my youth I was taught that nice girls don't ask for money.

Reluctantly I walked toward the bank, which was on the highway about two blocks from the Inn. In those days I got nervous every time a teller checked my balance, ever fearful lest I had added wrong and there was nothing in my account.

That was the first time I met Dennis Lightfoot, the new bank president. "Hello. I'm Virginia Cornell, C.D. Miller's daughter." I hoped my forced smile didn't give me away.

Dennis rose from his chair, extending his sizable paw in greeting. And he kept on rising because he was a very big man. Dennis looked just like what he had been — a champion wrestler who had put on some pounds now that he wasn't in training. He laughed easily, a deceptive laugh that his erstwhile wrestling competitors might have misjudged as belonging to a really nice guy, an easy mark. In his high school days, Dennis was probably still laughing uproariously when he slammed opponents to the mat and half-nelsoned them. On his desk was a picture of himself with a little girl. When I asked, he said she was his daughter, Tracy.

"What can I do for you?"

"We need a cashflow loan to get us through until ski season."

"How much you need?"

"Five thousand ought to do it. At seven percent, no points." I glanced at my note.

Dennis emitted a rippling little murmur that arose from somewhere near his navel. It rumbled into a chortle as it worked its way up his throat. As it erupted from beneath his moustache he threw his head back and allowed his gigantic bellow of amusement to explode its full impact against the exposed beams of his office ceiling. Then he took another drag on his menthol Salem.

"That's what your father told you to ask?"

"Yes sir," I replied, conscious that it felt odd to call somebody "sir" who was more than a decade my junior. For the life of me, I couldn't fathom what he found to be so funny.

When he got the heaving of his belly under control and was wiping the tears from behind his glasses, he pushed a small stack of papers across the desk: "Fill out this financial statement and tell your father it'll cost him eight and a half percent. A hundred and fifty up front."

Chastened, resentful of being caught in the crossfire between two men and sure that I had flunked some kind of litmus test, I trudged back to the Inn. What was so funny about asking for a loan? Eventually, Father completed the negotiation with Dennis over the phone — without me.

In time, I would come to know Dennis much better. A few years later he finally told me what the big joke was that day. He said that my father was one of his first customers at the Bank of Winter Park. Although only about half the size of Dennis, my father's presence was so forceful and intimidating to the young banker that when the little bald man strode into the bank office to dictate — with considerable authority — the terms of a loan, Dennis was so taken aback that he gave him what he asked for. In the years Dennis was bank president my father was the only person who imposed — and received — such favorable terms. Dennis was never able to summon the courage to turn Father down — in person. But, said Dennis, he found it easier to deal with C.D. Miller over the telephone.

❄ ❄ ❄ ❄ ❄

I just couldn't keep putting off going up on the roof much longer. Mountain roads don't bother me much. While being hoisted aloft on a ski lift, a person looks uphill, not down. But a rooftop . . . I kept remembering my brother's advice, "Never let the cook get you by the balls." Increasingly, I feared that roof would get me by the balls.

Around the time the plywood was delivered my dreams became very turbulent. In one of them I stood on the roof as its surface started to shrink. For each inch the area of the roof shrank, it lifted me up until I was standing on about one square foot at the height of the Washington Monument looking down, down, down to jagged rocks in the creek below.

Yet I was determined not to let Neil and Tonto know how terrified I was of going up there. After all, those brave fellows were lifting sheets of plywood into place, hauling rolls of roofing on their shoulders up ladders, trimming the eaves as they leaned over them, constantly risking life at the edge, so to speak.

The morning I planned my first climb to the roof, my heart was pounding like a snare drum in a parade. My stomach threatened to pump backwards. From his perch on the eaves above, Tonto was all gung-ho enthusiasm. "If you're afraid, I'd be glad to climb up the ladder behind you."

"No thanks, I'll manage." Suddenly I realized the fear of heights was nothing compared to the fear of having someone behind and below staring up at what I considered to be my all-too-ample rear end.

With a deep breath, I started to climb. Hand over hand, foot over foot, my knees shakily obeyed my orders to ascend. Just above towered the juncture I dreaded most — the spot where it was necessary to step from the ladder onto the roof. I dared not look down. But I did; at that exact instant a large arm from above grabbed mine beneath the armpit. My stomach felt like it was hurtling down an elevator shaft. In fact, I was too frightened even to scream. But I recaptured my composure in time to thank Tonto for his help.

As I stood up I felt as though I couldn't raise my chin above the level of my knee. I hated to stand because my legs were as elastic as rubber bands. And I couldn't look straight ahead because peripheral vision caused trees to slide by at dizzying speeds. I wanted to drop to my hands and knees and creep like a baby.

I expected the roof surface to be hard and slick but it felt like spongy, gritty carpeting. So, in addition to worrying about falling off, I had the uneasy sensation that at any moment the roof might cave in, sucking me into a bedroom below. With my luck, I'd fall right in the middle of a copulating couple.

With what I hoped passed for a purposeful stride, I found my way to the exact geographic center of the roof — as far as I could get from its edge in any direction — and plopped down. There I felt protected by a large stretch of black roofing, veined with tar.

"Biggest problem is joining the new roof to the old one at the ridge," said Neil, pointing toward the top. "If we don't do it right, water'll seep under the cold roof and we'll be back to square one."

"I think Dad said something about that in his plans," I replied.

"But I've figured a way to make a better bond," said Tonto, demonstrating his idea with a couple of pieces of scrap board.

I glanced nervously at a sheet of plywood Neil was carrying: rough and knotty. "That plywood looks terrible."

"It'll be okay. No reason to buy top grade for a job like this."

"See that chimney jack?" Tonto pointed. "I've figured a way to fasten the roof to it."

They were proud of what they were doing. I relaxed a little and allowed my eyes to lift.

The vault of sky was as blue as the thin air was pure. To the west, the first of the day's clouds were beginning to swell behind an olive-green hill. Opposite, toward the Continental Divide, a grove of aspens was turning bright gold against the great gray and green of their mountains. Far above soared a hawk, who seemed to be circling in order to get a better look — at me.

"What a view that must be," I thought to myself, wishing I could hire the hawk to keep an eye on things.

"Sure glad we waited until your dad left to do this roof," said Neil. "He's scared to death of heights."

Chapter 16

When White is Black

When it came time for me to finish my dissertation, Tonto came to my rescue. Any woman who is determined to write, to immerse herself in a difficult, tedious project, would do well to hire a hefty secretary like Tonto.

Its completion had been weighing heavily on me all summer; finally, about the first of September, I set up my typewriter in the Balcony House — just across the driveway from the Inn. When anyone insisted on seeing me, Tonto would curl his lip into the threat of a snarl, pull down the length of his Fu Manchu moustache and discharge a feral stare. The person generally admitted that whatever was on his or her mind could wait.

My work room was a pleasant one because years before my brother Dwight and his wife Jean had built it to be the living room of their personal apartment. Exposed pine beams, gleaming gold with age, supported a peaked ceiling. On chilly mornings I built a fire in a nice old rock fireplace. No telephone jangled its interruptions. I closed the draperies so I wouldn't be distracted by traffic on the road. The only noise was my buzzy old electric typewriter, the one with a manual return. I laid in a supply of the little brown Garcia y Vega cigars I liked to puff as I wrote, and set about sorting my research notes into chapters.* Even with so many distractions eliminated, it was hard to concentrate.

One distraction I couldn't ignore was my children. Their first day at school was particularly traumatic.

"Mother, they all laughed at this dress!" Tears flooded from the blue eyes of my normally perky twelve-year-old daughter. She stomped to her room, tearing at the buttons of the offending garment. Drew had worn her new plaid dress, a birthday gift from her grandfather, to her first day of school. I thought she looked picture pretty earlier that morning when she skipped down the road to catch the bus. But we quickly learned that this rural school would be quite different from the one back in Phoenix.

Yanking a T-shirt over her head she sobbed, "Everybody was in jeans and stuff. I felt silly. And they made fun of my green hair!" Poor kid, a dip in a friend's ineptly chlorinated pool had turned her flaxen hair to lime green.

"I'm sorry, honey," I tried to soothe her by rubbing her neck as she clung to me. I remembered, all too clearly, my own childhood — times I wore or said the wrong thing.

---

* Information about a dissertation properly belongs in a footnote, especially because that long and arduous exercise didn't amount to much more than a footnote to my life. Occasionally, somebody politely inquires about the subject of my treatise. The title was *Understanding Elizabethan Laughter, the Martin Marprelate Tracts.* Back at the university, one of my professors referred to these anonymous Puritan booklets, illegally published in 1588, as hilarious attacks on the Church of England. When I read the pamphlets I didn't get the joke. Through onerous linguistic research, I made an earthshaking discovery! Their humor centered on jokes about flatulence, produced from the windbags Elizabeth I had handpicked to be her bishops. Imagine my delight when I rescued for generations of scholars to come many forgotten words for farts. I concluded that religious controversy was friskier in the olden days. Even so, it is quite possible to write a very dull dissertation about such a lively subject, because I did it.

"And how did *you* get along?" I turned to ask Gordon.

"Oh, everything went OK." He glanced up at me through his tousled curly forelock. But I could see that it didn't. However, it was unlikely he'd complain; Gordon always wanted people to think he was a cool little dude who didn't bitch about every little thing.

Keith, with the superiority of an old-timer who had already attended this school the spring before, tried to explain the local folkways to his younger brother and sister. "We come from the East End, so we're supposed to be hippies and ski bums. Rednecks come from the other end of the county; you know, the ranchers' brats. We call 'em saddle soreheads. Drew," Keith lectured his sister, "you should dress more like a hippie."

"But you aren't hippies or rednecks," I pointed out.

"Doesn't matter," said Keith. "You've got to be one or the other." I noted with alarm that Keith's hair was lengthening in search of his shoulders.

So busy had I been, trying to learn my job, that I hadn't given much thought to how my three children would adjust to their new school. I had never attended Middle Park Junior-Senior High School in Granby, the nearest town of any size, seventeen miles west. In our small, rural system grades seven through twelve were jammed into the same building.

Through the rearview mirror, I now regret my failure to anticipate problems. My "new kids" would have trouble being accepted except by other "outsiders" — renegades whose only track records were earned on the field of trouble. Teachers didn't help much; they tended to prefer children from families they already knew.

But I had my hands full with the lodge because each day our mailbox was stuffed with letters of instruction from Father. Several times a week he phoned, adding to my list of things to build, clean out or buy. It seemed to me he was attempting to manage from afar — with me acting merely as his agent. Even with all the work he piled on, at the end of each conversation he would say wistfully, "I don't suppose you'll ever finish that degree."

Oh yes, I would. In spite of him and maybe to spite him.

Usually Father waited to phone until evening, when the phone rates were cheaper. Once after dinner he complained, "I called this morning but Tonto wouldn't let me talk to you." Bless Tonto, he was doing his job.

Each morning I carried a thermos of coffee across the driveway and set to work. Pounding that typewriter, smoking cigars, framing my thoughts in academic jargon — the previous summer's highjinks seemed far behind. Although it was dull slogging, I relished the luxury of working on just one thing at a time. How soothing it was to be alone, to have my little world organized around me, but above all to feel I was in total control of something, anything.

I mailed chapters to Arizona State; my professor marked them up. He criticized my writing, urged me to tone it down because it was too lively. "Preserve literary decorum," he admonished.

Resigned, I sank to the occasion, sat back and hurled semicolons at my manuscript. At some point it occurred to me I never wanted to get very good at that kind of writing.

I envied Tonto because, as correspondent for the lodge, he was free to express himself creatively. One day I picked up a letter he had written to the leader of a Wichita ski club, confirming reservations for a weekend in late January:

Dear Mrs. Allison (NRN):
In your last letter you asked how to get here from Denver. That is simple. Drive west on I-70 until you get to the buffalo farm. Turn toward Wyoming, look sharply for Mountain Ben's trap line which you will

follow to the East Portal of the Moffat Tunnel. Put your ear to the track to be sure no trains are coming...

Of course, the next paragraph gave sensible directions. The lady grabbed the bait and fired back a snappy letter of her own. While their correspondence did not soar to the heights of Heloise and Abelard, it made for amusing reading.

Meanwhile Bridget, with Carolyn's guidance, had been busying herself organizing my linen closets and cleaning supplies. She reported that our fleet of vacuum cleaners needed new belts.

"Tonto, send for some belts from the Kirby company. There's an address in the files." I tossed the order over my shoulder as I fled to the Balcony House. Out went his request:

Dear Kirby Vacuum Machine People:
    Your sucking machines won't suck.
Send belts.

His terse note tickled the Kirby people so much they phoned back long distance to assure him the belts were on their way.

Nor did Tonto ignore the junk mail. One day an advertising brochure arrived, addressed to the secretary of Millers Idlewild Inn. "Dear Madam," it began. It offered to send the secretary a gift of a very nice Scotch Tape holder if she would fill out a short form and return it to the 3M company. The form requested a description of her boss's copying system. Tonto wrote an intentionally cutesy note, declaring himself to be a male secretary. He tucked a sheet of carbon paper into an envelope, along with a complaint that it constituted the sum total of his boss's reproductive capacity. The 3M people sent a salesman, not to peddle a copy machine, but to try to figure out what was going on at Millers Idlewild Inn.

When a letter of inquiry arrived from a young man named Gary Bader, requesting a single room because he wasn't married, Tonto's return salutation began:

"Dear Master Bader."

But his life wasn't all fun and games. The outside world intruded in a very forceful way. On October 19, the Arabs embargoed oil shipments to the United States. At the sight of long lines at their neighborhood filling stations, prospective guests stampeded to cancel their reservations.

The phone rang constantly. "Can we get gasoline out there?" I don't know how he did it, but Tonto managed to soothe their fears — and hang onto their deposits. To my knowledge, nobody got stranded in Goodland on their way across Kansas.

At the end of each day, Tonto would read me his log: "Linen service called, wanted to explain their new rates, Bridget talked to 'em; got an inquiry from Houston for a group of thirty for March; salesman stopped in and wanted you to buy thirty dozen ash trays with pictures of the Inn on them." Sometimes he would throw in significant news: "And by the way, Spiro Angew resigned as Vice President today."

My eyes blinked as I did a double-take, "I thought it was Nixon we wanted to resign."

"Agnew beat him to it, something about bribes he took as governor of Maryland. Had nothing to do with Watergate." Watergate! I was so busy I rarely saw TV or read a newspaper. I might as well have been living on another planet.

Rarely did Tonto disturb my solitude. He had promised to keep the world from my doorstep; with only two exceptions, he did.

Tonto's first interruption came when he stuck his head in my door and announced, without ceremony, "The Army's here.

They've come to get Gordon."

Gordon? My second born? What had that rascal been up to now? For just a moment I panicked at the prospect my fourteen-year-old child might die in Viet Nam. Then I remembered the draft was no longer in effect.

In the driveway stood two smartly pressed olive-drab uniforms, next to a motor-pool green automobile. "Ma'am, do you know a Gordon Cornell?" asked the beetle-browed older man as he removed his hat, holding its stiff brim in front of his sucked-in gut. Maybe his shorter, blonder sidekick was in training; he didn't say anything.

"I certainly do. He's my son."

He sized me up; probably thought this woman with the long red pigtail was some kind of hippie peacenik. "Senior in high school, is he?"

"Lord no, he's only fourteen."

"You sure about that? You got his birth certificate?"

"Of course I do. But I don't know where it is. Believe me, he's a freshman in high school."

"We're here to talk to him. We're recruiters."

"Sir, you are not going to induct my fourteen-year-old son into the army. That is not going to happen."

Tonto stood to one side, listening; his grin was so wide his gold molar gleamed.

"How did you find out about Gordon?" I asked.

"He called us."

Perhaps I had underestimated my middle child's difficulty in adjusting to his new school.

I was waiting for Gordon when he got off the school bus, told him about my unusual visitors. "What made them think you wanted to join the Army, Gordon? Are you that unhappy?"

Gordon grinned impishly. "Oh Mom, I was just fooling around, dialing up some 800 numbers." Just introduced, toll-free 800 numbers were still a novelty. "Told them I wasn't old enough to join, but I might be interested later. They wanted my name anyhow."

Somewhat relieved, I asked, "Have you called anybody else on 800 numbers?"

"Oh yeah, do it all the time. I call up people, find out where they are. Did you know some of 'em are in New Jersey? Even Florida. We talk about the weather and stuff. They like to talk to me. I think they're lonesome. Especially at night. They think it's far out that I'm calling from Colorado. Don't be mad at me, Mom. It's free."

"So you're not thinking of running away from home?"

Gordon looked at me, astounded. "'Course not, Mom."

Tonto and I concluded the recruiters probably knew all along that Gordon was underage. But following up on his phone call gave them an excuse to take off on a pleasant day's excursion through the mountains on Uncle Sam's nickel — a prospect much more interesting than shuffling papers in their office or hanging out at some mall.

❄ ❄ ❄ ❄ ❄

About three weeks later, Tonto appeared at my door again. Said I'd better come over to the Inn right away.

"Can't it wait? I mean, I'm right in the middle of figuring out who was standing next to the Bishop of York, making wind."

"I don't think you want to miss this."

There, by the front desk, stood a man holding a bulky old leather briefcase. He wore a dark suit; a white polyester shirt and nondescript tie showed beneath his old-fashioned overcoat. When he doffed his fedora, his head was balding.

"Salesman," I thought to myself. "Weird salesman."

His lips expanded into an infectious smile as he politely extended his hand, "Hello, I'm Bob White, but as you can see, I'm black." Very. He might have been the only black person in

Grand County at that moment.

"I solicit for the blind and I'm a friend of your Daddy. Here, let me show you." He pulled a battered leather photo album from his briefcase and proceeded to thumb through pictures of blind children, of all races, enjoying themselves at a Christian summer camp in the woods.

Rap music hadn't yet been invented, but Bob White, articulated — in bouncy rhythm and frequently in rhyme — his appeal on behalf of the "little-bitty blind children." Evidently he believed that a contributor should get more than gratitude for a donation, because he was a one-man show — gesturing, rhyming, charming us with his syncopated patter. Had he broken into a buck and wing and tap-danced his way into the dining room I wouldn't have been surprised. His routine achieved its desired effect, because I could hardly wait to reach for the check book.

"Thank you very kindly," he beamed as he folded the check and tucked it into the pocket of his suit jacket. "By the way, your Daddy usually let me spend the night here."

"That's fine with me, stay as long as you like," I replied, because an extra body was never a problem in off-season. "Would you like to eat dinner with us?"

"Oh no, I'm a vegetarian," he explained. "I just like to stay in my room, say my prayers and read a little."

I made stew for Neil, the kids and myself. Afterward Drew was happy to help Neil with the dishes. He made it a point to meet her school bus often in the afternoon and cheer her up with an encouraging hug after the ordeal of school; she found his ear much more sympathetic than those of her brothers.

Bob White sat in the living room, scanning an old *Reader's Digest*. "Have you been collecting money for the blind very long?" I asked.

"Fifteen years," he answered proudly. "I'm their best representative."

"I can certainly believe that."

"Miss Virginia," he looked around, "Where is your husband?" He had noted children calling me Mom.

"I'm afraid I'm divorced. Have been for three years."

"Oh, that is so sad, so very sad." A look of considerable pain crossed his face.

"And Mr. Tonto?" Bob White gestured toward the office, which was shuttered now. I probably blushed, "No, nothing happening there."

A sly smile flashed across his pleasant face. "You know what else I do, traveling through the highways and the byways like I do?"

"I couldn't guess."

"It's like this. I was over at a little town — Dove Crick. Called on a nice waitress, works at a little restaurant. Always very kind to me. Then two days later, in the hardware store in Mancos, I called on the owner, man I've known many a year. He was sittin' there, eatin' cold beans out of a can. 'Where's Miz Alice?' I asked. Told me his wife died — year ago, cancer it was. That man looked so sad.

"So I got this idea. I circled back to Dove Crick, asked the waitress if she'd mind meetin' somebody. Said she wouldn't. So I introduced them two. Praise Jesus, if they didn't hit it off and get married. Happy as can be. Six years in March."

In the course of his travels, maybe to relieve the boredom, Bob White played matchmaker. He claimed half a dozen marriages resulted from his efforts. "Maybe I'll find somebody for you," he winked.

I shook my head — "That would be a pretty big assignment" — and thought no more about it.

A couple of days later Bob White burst in the front door, a bit out of breath.

"Miss Virginia? I've been talking to a very nice gentleman. But I must ask you. Is *age* any matter with you?"

What could it hurt to play along? "No, I'm not prejudiced," I tossed back. I figured he had located some mountain geezer, old as the hills, who needed a maid and cook.

"And would the presence of a little child bother you?"

"You know I have three, what's another one?"

"I'll be back," he promised, hurrying out the door. What was he up to?

When I looked over the registration counter, I saw that Tonto had overheard and his molar was gleaming again.

A half an hour later, the phone rang. It was my banker, Dennis Lightfoot. "Virginia, I think you'd better come down here. Something has come up." He sounded severe. Oh dear, they couldn't have called my note yet. Was our account overdrawn?

When I entered Dennis's office, there sat Bob White in the borrower's chair by the desk, next to the picture of Dennis with his daughter who — I had since learned — lived with her mother. "Now don't you two take it wrong, but I think you ought to get to know each other," said Bob, beaming nervously.

Dennis and I looked at each other, swallowing our almost unstoppable urge to roar with laughter. Neither of us would have wanted to hurt Bob White's feelings. The wrestler and the professor? No, there would be no match for us; Dennis and I were not long-lost soul mates.

"Bob, when you asked if age made any difference I didn't know you wanted me to raise another kid! Why Dennis is almost young enough to be my . . ."

"Banker!" shot back Dennis quickly.

But I thanked Bob White every year when he came around again, soliciting funds, because from that day onward Dennis and I became very good friends. Every time we met, over business or pleasure, one of us would deliver the obligatory opening sally: "When's the wedding?"

Although connubial bliss continued to elude me through that autumn of 1973, despite all distractions I did manage to complete the draft of what eventually became my doctoral dissertation. As of the following July, guests at Millers Idlewild Inn could ask to have their hummingbird feeders refilled by Virginia Miller Cornell, Ph.D.

Winter 1973-1974

Chapter 17

White Christmas

"Let it snow, let it snow, let it snow," go the lyrics of an old song. Toward the end of 1973 it snowed; it snowed some more and then it kept right on snowing. Before the introduction of artificial snowmaking, we worried through every autumn about whether the ski area would have enough base to open for the Thanksgiving holiday. For turkey day in 1973 we shared our feast with about twenty guests, who were staying in the main lodge. The Inn wouldn't get really busy until mid-December.

One by one, we opened up the cabins, frantically working to get ready for Christmas. I was anxious for everything to be just right. My nerves jangled in harmony to the telephone — which rang continuously as the outside world heard about the enormous amount of snow dumping on Colorado.

As guests registered and staff members arrived, Myrtle and Roger tried to outdo each other, preparing cookies and treats for the Christmas holiday. When skiers returned in the afternoon, the Inn was filled with the smells of gingerbread boys and cinnamon cookies. We set a pot of hot, spiced cider on the burner of a little sheepherder's stove in the living room to welcome cold skiers when they came home from the slopes.

Neil pruned the Christmas tree we had cut out of the forest a couple of weeks earlier. He wove a very nice wreath from some of its lower branches for the big front door. Over the oxen yoke light fixture in the lounge he draped boughs.

Although we had tried to anticipate a guest's every need, inevitably the first guests to check into a unit requested more towels, more blankets, less heat or more heat. As the onslaught of winter business swelled, dozens of little problems popped up — from storing a diabetic guest's insulin at just the right temperature to a crisis that arose when two mothers laid claim to the same baby crib.

"We'll just do what Solomon did," said Tonto.

"Offer to chop the baby in two?" I asked.

"No, chop the crib in two and give each mother half of it."

I was determined guests would find the Inn, under my management, every bit as good as it had ever been — if not better.

Neil and a new employee named John Brandenburg began trundling carts and carts of firewood, stacking them neatly, to fuel those thirteen fireplaces and two saunas. The kid we called J.B. was just out of high school. Lanky, skinny as a coat hanger, he was the fair-haired son of former guests. Of course he was attempting to grow a beard; all my male employees tried — after all, a beard was certifiable proof of manhood.

❄ ❄ ❄ ❄ ❄

"Hey, you made it!" I greeted the aptly named Good family when they returned for their eighth Christmas holiday at Millers.

"We felt lucky to get through Western Kansas without getting stranded," answered Karol Good. "We've never seen so much snow this early in the season."

"Any trouble getting gas?" I asked.

Richard Good patted his tummy and deadpanned, "Always have plenty of that!" I laughed at his quip; almost everybody got gas when their stomachs distended in the altitude.

My father frequently cited the Goods as a fine example of a family with the right idea. All year, they saved from the earnings of Dr. Good's dental practice in Chanute, Kansas. Except for the odd gag gift and ski equipment, family members didn't exchange presents. They spent their money enjoying a glorious holiday — and each other.

For the four Good children, Christmas at Millers meant memories. One year they brought along the children's pet gerbil because she was inconveniently pregnant. She celebrated Christmas, appropriately, by birthing a litter. When their oldest child, Diane, applied for work by mail earlier that fall, I didn't hesitate to hire her. Diane wrote she was finishing two years of junior college and declared herself ready to "get away from it all."

But when I saw the girl I remembered as a bubbly teenager I was alarmed. Behind her black plastic-rimmed glasses, the tall brunette looked tired, melancholy. I hoped her only problem was post-final fatigue.

"Do you want to stay with your family in the cabin or settle right into the bunk room?" I asked.

"The bunk room, please, the bunk room," she responded, kindling her first ray of enthusiasm.

I opened the door to a bedroom off the Recreation Room to reveal the incredibly messy space Diane was to share with three other girls. I motioned to a lower bunk, then gingerly lifted a pair of crumpled long johns and some stiff jeans slung over her bedspread.

Only one corner of the room was tidy. It belonged to Sally, the sole "maiden" who returned for the winter. Sally marked off her domain with masking tape and a sign that said "KEEP OFF."

I could see that Diane was attempting to hide her revulsion at the condition of the room. But because this was to be her first real job away from home she didn't complain, didn't want to be known as a whiner.

"The girl in the upper above you is named Alice Simmons" (NRN), I explained. "Everybody calls her Chub. Don't know why, she's not fat. She must be out skiing. You'll meet her when she comes back in an hour or so. Diane, is anything wrong?"

"No," she sniffed. "Just finished finals; guess I'm pretty tired."

Diane was the last employee to appear; by then I noticed a familiar pattern. The date of all arrivals coincided with the date of their finals; every one of them was exhausted from pulling late-nighters.

"We'll have a staff meeting in the dining room," I told Diane. "Right after the dishes are finished. Please be there. Go ahead and put your stuff away." I pointed to her chest of drawers. "More hangers in the laundry room, if you need 'em."

"I'm bushed, but don't want to sleep. When do I get my lift ticket?" asked Diane.

That phrase was familiar, too. "After you get your job assignment," had become my standard reply. I quickly learned my employees' top priorities were not the hard work of shoveling snow, splitting wood, making beds and doing dishes for dear old Millers Idlewild Inn.

Skiing! It was the only reason to descend to such menial chores.

❄ ❄ ❄ ❄ ❄

From my years in teaching, I realized I'd better come across as hard-nosed and firm in the beginning. You can always soften up, but it's difficult to retrench without seeming petty and mean. I had already learned how hard it was to stifle my natural inclination to mother my young staff. My experiences with the maidens had taught me a little bit about personnel relations. Not enough, but a little. Managing fourteen employees — many of whom had never held a job before — would become my most difficult challenge.

I started the meeting: "You all know your deal. You get a hundred dollars a month, lift ticket, meals, tips shared from the pool."

As I looked out at the ski bums, most of them newcomers, I realized although I knew their names I referenced them by their sweatshirts. All of them were labeled — either with the college they just attended or the one they wanted to attend. Brand name identification, I suppose.

"What if somebody offers me a tip? Can't I take it?" asked Brad Allen (NRN) with the hint of a sneer in his voice and Central Illinois on his chest. Although the youngish-looking sophomore with curly brown hair had been eager and pleasant when I interviewed him earlier in the month, his true colors were emerging. I knew his type from my teaching years. He grew up with nice parents, nice family in a nice neighborhood. Because nothing much had gone wrong in his life he held it against his parents that his life had been boring! The sulky Brad would bear watching.

"It's OK to take a tip if you do a big favor for somebody and they offer it. Otherwise, tips get pooled because some people working behind the scenes, like J.B. and Bridget, don't get noticed."

"If anybody asks, tell 'em to leave tips with me when they check out," noted Tonto. "I'll divvy them up every payday."

"Tips are pooled equally with shares going to Myrtle, Roger, Bridget and Tonto but not to me," I explained.

Neil, J.B. and Brad talked about sharing the early morning snow-blowing chores — something we needed a lot of that season. In successive, drier years, I would come to appreciate what an abundance of snow fell in December of 1973.

I noticed that Chub, an athletic-looking girl whose strong shoulders hinted she might have been a swimmer for the Colorado State team, was sniffling and coughing. Besides sweatshirts, each ski bum brought whatever contagious germ topped the charts back on their campus. For Christmas each year, because new employees were just getting to know each other, they traded flu bugs in lieu of gifts.

Diane was lucky. Her family was with her. The double whammy of flu and holiday homesickness usually caused my employees to choose blue for their favorite Christmas color.

Sandy Morgan (NRN) spoke up. "How long do we have to hang around every day before we can go skiing?" The wispy girl with a perpetually red nose had attended an impressive prep school. The organic shampoo she touted left her long dark hair in an unruly mess. I was glad Bridget made little bandannas to tie over the girls' heads when they served food.

"Not a matter of hanging around," snapped Roger, who had helped me formulate the rules. "You can leave just as soon as your work is finished and checked. If you get done early, help somebody else. Nobody leaves until everybody is finished."

Brad wasn't paying attention. He wadded paper napkins, aiming at the big fireplace as a target.

"Are you getting all this, Kareem?" I asked. He scowled.

Then I turned to the others, "You get one day off each week. Here's the schedule Bridget worked out."

They studied the duty roster to see who was changing sheets, running vacuum cleaners, assisting the cook. Bridget's schedule was tight, but if everybody carried his share of the load, it should work. I heard Brad mumble, "Shit, I have to run a vacuum cleaner. That's girl work."

"Most of the jobs around here can be done by either sex," I shot back.

When I closed, I warned them, "It is very unfair that the busiest time of the entire ski season happens when you are trying to learn your jobs. You might want to put off skiing until later because the slopes will be much less crowded after New Year's. The work load will be a lot easier, too. Bear with me."

I hoped I had covered everything; it was time to switch gears, to turn my attention to the guests. "We're going to decorate the Christmas tree. Want to help?"

Several guests were seated around a card table in the lounge working a jigsaw puzzle. They looked up, with interest, toward the handsome spruce. Such a pretty tree. Given the slow pace at which trees grow in the mountains, that tree was probably as old as I was.

"I know, let's string popcorn and cranberries," piped up a teen-aged guest from Louisiana.

"All we have are the jellied cranberries in the can, hard to keep them on the string," I joked. "But Sally will pop up some corn."

Among the diverse crew decorating the tree that night were many of those I called my Christmas orphans. The balding insurance executive helping Neil steady the tree in its stand said, "My ex-wife has custody. She takes the kids to visit their grandparents. I never get to see them at Christmas."

A chubby little woman whose graying, close-cropped curls seemed to corkscrew themselves straight into her brain sighed, "Ralph just can't stand to stay at home since little Jimmy died December 23, 1959, at 11:32 p.m." She had taken it upon herself to try to untangle strings of lights while her husband sat in one corner, his nose stuck in a *National Geographic*.

A jovial accountant from Chicago picked out ornaments. "My wife's family get to drinking and everybody fights. It's just easier to leave town."

"This is fun," said a willowy co-ed from Houston. "First time I ever decorated a Christmas tree." Everybody turned to stare at her.

"Hey, I'm Jewish."

Somebody always got the bright idea of stringing popcorn. Although I knew that project was doomed, I didn't want to dampen enthusiasm.

"Every time I stick a needle into a kernel it shatters," complained the curly-headed lady.

"I was afraid of that," I replied, "Popcorn stringing is one of those picturesque, impractical little customs — the kind of thing you see in magazines."

Although my father kept the rates low at Millers, saying he wanted the common man to be able to afford to ski, I was always astounded at how many of our guests were quite wealthy.

Patsy Nason darned her husband's glove liners with the thrift of a New England farm wife while she chatted with the tree trimmers. You never would have guessed that her husband Ross was CEO of a large chemical corporation. They took two ski holidays yearly, one to Millers Idlewild Inn and the other, significantly more expensive, to Montreux, Switzerland. Yet I remember one year they agonized for a week about whether or not Patsy should invest in a *used* pair of Scott boots. My dad once asked Ross why he came to Millers when he could obviously afford to go anywhere. "C.D., everything in Switzerland is correct, very nicely done. But here I can put my feet up in front of the fireplace and take a nap."

Janet Staples stood back and gave advice about placement of ornaments. Janet and her husband John, school teachers from St. Louis, had been twice-annual guests for many years. Often they were our only black guests, which didn't seem to bother them or anybody else. Janet was a big woman who didn't ski but went to the slopes every day to act as a one-woman base area to her wiry husband and their three strapping college-age sons. John was determined to win a Gold Medal in NASTAR skiing — a national amateur competition. Toward that eventually realized goal, Janet served as family cheerleader, holder of coats and stopwatcher.

Inevitably, the discussion turned to the expense of the sport. Karol Good pretty much summed it up. "Unless you can take a hundred dollar bill, march into the bathroom and flush it down the toilet without wincing, you have no business taking up alpine skiing."

Everybody chuckled and nodded. Her observation caused me to reflect that I could never have afforded to take my own children skiing were it not for the fact we lived and worked at the Inn. Just then, I wondered if my kids were decorating a tree in Arizona.

I was a Christmas orphan, too. When I hired Bridget it was with the understanding she could go home to Phoenix for Christmas. She volunteered to take my children with her in her big VW van so they could spend the holiday with their father. Being apart from my kids made me sad, but I knew — from spending many Christmases at the Inn — that I would be far too busy to pay much attention to them. Bridge was very brave to offer. I thought at the time she was either the best friend I ever had — or else the craziest.

"You're doing a good job of running this place," Janet told me. I was happy when other former guests agreed.

"There's only one thing I miss," said Patsy.

"What's that?"

"Your dad's wake-up call."

"You mean, 'It's Alarm Clock Time?'" I tried to mimic my father's toneless chant. The other guests nodded.

"Sorry. I don't think I could do it justice." I winced.

"Nobody could," said Patsy.

SKI LODGE

❄ ❄ ❄ ❄ ❄

Throughout the week before Christmas, it kept right on snowing. Brad complained because he had to arise early to run a snowblower along the paths and sidewalks. But the guests were ecstatic. Every morning they scampered to the bus, eager to be the first skiers to break deep powder on the hill.

"Lady," said Neil one morning, his red beard sprinkled with snow, "if it keeps on snowing like this we'd better shovel the roof." Neil was very good at anticipating trouble.

"Dad says we'll never have to shovel again," I reminded him. "That's why we put on the cold roof."

"I dunno, you better ask him." His duty done, Neil squared his shoulders and hurried to his next chore.

When I mentioned it to Father that evening he snapped back, "No need to, no need to shovel it again, ever."

"Dad, we've had thirty inches already this week."

"Nope, don't do it."

Neil shrugged. "OK, if he says so. I'll be busy enough shoveling all the other roofs."

Finally, on Christmas night, it stopped snowing. The sky cleared, the temperature plunged.

How cold was it?

When it is merely cold in the mountains, say zero degrees, snow underfoot crunches with a hollow sound. When it is thirty-five below zero, snow shrieks bloody murder when you walk on it.

Father used to tell the guests: "One year it got so cold that the mercury in the thermometer went down to freezing, fell below zero, bored a hole in the bottom of the glass tube, drilled through the floorboards of a cabin and killed two pack rats in the basement."

Some Southern belle was sure to ask, "Is that true?"

It was so cold that when I ran an errand out to one of the cabins the hairs in my nose froze together, my lips turned crisp and my eyes watered. When I raced back for the warmth of the Inn, I ended up gasping for breath because the super-cold air pierced my lungs.

It was so cold that not one car in the parking lot started first thing in the morning unless it was jump-started by Jim Fulton — a local entrepreneur who drove a romantic sleigh ride by night, then started cars in the harsh light of morning.

However, the sun shone brightly on those clear days, so when people got to the slopes they often didn't notice. It's surprising how warm the sun can feel on your back, even when the temperature stays below zero.

Father reminded me to caution skiers about the dangers of frostbite, to warn them to watch for patches of white on each other's cheeks. Unfortunately one girl, more dedicated to fashion than safety, wore a cute little stocking cap, her gold hoop earrings poking out from below. That evening she asked, "What do you think is wrong with my earlobe?" Her dainty lobe was swollen to the size of an angry walnut. We concluded that the wires on her earrings had conducted cold into her pierced ears, increasing the severity of frostbite. I often wondered if she lost her earlobe.

The Frank Morton (NRN) family from Florida checked into the Alpine Fir cabin on December 26. The disturbingly handsome father was an airline executive and ex-pilot. Dark, he had a brooding, Heathcliffian look about him. He, his beehive-topped wife and two scrubbed sons had brought along her just-divorced sister with two children.

A couple of mornings later, after breakfast, Annabel Morton appeared at the office window, "Somethin's happened to our water." I looked up from the maintenance roster and managed to stanch an oncoming giggle at the sight of the woman's elaborate hairdo. The cabin girls had reported that the lady had brought along a six-pack of hair spray!

"Do you suppose those pipes got frozen?"

"Let's see. You're in the Alpine Fir. Didn't Tonto explain how to bleed the pipes?" At check-in, cabin guests were cautioned to leave a spigot in their cabin dripping a little at all times. With that precaution, pipes rarely froze.

"Tonto did tell us but we forgot to tell little Jimmy Ray, my sister's boy. Guess we yelled at him too often to turn off the water back home. Last night he went around and turned off all the faucets like we taught him back in Tampa."

"Helpful little bastard," Tonto asided from the corner of his mouth.

When Neil came in from outside, his glasses steamed opaque with the cold, I sent him to tackle Mrs. Morton's problem.

The first thing he did was to check the heating wires attached to the pipes, where they passed through the cabin's foundation. They were functioning. Next he fired up a blowtorch and passed it along the line, a dangerous gamble when working beneath an old pine building, because it could have started a fire. It usually thawed the pipes. But not that day.

When the Mortons returned, I explained that we had put in a call for a plumber, but in the meantime we had placed buckets of fresh water in their cabin so they could brush their teeth and flush toilets. "Feel free to use the sauna showers," I advised.

During Christmas week it would be easier to capture one of Santa's elves than to get a plumber. By the time I called for help, we were well down on the local plumber's priority list. I suspect some of the plumbers left town and fled to Mexico where they sat on the beach chortling at the thought of their phones ringing off the hook back home. Who could blame them? Who really wants to worm his way into a frigid crawl space beneath an old cabin to warm up pipes?

The next day we still hadn't seen a plumber, but the freeze-up had extended to a second cabin, the Englemann Spruce. Try as we would, we couldn't bust through the ice blockage.

After dinner that evening I noticed that Frank Morton was standing at the front desk. From the tension in his neck, I knew cross words were being lobbed at Tonto. As I approached I heard, "I'm not paying hundreds of dollars *not* to take a shower!" He held his breath long enough that his chiseled features seemed to harden before my eyes.

I felt just terrible for the Mortons; Millers Idlewild Inn, with myself as manager, was ruining their precious vacation. They'd probably demand their money back, go back to Florida, tell everybody how awful the Inn was. Even though I could do nothing about the pipes, I also couldn't quit worrying about the situation.

In desperation, I called my father — who smugly reported that it was seventy-five degrees in Texas.

"Don't call a plumber, call a welder," he advised.

"A welder?"

"He'll clamp onto the pipe at either end, pass a DC current through the pipe, using it as a resister, and it will warm up and pop open."

When I told Neil he nodded. "Well, I've heard of that. They call it the atomic bomb of pipe thawing."

The welder turned out to be nearly as busy as the plumber. But when he finally arrived, during dinner the next evening, he set about hooking up his equipment. Neil stationed himself at one end of the line. Because no other employee was available — all the rest were busy waiting tables and doing dishes — it fell to me to stand out in the ferocious cold and hold the flashlight so the welder could see what he was doing.

Happily, before long, water was gushing through the pipes into the Alpine Fir and the other cabin. It was a wonderful sight, but my fingers were stiff and my feet numb by the time we finished. I've often wondered if a welder can use that ploy with newfangled plastic pipes.

As I sat in the office, trying to warm my hands sufficiently to sign a check for the welder, the phone rang.

It was my ex-husband in Phoenix. "We've got a real emergency here." The timbre of his voice was ominous; my heart sank. Oh no, something had happened to the children.

"What's wrong?"

There was a long pause, as though my husband couldn't get whatever terrible information he had to impart out of his mouth. Finally he sputtered: "Gordon won't take a bath."

"What?"

"You heard me, Gordon refuses to take a bath. What shall I do?"

In that moment I didn't pause to remember the times when Gordon, or his brother and sister, had reduced me to the point of exasperation, too. How could the man I referred to as "my *last* husband" possibly know that I was already hot under the turtleneck?

"Look. If you can't get one fourteen-year-old boy to take a bath, God help you!" Maybe for the first time in our turbulent relationship I slammed down the phone in his ear.

Almost immediately I broke into uncontrollable gales of laughter. I'm not sure my last husband ever saw the humor in the situation. How preposterously uneven problems can be! I had managed to maintain my equilibrium when surrounded by complaining guests, inefficient employees, frozen pipes. But the poor man had cratered over a balky child.

Although I welcomed a good laugh, I dreaded the tongue lashing I thought Morton would give us when he checked out — debated in my own mind whether we owed him a refund.

Because I didn't want Tonto to take the brunt of Morton's wrath, I stood with him when the man came to the office to pay his bill.

"Sorry about the pipes," said Tonto.

"Oh, I didn't care for myself. The women got excited about it."

"I surely hope you'll give us another chance some time," I said. "We could reserve you into in a different cabin."

"Different cabin? I hope not!"

"Oh, you liked it?"

"Same thing always happened every year when your dad was here, too. We've had that cabin six years, wouldn't want to be anywhere else. Book us again for next year."

❄ ❄ ❄ ❄ ❄

Throughout the week between Christmas and New Year's a steady stream of people tromped into the Inn — seeking a room for the night.

"We're sorry, but most of our accommodations have been reserved since August," Tonto would explain, over and over.

"Couldn't we just sleep on your couch?" Of course, we couldn't allow our lounge to become an overnight depot for people who didn't plan ahead. Denver, where there were plenty of motels, was only two hours away. It would be very unfair to guests who had anticipated their vacations since summer to crowd the Inn with latecomers.

Weary of explaining, Tonto turned to me one afternoon. "Do you know who the most underappreciated person in the Bible was?"

"No, who?"

"That Innkeeper in Bethlehem. Here comes Mary and Joseph — with a jackass yet. He did his best, offered them a place to sleep in the stable. No wonder there wasn't any room in the Inn. Didn't they know it was Christmas?"

Chapter 18

There's Always More

My fingers trembled with the cold as I fumbled to zip up my bell-bottom jeans. Normally my tiny bedroom — formerly my father's den — was warm, but not that first morning of 1974. When I scraped a little hole in the window frost so I could read the thermometer mounted outside, it said forty-two degrees below zero! No wonder I felt cold. I hoped no pipes had frozen overnight; I also hoped the new year would be less eventful than the one just completed.

We never had a big celebration at the Inn for New Year's Eve. Most people just turned in so they could enjoy the next day's skiing, or went down to the highway to celebrate at a bar. The last couple of weeks had been so strenuous; I, too, wanted to fall into bed and sleep. So of course the phone rang a little before eleven, with some drunk in Kansas City demanding I summon his friends — guests staying in the farthest cabin, the Juniper — so he could wish them Happy New Year.

"You want to hold the phone while I get dressed, walk outside in forty-below-zero temperatures a quarter of a mile and wake him up?"

"Oh well, guess I can wait to tell him when he gets home. Have a Happy New Year yourself!" I wondered, would my dad have gone to get the guests?

I had a tough time getting back to sleep. Why hadn't my kids and Bridget returned from Arizona? "I'll be back in time for New Year's Eve," she had promised. Something must be wrong.

It was 6:30 in the morning when I hurried down the stairs and into the kitchen. Myrtle glanced up, her glasses speckled with grease from the bacon she was frying. She shrugged her shoulders, barely acknowledging my presence. "Nobody's here."

Nobody was breaking eggs for Myrtle, nobody had turned up the gas under the coffee urn, nobody was filling juice glasses.

"Hung over, probably," was all I said. But as I fussed with the coffee urn, water wasn't the only thing approaching the boiling point.

As soon as I measured the ground coffee I went looking for my employees. I thoroughly expected to find them sacked out in their bunks. But their rooms were empty. I had no staff! My ski bums had vanished as certainly as 1973 was history.

The afternoon before, a couple of them had asked permission to take the evening off. They proposed to get rowdy at my nephew Andy's house trailer, two miles away in Fraser. "OK by me," I replied with the added warning, "Just don't indulge so heavily you won't be fit for work in the morning."

I thought it would be a good idea if the kids got off by themselves; they had been working very hard. Middle-class kids — some people would even call them rich kids — it came as a jolt when they learned *employees* celebrate Christmas Eve and Christmas Day by making other people's beds, carrying their wood, washing their dishes. "Bummer!" was the word heard up and down corridors that day.

Their noisy party, probably accompanied by Pink Floyd as loud as the stereo could play it, would be better held elsewhere. Besides, I didn't want to have to explain away the "funny-smelling smoke" that would almost certainly be a by-product of their revelry. Even Diane, straight as an arrow, decided to go. This was the same Diane who one day ran out of a guest's bathroom screaming in horror at the sight of a hookah — a water pipe with several four-foot hoses — sitting in the bathtub. No doubt it was used by the college students, who rented the room, for smoking marijuana.

Neil was the only one who declined the invitation. "What if there's a fire? How would they get ahold of me? Andy doesn't have a phone."

Why couldn't all my employees be as dependable as Neil? I fussed to myself as I mixed apple juice and poured it into glasses. My hands weren't too steady. I wanted to detonate my righteous indignation into a scream of rage. But I was too busy mixing Cream of Wheat, pouring milk into pitchers and following Myrtle's orders to indulge my tantrum. Her own fury was expressed in an exhalation of syncopated sighs which I read as *lazy-good-for-nothing kids* sighs, *sorry-for-herself* sighs, *the-boss-is-incompetent* sighs.

Fortunately the tables had been set the evening before. When it came time to serve, I discreetly asked a guest at each table if he or she would mind stepping into the kitchen to pick up a platter of eggs, hash browns, bacon and toast.

"Kids had a big party last night?" They laughed. To my relief, they good-naturedly grabbed serving bowls and platters, then went on to pour their own coffee.

"Just like when I went to scout camp," chortled one fellow whose sideburns grew clear down the side of his face and clamped together beneath his chin. "Hope I don't have to swab out the biffies."

Beneath what I hoped was a "kids-will-be-kids" smile I was embarrassed and humiliated. Just like my own kids — and by the way where were *they*? Give them an inch . . . Why was I becoming a patsy-cake? Why couldn't I demand, and get, obedience from my staff?

When the phone rang halfway through breakfast I instantly thought of my children, then realized Tonto hadn't come to work, either. I glanced up to see that the louvered office windows were still shuttered. I knew there were six bills to be figured before check-out time. That jerk! He was probably the ringleader of this insurrection.

I groped with my master key to unlock the office. Safely out of sight of guests, I yanked the phone off its hook with such fury I almost pulled the fixture from the wall. I heard a sheepish voice at the other end. "Uh, Virginia, we're late."

"News flash, Tonto. I already noticed." I started to unload. "I warned you guys not to get so wasted you couldn't show up for work. Where the hell are you?"

"I walked up to the phone booth at the New Fraser Market. It's fifty below in Fraser. Nobody's car will start but we're working on it. Gosh Virginia, we feel just awful about this. We'll get there as fast as we can."

"I'll send Neil." We kept the van in a heated garage, so it would start when nothing else did.

Before long, Neil brought back a chastened, tired, hungover crew. "We decided to sack out at Andy's last night because we didn't think we were in any shape to drive," murmured Sandy, whose eyes refused to open more than half a slit.

"Good plan," I agreed.

"Somebody unplugged my engine heater," fumed Brad, who never accepted responsibility for *anything*.

"Bad plan," I said.

"There's always more!" said J.B., with a silly grin that led me to believe he was still a little cooked.

"There's always more!" echoed the others, breaking into giggles. I was too upset to ask them what *that* was all about.

Before me stood a pale, sluggish-looking bunch. However, they turned to and slowly sorted through the stacks of dirty dishes guests had piled helter-skelter in the kitchen.

Myrtle greeted them silently, with a look somewhere between ice and granite.

"Heard anything from Bridge?" asked Tonto, an edge of worry in his voice.

"No, not a word. She should have been here by now." He wanted Bridget. I wanted my children.

For the first day since the ski bums came to work, when their chores were finished nobody went skiing; instead, they all went napping.

❄ ❄ ❄ ❄ ❄

I hated presenting people with bills. I knew my sentiment was irrational, but somehow it didn't seem right to charge people to stay at the Inn — I tried so hard to make every guest feel at home in what I considered to be my home. If I could, I always tried to get Tonto or someone else to go over the bill with the guest. I was always a little surprised when nobody objected.

Every time I glanced out a window, watching eagerly for Bridget's van to pull into the drive, the only thing I saw was my dog Pepper and Myrtle's three-legged mutt, sitting on top of a pile of snow. The mound had been created when the snowplower pushed all the extra snow into one place. The dogs had discovered a perfect perch from which to watch the world go by, and occasionally bark at it.

Tonto and I fretted at the failure of Bridget's habitual punctuality. There was a lot of bad country between the Inn and Phoenix, especially in winter. He phoned the police to ask if there was stormy weather in New Mexico, whether there had been a blizzard. But our Highway Patrol dispatcher replied New Mexico was out of his jurisdiction — as though the world ended at the top of Berthoud Pass.

All day, the hands on the clock moved very slowly. Finally, just after dark, I heard a car door bang, followed by the voices of my children as they trooped through the Rec Room. Behind them lagged Bridge, lugging the kids' suitcase. Her teeth were chattering from the cold; her VW van had a lousy heater.

At first she said nothing, as though she were in a catatonic state. Then she bawled, "I want Scotch!" Tonto pulled a bottle from behind his desk and ran for some ice from the machine in the Rec Room.

"My God, it was awful. Just awful."

Oh dear, I knew I shouldn't have let her drive cross-country with my quarreling children. "You kids — " I turned to them, raising my shoulders, inhaling rapidly in preparation for the blistering lecture I was about to deliver.

"No, no, the kids were fine! But we almost got thrown in jail!"

"Jail? What for?"

"I'll tell you." By now Bridge had gulped her way through her second shot of Scotch; Tonto was rubbing her icy hands, rigid from clutching the cold steering wheel hour after hour.

Finally, a coherent account began to emerge. "We were between Gallup and Albuquerque. It was snowing a little, but the wind was blowing really hard. I could hardly keep the van on the road. Suddenly, from behind me, I see the gumball machine," she said, gesturing to imitate revolving red and blue lights atop a state trooper's car.

"I asked myself, could I have been speeding? Pretty hard to do in a VW van loaded with three kids and all our gear. So I pulled over. I reached into my glove box for the registration.

But instead of coming up beside the van the guy opens the door of the patrol car, crouches behind it and yells at me through a bullhorn, 'Come out with your hands up!'"

My tired-looking kids nodded to confirm her account.

"The boys were asleep under blankets in the back, barefoot. They were waking up, trying to figure out what was happening.

"That loudspeaker, or whatever it was, said, 'I've got a shotgun leveled right at you and if you aren't out in sixty seconds I'll fire!'

"It was just awful, Mom," said Keith.

"I was so scared I decided I would climb across to the passenger's seat to Drew's side. I hauled her out that door so she would be in front of me. Sorry Virginia, I know she's your kid but I put her between me and the patrolman. Figured he wouldn't shoot a little kid."

I gasped with horror at the thought of my child between Bridge and a gun. But I was too astonished to object. "That's right, Mom, she did." Drew glanced up at Bridget. Maybe until that moment Drew hadn't figured out Bridge used her as a shield.

"All this time I'm trying to figure out what's going on. I decided they must be looking for drugs. Then I remembered everybody I saw in Phoenix said 'Here, take this to Jake.' They kept handing me little envelopes and baggies and winking. I just tossed everything into a bag for him, didn't think much about it.

"So we were standing outside in a blizzard, freezing to death, and this patrolman ordered us to take everything out of the van."

"Wouldn't they tell you what they wanted?" I asked.

"No," she nodded her head vigorously, "So I said, 'Sir, you can't keep these children standing in the freezing cold with no jackets or shoes on. What do you want with us?'

"In the meantime, more patrolmen arrived and they all had guns — trained right on the van. Finally somebody started thinking maybe they weren't looking for a woman and three children. They checked my driver's license, and when I explained these weren't my kids, they insisted on seeing *their* IDs. I tried to explain that children don't even carry library cards."

Bridge's elbow rested on Tonto's desk, she cradled her chin in her hand. "Talk about paranoia! One guy was looking in the back of the van, picking up suitcases and backpacks and putting them down. I just knew that duffle bag full of stuff for Tonto was sitting back there throbbing, absolutely throbbing! It was alive. I even wondered if your kids had any drugs with them.

"Finally the guy said, 'OK, you can go.'"

"Well, what were they looking for?" asked Tonto.

"Somebody robbed a bank in some little town then made their getaway in a blue and white van."

"What kind of a dumb robber would use a VW van as a getaway vehicle? Especially in New Mexico on the interstate?" asked Tonto.

"Beats me, but I guess I finally convinced them I wasn't the one."

On her third Scotch, she was mellowing considerably. Most of the staff members were gathered in front of the office counter, taking in the story.

"Mom, I thought they were going to kill us," said Gordon.

"Yeah," agreed Keith. "I was never so scared in my life."

"When we got to Albuquerque I was so shook I rented a room and spent the night instead of driving through like I planned. Sorry, El Cheapo No-Tell Mo-tel didn't have a phone so I couldn't call you," explained Bridge.

"There's always more," said J.B., thoughtfully. When I turned to ask him what he meant, he was gone.

❄ ❄ ❄ ❄ ❄

A couple of days later it was Tonto's Thursday off. He announced he was going skiing. Despite his bulk, he had survived his first three days on skis and was intent on learning the sport. In his absence, I needed to stay near the telephone, so I assigned myself the chore of undecorating the Christmas tree and packing ornaments.

The tree chore went very slowly because I was constantly interrupted by the phone, the linen delivery man, the Pepsi man. Then I stopped to recycle leftovers for lunch, one of my daily chores. Avid skiers, like Sally, didn't wait for lunch. She grabbed a cold scrambled egg sandwich to gobble on the ski lift. Others stuck around long enough to wolf down their hash.

By midafternoon, I was still cramming ornaments into boxes. Nobody ever says, "Oh goodie! Let's all un-decorate the tree!" Our pretty little spruce — responding to the indoor warmth as though it were spring — sprouted soft blue tips of new growth at the end of each branch. What a rotten trick we had pulled on that beautiful tree.

About three o'clock, Neil was stowing boxes beneath the stairway when Sally rushed in, a stricken look on her face, "Tonto broke his leg."

"He what?" I gasped.

For once, Sally was not giggling. "I was skiing with Bridge and Tonto. He was really slow and we were getting cold so we told him we were going down to Snoasis (the warming house halfway down the mountain) to get a hot chocolate while we waited for him. Just as we skied off he fell down. We heard him yell out, 'Don't leave me,' but we thought he was just kidding. We were sitting there, sipping our chocolate, wondering what had happened to him. We looked out the window and saw them hauling Tonto down the mountain on a sled with ski patrolmen in front and in back. He's at the doctor's now with Bridget, getting X-rays."

"Is it bad?"

"Can't tell yet."

All I needed was for my lovely male secretary to break his ever-loving leg. I had visions of the gory compound, complex fractures I remembered from my junior high first aid book. Traction. He'd probably have to spend a month in traction!

❋ ❋ ❋ ❋ ❋

After dinner, apprehensive about what I might find, I went over to Tonto and Bridget's apartment.

To my relief, my secretary was not in traction, nor was he suffering particularly. Tonto sat on a big chair, his foot elevated so his bare toes, sticking out of the cast, could toast before the fireplace.

Nearly everybody on the staff was there, too, offering exotic remedies for relief of pain. Sally and Sandy had busied themselves cutting centerfolds from *Playboy* with the object of decoupaging his cast.

"He didn't want autographs and all that hoo-haw," explained Bridge.

As Tonto sipped Jack Daniels, he assured me the break wasn't bad and he would be back at work very soon. He fondled a couple of prescription bottles.

"There's always more," chanted J.B.

"OK guys, what's with this 'always more' slogan?" I asked.

"Well, it was New Year's Eve," began Tonto.

"J.B. thought we were running out of beer. I told him, 'It's OK, J.B., there's more beer.'

"Then a little while later J.B. asked, 'Are we out of chips?'

"I said, 'It's OK, John, there's more chips.'

"Later he says, 'How about brownies?'

"There's more brownies."

"Seemed like every time I turned around he was asking me if there was more of something. Finally J.B. turned to me with this profound look of cosmic understanding on his face and said, 'That's right. There's always more. There's more beer, there's more chips, there's more pop, there's more snow, there's more good stuff, there's more trouble, there's more happiness. There's always more!' Whatever there is in life, There's Always More!'"

"There's Always More," chanted everybody in unison.

Thus was born a phrase that echoed through the rest of the season — and beyond.

Chapter 19

And Yet More

It might have been a new year, but my problems promised to be the same — at least as far as the staff was concerned.

While I was pouring a bushel of wheat into the top of the flour mill, listening to the whirr of the machine cracking wheat for our morning breakfast cereal, I looked up to see Brad Allen standing there. The kid always shambled to work late; Neil complained that every time he got his hands on a snowblower it broke down and needed fixing.

His gray, sweatshirted arms were crossed; his eyes shone with hostility. "Buddy of mine's got a good job in Breckenridge," he mumbled. "Says he can get me hired on. I'm givin' you notice. I'm leavin' day after tomorrow."

"Hey, you said you wanted a job for the season," I objected.

"Well, I'm givin' you notice. So today's my day off and I'm going skiing," he turned on his heel.

"Turn in your lift ticket and pack your gear," I responded. "You're outta here."

"Can't I go skiing today?" he whined.

"If you want to buy your own lift ticket you can."

He muttered something about a sweat shop as he slunk toward his room to pack. Closest that kid ever got to sweat was his shirt. But a moment later I was racked with anxiety. What would his parents think? They had been repeat guests. And how could I find another employee on such short notice? Fortunately, business slacked off a little after the first of the year and wouldn't pick up again until in February.

A glance at my watch told me it was time to check the progress of the housekeeping staff. As I went in and out of bathrooms lifting lids and nosing about, the first person I saw was Diane. The girl's mood was improving — slowly. I finally put together that she was rebounding from an unhappy love affair with a fellow she met while studying in Switzerland. Not only did they break up after a torrid interlude, but he almost immediately married her best friend. Not the sort of thing to cheer a girl up during her semester abroad. I felt sorry for her, but had to remind myself I wasn't running an asylum for the lovelorn.

When I glanced through the bathroom door, I saw Diane kneeling before a toilet, preparing to clean it. A diligent girl, she was fastidious — if not cheerful — when she went about her chores. Just then she looked like a sad postulant at prayer.

When she glanced up to see me watching I quipped, "What strange gods we people worship." She blinked back at the white throne, startled, then laughed. Humor was one of the few ploys that always seemed to work for me.

I was concerned about Sally. She hadn't been feeling well, complained of a bad stomach and diarrhea — not uncommon in the mountains. Certainly she had lost weight. I feared she might have to go home. Why did calamity always befall my best workers?

"Anybody seen Sandy?" I asked. The girls shook their heads no and looked disgusted.

"She's probably off with her book hiding somewhere, leaving us to do all the work," complained Chub.

Evidently Sandy, our resident hippie girl, had figured a way to wriggle through my rules. Since nobody could go skiing until all work was completed, she would just let everybody else make the beds and empty the wastebaskets. She counted on them to work extra, finish her chores.

I was determined to find that girl — to set her straight. My search led me to her room, then to the boys' bunk room, which they called the Spoon Room for some reason that nobody remembers. No Sandy. I checked several unrented units. I finally found Sandy stretched out asleep in the darkened women's sauna, her naked body covered with a towel. The sauna fire had been out since the night before, but the room remained warm and cozy. Evidently she had decided to take a shower, wash her hair — organically, of course — and relax.

The sight of her, asleep and shirking, sent my teeth to gnashing. When I spotted her hairbrush, a scene from Erskine Caldwell's *God's Little Acre* flashed through my brain. As Sandy awakened, startled at being caught, I grabbed her hairbrush, lifted her towel and spanked her on the bare bottom — about four smart whacks.

"Get up and go do your work," I ordered.

"How dare you! Nobody ever laid hands on me in my entire life!" she wailed.

"Then it's high time," I replied as I stalked back to my flour mill.

I shouldn't have done that, but it felt good just the same. My employee relationships were not going by anybody's book. Fortunately, Sandy did settle down. Although she was always a bit lazy, she never tried a trick like that again.

A couple of days later, Chub intercepted me in the hallway. "Can I talk to you?"

"Something simple or serious stuff?"

"Serious stuff."

Lately, the popular Chub hadn't been herself. I couldn't tell whether she was ill, maybe with the same stomach problem that plagued Sally, or had suffered some reverse in her love life — an all-too-common malady among the staff. "Come on up to my apartment."

Chub sat on one of my padded benches, flexing her powerful shoulders as she twisted a Kleenex into a thousand bits. "I'm leaving."

"Leaving? Why?"

"Gotta get an abortion."

"Abortion?"

Chub? The rough, tumble ski demon who beat the guys in informal "Downhill Racer" competitions? Although abortion had been legalized, I had never talked to anyone who had actually gone through with it.

"Was it somebody on the staff? Do you need help? Do you want me to talk to him? What can I do?" My words tumbled forth with more speed than direction. I realized how ridiculous I sounded, a poor imitation of a hillbilly father reaching for his shotgun.

"Nothing you can do. I've talked to my dad. He's driving up to get me this afternoon. It happened before I got here. An old roommate. But I won't be back. I've got to get my head together."

"Why didn't you take the pill?"

"I dunno. Never got around to it. I'm sorry to go, but I just can't cope any more."

Abruptly she stood up and went to her room to pack. In the abstract, I supported Chub's right to do what she was about to do. But I was furious with her for being so careless. What was so damned difficult about going to the clinic and getting a prescription?

Obviously, I was the last to know of her decision. The other employees liked Chub, sympathized with her plight.

❈ ❈ ❈ ❈ ❈

When the phone rang a couple of mornings later I answered it myself because my lovely male secretary was still on the mend. Father sounded excited. "Zidzy. You said somebody quit. I've hired an employee for you."

I bristled. "Thanks, Dad, but I think I'll hire my own employees. I want to find someone who was never a guest; maybe he won't act like he's on vacation all the time."

"It's Heather Wendelken!" In his excitement, he ignored me. "Clyde called. She can get there in a few days." Although I only met her once, I remembered Heather as a cute little blond whose granny glasses perched atop her turned-up nose. Her father, an attorney, absolutely doted on his only child. From the time Heather was old enough to ski, those two came to the Inn at least twice each winter. Her mother — who hated snow and wasn't very well — stayed behind in Wichita.

"Dad, don't you think Heather could have called me herself if she wants a job?"

"No need to, Clyde and I took care of it on the spot." Just like that, Heather's dad and mine made a deal!

I was getting set to unload on my dad with the vigor of Neil scooting snow with a shovel, when my mother came on the phone, forcing me to calm down. Mom, with her sixth sense, probably knew to grab the receiver before I exploded at Dad. "You'll really like Heather."

"Mom, I know you and Dad think a lot of Clyde and Heather, but the only time I met her I had the distinct impression that she's used to getting her own way. I've got enough prima donnas around here."

"Now, Virginia, your Dad and Clyde have been friends for a long, long time. Clifford always told Heather she could have a job any time she wanted it. She just finished her senior year at the University of Arizona. Needs something to do until spring."

There was no use arguing. I might win against Father, but never when Mother sided with him.

"You'll see. You'll like her."

When Dad came back on the phone I changed the subject, "Dad, I think we should shovel the roof."

"No need to, don't do it."

When I hung up, I wouldn't have been surprised to feel smoke issuing from my ears. I leaned my head against the wall and banged my fist in frustration against the door frame.

Chapter 20

Heather on the Hill

I was looking over the chart, listing Saturday's arrivals, when I looked up to see four rumpled people standing in front of the desk.

"This that Millers Idlewild Inn place?"

"You've got it, sir," I replied. The husband wore dark-rimmed bifocals with smudged lenses. His pallor was that of someone who worked in a bank or an office. It was easy to see these people had driven all night; the man's chin sprouted fresh whiskers. Beside him stood his rail-thin wife, whose black eyebrows had been plucked so severely they looked like a pair of parentheses that had been pried apart. Their two teen-aged daughters stood a few feet away, scanning the postcard rack.[*] They looked at the bulletin board tacked full of brochures for sleigh rides, for the inner tube hill, plus a "Crisis Hot Line" 800-number someone had stuck on it.

"Name's Franklin and we have a reservation."

"Yes, Mr. Allen Franklin (NRN) from Decatur, Illinois," I

---

* Hanging from a string by the postcard rack ws a rubber stamp I ordered made. It said:
  **Having a Wonderful Time
  Wish You Were Here**

replied.

"I'm not sure this is the right place." His wife spoke in a Chi-caw-go accent. "This doesn't look right to me at all." In what I perceived to be an habitual attempt to become invisible at the first hint of conflict, the daughters slipped away into the lounge.

"Your reservation looks in order; fortunately, your rooms are made up. But we were expecting you later in the day."

"We drove all night to get here. I thought this place would be more — more modern." The woman looked more than tired; instinct told me she hadn't rested for about twenty years.

"I believe our brochure advertised Millers Idlewild Inn as rustic," I replied, forcing a smile. Always I dreaded taking first-time guests to their quarters. It was easy, at first glance, to mistake the Inn's raffish charms for dowdiness. "Let me show you to your rooms."

Now I remembered. Tonto told me of several phone calls from the travel agent who made the Franklins' reservations. "My client wants your least expensive accommodations."

"My client says she is bringing four people and wants me to ask for group rates."

"My client wants to know if you will rent your rooms without the meals."

Tonto patiently explained that four people got family plan, but not group rate; that we rented no rooms without meals. He finally booked the Franklins into our cheapest family-sized rooms on the lower floor of the Balcony House.

"Follow me." I tried to assume my professionally cheerful innkeeping voice, but my shoulders tensed for the worst.

As I opened the door to their rooms, the wife put her hand to her forehead dramatically, her chin jutted sideways.

I nattered away, explaining meal schedules and how to redeem lift tickets. "You can pull your car into the driveway to unload. By the way, we are going to do something really neat this week — ski down Seven-Mile-Trail in the moonlight."

As I recrossed the driveway to the Inn I sighed. I had just glimpsed those rooms the same way my new guests undoubtedly saw them: the ceilings were low, the bathrooms damp and the wallboard buckled ever so slightly. The bedspreads matched each other, but nothing else. No amount of paint could brighten the basic dinginess of a long room with one tiny window.

About five minutes later, the husband was back at the front desk, his wife at his heels. The poor man stood there in an embarrassed silence until his wife jabbed him in the ribs. He blurted, "We won't stay in that dump." He was sweating in spite of the cold.

"Well, I have other accommodations available, but they're more expensive," I explained, distrustful of my emotions which were somewhere between sad and mad.

His wife took over. "Let us see them." Ever the obliging innkeeper, I unlocked an upstairs suite in the Inn and showed it to her. Then I led them across the creek to show them a vacant cabin.

At that moment a long freight train came barreling down the tracks — forcing me to raise my voice. "Doesn't happen very often," I yelled, although that wasn't quite the truth. The Inn's property abutted the main line of the Denver and Rio Grande Railroad. Most guests adapted quickly to the presence of noisy trains, even to the point where they enjoyed watching them. But new guests were often appalled.

"We'll take the cabin, but we think you have advertised falsely so you should give it to us for the same rate as those first awful rooms you showed us," demanded Mrs. Franklin.

"I'm sorry, but the rooms in the Balcony House are a lot cheaper than the cabins. You requested the least expensive thing."

"Then we want our deposit back." Mrs. F. had taken over

completely. Her husband was no longer just deferential; he had joined his daughters in their attempt to fade into the knotholes in the wall.

"No refund on deposits. That's our policy." Mad was winning out over sad. "However, if you'd like to stay a couple of nights until you use your deposit, then move elsewhere; that's all right with me."

"Our travel agent will hear about this," hissed Mrs. Franklin. My guess was her travel agent had already heard quite a lot. The couple retreated to the Balcony House to talk it over.

The next thing I knew the Franklins were unloading their car — moving their luggage into the same rooms they had originally reserved.

❄ ❄ ❄ ❄ ❄

Dwight dropped by that morning; he had not lost his knack for showing up when I needed him.

While I poured a cup of coffee he listened patiently, as I bitched about the family from Illinois — or hell — or wherever.

"You did the right thing. They were classics. Tightwads, too cheap to fly or rent a motel on the way. So they arrive exhausted, dizzy from the altitude. Probably figured if they made a scene they could talk you into something for nothing. Tell you what, Ginger. When people aren't happy with your rooms, ninety percent of the time it's because they've got marital troubles. Domestic problems.

"Probably she wanted to go to the beach, but he and the kids voted to go skiing. So she's going to make them pay because she didn't get her own way. They'll probably settle down. When they get some rest they'll be OK."

I accepted his advice, gloomily. "Seems like everything's coming apart."

"Like what?"

"Tonto broke his leg. Not too bad, but he isn't back to work yet. One of my ski bums quit to go to Breckenridge and another's getting an abortion. Sally seems to have picked up some parasite or other."

"Not too bad, I'd say. Normally you expect about a thirty percent turnover after Christmas." He bit, appreciatively, into a cinnamon roll Myrtle had silently slipped in front of him. "Myrtle, you're such a sweetie," Dwight said, grinning. She smiled back, shyly.

"Should I try to talk kids into staying if they want to quit? What'll their parents think? I'll bet we'll never get them back as guests."

"Naw. Don't treat them like your own kids. Chances are, if you asked their parents, they've been making trouble at home, too."

"Dad called, informed me he's hired a new employee. Without even consulting me. Got any ideas for keeping him out of my hair?"

"Get yourself another line of work. Sorry Ginger. Dad goes with the job and you knew it when you signed on."

Just then Neil rushed by, bent on an errand. When he saw my brother he stopped in his tracks. "Hey, Dwight."

Dwight had been upset with Neil when he rolled the scraper the summer before, but he liked Neil and was never one to hold a grudge. He stood and slapped Neil on the shoulder, "Hail to the chief."

"Chief?" asked Neil.

"Everybody says you're going to be the next fire chief. You'll be the youngest one since I did it almost twenty years ago."

"Nobody told me," said Neil, a pleased look creeping over his face. "Lady, Sandy says the couple in the Columbine broke down another bed last night."

The Columbine was a small suite, which until very recently had been furnished with two double beds. "What, again? So, don't just stand there, go fix it."

"But, but, you don't understand . . ." He looked like he wanted to say something but decided against arguing and hurried off.

"I wish all my employees were as reliable as Neil," I said. "This job would be a piece of cake."

Because the Columbine was right above where we were sitting, we heard a series of loud thumps, bangs and thuds. "Neil must be taking the bed apart so he can fix it. There's a real heavy couple from Topeka in the Columbine. Shaped like gourds, both of them." I outlined a large pear shape with my hands to indicate their degree of roundness. "Don't know how the two of them manage to fit into a chair on the lift. Neil told me yesterday one bed was broken, but I didn't go up to check the damage."

My father was very particular that we furnish rooms with firm, good-quality mattresses set into sturdy wooden bedsteads. An attractive, knotty pine headboard stood at the top of each bed.

I assumed Neil would shore up the damage or strengthen the frame by nailing on a new board for support. But when Neil and J.B. appeared, the splintered boards they carried in their arms more closely resembled kindling for the fireplace than anything that had ever been furniture.

My brother's mouth hung open; he was intrigued: "How did they do that? Do you think he was jumping on her? Or was she the jump-er and he the jump-ee? Why don'tcha ask 'em?"

The mental picture was too much for me, too. I started to laugh at the thought of two 'punkins' chasing each other around the bed, then crashing onto it in the heat of passion.

"What'll I do? I can't fix these. I'll have to burn 'em," said Neil.

"Not much you can do," advised Dwight. "Just set the box

springs on the floor until they leave. Tell 'em to have at it, whatever it is they're doing, and hope the floorboards hold together."

"Should I say something to them?" I wondered who would be more embarrassed to talk about what happened — the jumping gourds or myself.

"Don't say a word. Believe me, the subject won't come up. If you say anything, they'll claim your beds are no good. Just act as though nothing happened."

Just then we looked up to see Tonto crutching his way through the front door. "I'm sick of sittin' around. Might as well work as be bored out of my mind."

I was thoroughly happy to see him; I was royally tired of running to answer the phone. "How's the pain?"

"In my leg, not bad. Couldn't get much sleep, last night though."

"Because it hurt?"

"No, because Sally and Bridget decided to paint a coat of lacquer over their decoupage and it didn't set up. I had to hang my leg out of the bed the whole night so my cast would get dry. My toes got cold." He pulled up his pant leg to reveal two provocative centerfold models hugging his cast.

Dwight admired it. "Hey Sport, think those girls will make it up your leg?"

❆ ❆ ❆ ❆ ❆

During the days leading up to Heather's arrival, I continued to bitch — but only to my children when we were alone in our apartment. "She'll probably be just one more problem for me to deal with!" I lamented.

But I said something quite different to some of the lazier staff members. "It's about time we got someone older, more mature and responsible around here. Somebody who'll take time to attend to little niceties, like emptying vacuum cleaner bags without being told."

Diane, whose girlhood path had crossed Heather's several times at the Inn, looked forward to her arrival.

When Heather drove up in her immaculately maintained Volkswagen bug, light blue with a sun roof, she immediately asserted herself as a person to be reckoned with. She walked into the girls' bunk room, took one look around and announced, "Let's clean up this pigsty." Because Diane and Sally had been struggling to do just that, her declaration was welcome. Sandy, who viewed her mess as being somehow organic and therefore excusable, found herself outvoted and agreed to try to keep her belongings tidy.

Diane hugged her and squealed, "Good thing you got here today. We're skiing down Seven-Mile-Trail tonight."

"You'll be Dining Room Manager," I explained to Heather. I figured since she was a little older she might enjoy responsibility. I had learned that trick from my father, who loved to bestow titles. He was forever handing out paper promotions. I remember one time when he told an employee, "I have just promoted you to Snowblower Foreman." The kid felt very good until he realized no mention had been made of an increase in salary.

Dining Room Manager *was* an important job. So much of the Inn's "atmosphere" was centered in the spacious room with low beams. While they ate, guests could look past my pots of red geraniums through two enormous picture windows. At breakfast, they could watch birds at the outsized birdfeeder which Myrtle kept supplied with suet and birdseed. At night, the tiki torches and some floodlights illuminated the postcard-pretty creekbed.

It was extremely important that the organized, but chaotic, mayhem in the kitchen be offset by a relaxed feeling in the dining room. I hoped Heather would have a good eye for the details that would make our simple fare seem charming.

After dinner, Roger started training Heather in proper headwaitress etiquette. They, too, knew each other from previous years. I was halfway listening as I sat at a dining room table, fretting over a grocery order. Seemed like the price of everything was skyrocketing — except for our room rates, which had been set and published almost a year before. Inflation was threatening to eat up more profits than the employees.

"Make the girls keep their hair under bandannas," Roger told Heather. "Fill the sugar shakers every evening. By the way, if you haven't already figured it out, I'm gay."

For just a moment Heather looked startled at his off-hand declaration but just smiled. I had wondered how, or whether, Roger imparted that delicate information.

He did not pause, just kept up his rapid-fire instructions. "Be sure to shake out the bread baskets over the fireplace before you put them away. Refill the catsup and mustard farters every time they are used." Heather looked startled; the kids had referred to the red and yellow plastic squeeze containers as "farters" for so long I sometimes forgot and called them that in front of guests.

His training session droned on until I heard a big boom that sounded like a cross between a barking dog and a bursting balloon. When I looked up I saw Heather, her hand on her tummy, a pleased look on her face.

Diane laughed. "When it comes to belches, Heather's is far out!"

"Enough for now," said Roger, who perceived, correctly, the lesson had gone on long enough.

"You skiing down Seven-Mile-Trail with us tonight, Lady?"

"You bet. Fifteen-minute drill!" I called out.

I didn't have to tell anybody to hurry. On the several nights each winter when we went for a moonlight run from near the top of Berthoud Pass to the bottom, everyone was eager to go.

Seven-Mile-Trail wasn't really a trail — it was an abandoned road built for Model T Fords early in the century. And although the distance on the highway that replaced it was seven miles, the trail was only about four.

Tonto's leg had improved enough that he could drive, but not ski, so he volunteered to bus everybody to the top in Bertha, the Inn's old red twenty-four-passenger school bus. He would wait for us to emerge from the woods, about an hour later, at the bottom. Most of the staff, plus some of our more adventurous guests, were eager to go. I was surprised to see the Illinois malcontents climb aboard. Perhaps Mrs. F. decided her family should take advantage of our late night ski because it was free. They hadn't departed when their deposit was used up after all; maybe they checked the rates at other lodges and concluded they had a bargain. Their daughters were obviously happy; they had taken up with some college boys.

"Do ya'll think I can do it?" queried a Dallas lady from beneath her bunny fur hat as she slipped her skis in the rack.

"Nothing to it," Roger assured her. "It's easier skiing than anything at Winter Park. We wouldn't take you if it was dangerous." In those days people didn't automatically sue over unfortunate little mishaps like avalanches or broken legs.

One of our guests, a senior pilot for Braniff who would shortly become known as "Errol," plopped into the seat next to me. A tall Georgian with an arrogant air, he came to the Inn frequently. He loved to ski so much he sported what skiers call the "raccoon look." He was deeply tanned, except for the stark white area where his eyes were protected from the sun by goggles. He saw to it that during the winter months his itinerary often required a two- or three-night hiatus in Denver.

"Have you ever skied down Seven-Mile?" I asked.

"First time for me," he replied. It was dark in the bus. The pilot tucked his arm under mine with a possessive gesture, then snuggled closer. I wondered, had he been drinking? Seats on the bus were small — after all, they had been designed for children — so it was difficult for me to wiggle away from him. I remembered hearing him brag at the dinner table about his wife's social connections in Atlanta.

"You should bring your wife some time, I'd love to meet her." I doubted his wife was the conversational subject he had in mind.

"She's not much for snow. Won't go anywhere cold. Sometimes in the summer, even though our house is totally air conditioned, she sleeps under an electric blanket."

"Let me guess. You met at her sorority while you were in college."

"Something like that. Are you sure I'll be OK on my Rossignols? I don't own any cross-country skis."

"This will be the first time I've tried it on my new skinny sticks." I told him. "Always did it before on alpine skis. You'll be fine."

Near the top of the pass Tonto halted the bus while everybody grabbed hats, mittens and assorted gear.

"Follow me," shouted Roger. "The only hard part is right here at the top. After the first fifty yards, it's a piece of cake."

Compared to heavy alpine gear, cross-country skis felt like thin, wet noodles. I slipped my boots into their bindings — flimsy things, fastened only by a hinge at the toe. I stepped over the cabled highway guard rail and pointed my skis straight down the steep slope. I hoped the deep snow would slow me down because I knew how difficult it was to make any kind of a turn on light skis in deep powder. Near the bottom, I hit a submerged rock or tree stump. With no heel straps to secure my feet on the skis, my toe hinges hurled me forward fast — with the force of a mousetrap spring. My face planted itself firmly in an ice-cold snowbank.

The pilot, whom I had planned to outdistance, was promptly at my side. "You OK?" he asked.

"Will be," I sputtered, "soon as I clean the snow out of my glasses."

He grabbed me under one armpit and lifted me as he shoved his hip flask to my lips. I tasted cognac. "Sure you know where we are?"

"Quite sure."

Light from a full moon reflected against the bright snow, rendering the scene bright as day. It was as though we were skiing through a black and white movie; however, when we slid into the shade of tall trees it felt like somebody suddenly turned off the projector.

It was easy to forget the several places along the trail where lurked dips, two to four feet deep. Difficult to anticipate, they were often hidden in shady stretches. Each time I hit one, I pitched forward on my hinges into another face plant. The other skiers' stable bindings held them firmly secured to their weighty downhill skis; when they hit the same dips their skis flexed, carrying them safely through the ruts.

Although I wouldn't have admitted it, I was miserable. Cold snow clung to my hair, to my eyebrows, was stuck behind my glasses, plastered in my stocking cap, and worst of all, filtered down my neck. I felt frozen, a permanent snow angel. With my every tumble, my companion and I lagged farther and farther behind the happy voices we could hear shouting downtrail. The man was patient, helpful. But I had the ominous feeling he wasn't the sort to work for charity.

"By God, I know we're lost," the pilot complained. He swilled more cognac — presumably for aid in navigation.

I reassured him. "How could we be lost? We're going down a trail and down is the only direction we can go."

"I'll swear we saw that same tree a little while ago."

"What's the matter?" I started to laugh. "I'll bet you don't know where you are if you don't have dials, compasses, flashing lights and gadgets in front of you." I giggled at the thought that the same man who could navigate a 727 from Miami to Houston had been robbed of his innate sense of direction by technology.

He didn't see the joke. "Any bears around here?"

"Not this time of year. They're all asleep. In their warm little dens. Just like you will be an hour from now."

The guy was really getting worried. "Hear that?" He cupped his ear and pointed down the trail. "What is it?"

What he heard was Heather's stentorian belch, but I didn't let him in on the secret. The man's eyes were round, wide and open — and not just because of the dimness of the moonlight.

When we skied beneath some particularly low branches I realized we were close to the end of the run. I, for one, was damned glad. I had fallen more often that night than I had all the previous times when I skied Seven-Mile. I vowed never to attempt it again on cross-country skis.

Almost within sight of the bus we were bushwhacked — literally. A sudden shower of snow rained down from the trees. J.B., growling like no animal I ever heard, flung his elongated body across the trail. Other skiers joined the ambush. "We're abominable snowmen! Abominable!"

Heather belched. "Except for her," giggled Sally. "She's abdominal." Staff and guests were laughing so hard they could barely stand.

I immediately realized what was happening and who was making it happen. But the pilot was so terrified he extended his ski pole like a fencer and started lunging at our assailants. Alas, fancy footwork is nearly impossible on long, heavy skis. One ski thrust itself straight up in the air and he fell over backwards, still flailing away with his pole. To this day I can't remember the guy's name. That evening he received a permanent nickname. "Errol," for Errol Flynn's swordplay. He seemed to fancy his new moniker, used it when calling for a reservation.

As we returned our skis to the rack I heard a woman's voice, "That was the most exciting thing that ever happened to me!" I was surprised to hear this announcement from the lady from Chi-caw-go. "In fact, this is the best vacation we've ever had anywhere. We're coming back!"

So long as I was moving, the cold didn't bother me too much. But on the fifteen-minute ride home, it was all I could do to keep from shivering. I knew if I started shaking, Errol would attempt to share his big down jacket with me.

I preferred to remain frigid.

Because they were tired, everyone was pretty quiet. But I overheard Diane regaling Heather with tales of the New Year's party. "And I was the only person who knew how to alter the marijuana brownie recipe for high altitude!"

"Did you eat any?"

"Course not, but everybody else did. They said they were good — just before they fell asleep. You'll never guess what else happened? One night I went to bed early. I woke up when I heard some whispers. The bunk above me sagged so bad I could hardly turn over. There were two people up there! But I didn't say anything." My thoughts flew back to Chub.

As we unloaded, several people ribbed Heather about being the Abdominal Snowman. She rewarded them with another detonation. Heather proved to be efficient, organized, charming to guests and a hard worker. But what won me over initially was her uncouth belch.

Roger brewed hot buttered rum and I ladled it out to tired guests who immediately shuffled off to bed. As I was stacking dirty cups on a tray the pilot grabbed me around the waist, from behind. Startled, I almost dropped my tray. "Want to visit my room?" he whispered.

"Don't need to," I assured him. "I know just what it looks like."

View of Millers Idlewild Inn from Vasquez Road. Construction began in 1946 and never really ended. Here, the Inn is shown as it looked early in the 1950s. By the time I arrived in 1973 the building was twice as large; its log-slab exterior had been painted reddish brown. From the beginning the roof on the street side of the building was covered with slick, corregated silver aluminum, so snow slid right off. My father loved signs and put them everywhere!
Miller collection

Millers Idlewild Inn was the brainchild of my father, Clifford Dwight "C.D." Miller. He greeted guests with a smile, a joke and an inexhaustible fund of philosophy.

"You are a stranger here but once," he told them. Endlessly curious about people, he always had time to interrupt his chores and "chew the fat."

Miller collection

Gertrude "Trudy" Miller spent years of apprenticeship as "just a housewife." But they served her well when she ran housekeeping, food service and serviced as gracious hostess at the Inn. She treated each guest as someone she had personally invited into her very own home.

Miller collection

One year two very authentic looking gorillas showed up to surprise me on my birthday! My brother Woodie, right, rented gorilla costumes for himself and my brother Dwight. I had no idea who was inside those very realistic monkey suits. Here I am with my brothers — after they were unmasked.
photo courtesy Roger Roeck

Before we left Arizona Keith, Gordon, Drew and I posed for a portrait. My children learned to ski so fast that they immediately left me in their powder — a source of continual pride and embarrassment.
Cornell album

C.D. dons a Green Bay Packers sweatshirt and hat, gifts from his Wisconsin guests. Although he never waited until happy hour to be cheerful, my father looked especially pleased. Perhaps it was because a couple of days later I would take over management of the Inn in February, 1973.

Miller collection

On the eve before I took charge, my feigned self-confidence didn't fool the camera. I am seated between my father and my barely visible mother

photo courtesy Carolyn Manganello

Neil Brubaker, the amiable red-headed youth who drove the ski bus, kept the pipes thawed, shoveled the roofs and looked after all the maintenance. His patience and good humor made him a spark plug to other staff members.
Miller collection

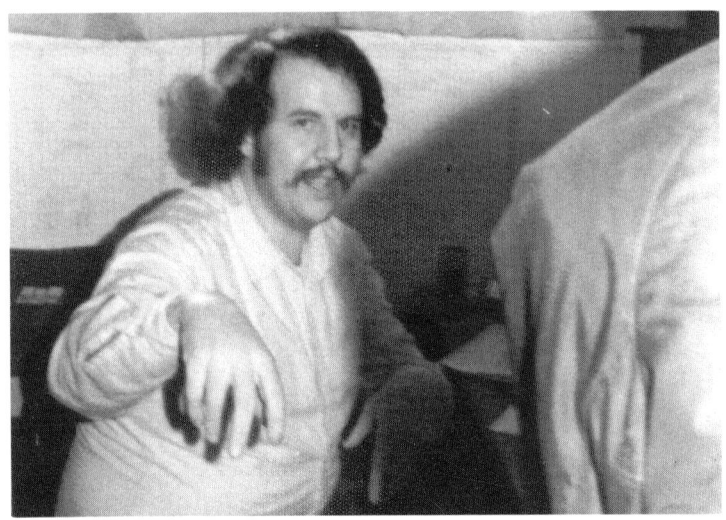

Tonto, the Inn's secretary, at his post in the office — gesturing toward Neil. In those days, a male secretary was even rarer than a male telephone operator.
photo courtesy Sally Jane Ludlow

Carolyn Taylor helps out in the office. Her look of exasperation leads me to believe she was trying to balance my accounts. She taught me that check books were not an appropriate place to practice creative writing.
photo courtesy Roger Roeck

Firm but good-hearted, Myrtle Ashton presided over the kitchen and fed the heartiest meals west of the Continental Divide. Everything was made from scratch. For Myrtle, cooking was easy. The hard chore was whipping a fresh batch of raw ski bums into shape every season.

photo courtesy Sally Jane Ludlow

Roger Roeck and his roommate Russ Stratton in their apartment in Denver. Three days a week, Roger cooked on Myrtle's days off. Because I didn't have an extra room for him, Roger slept in my father's cramped, smelly old darkroom.

photo courtesy Roger Roeck

Each autumn, everybody in town gathered to celebrate Halloween — the last big bash before ski season. Staff members and friends are seen just before departing for a party at the Swiss House of Fondue. Here, Bridget and Tonto, togged out as a Girl Scout and Boy Scout, pledge an evening of mayhem.
photo courtesy Sally Jane Ludlow

Outfits were home-made. On this occasion, people drew names and made costumes for each other. For her evening as a ballerina, Sally's dainty tutu was worn above her waffle stompers. Steve Smith, a neighbor, was a friar. And Flossie made a fine Brunhilde!
photo courtesy Sally Jane Ludlow

Roger and I traded roles. He shaved his moustache and beard, wore my glasses, cowboy ski hat and favorite shirt. I applied his moustache, beard and the inevitable chef's hat.

photo courtesy Sally Jane Ludlow

On another "dress-up" occasion I was snapped as I stood on the stairway. Behind me was a clock that said "R&F Spaghetti." The "R" stood for Raverino and was a gift from the Raverino family from St. Louis — frequent guests. My photo-gray glasses protected me in bright sunshine, but stayed permanently gray, even at night.

photo courtesy Roger Roeck

Sally Sawyer gets set to break a few eggs. When working in the kitchen she liked to wear Roger's hat along with her waffle-stomper boots.
photo courtesy Roger Roeck

Neil checks his daily list of chores with Tonto. Next to his left elbow is a stack of room keys which we chained to small logs. They were intentionally lumpy so skiers would not take them to the slopes and lose them.
photo courtesy Sally Jane Ludlow

I never became an expert skier and tried to avoid competitions. Occasionally, as at the annual Elbert Cup race to benefit handicapped skiing, I got suckered into entering. I could not hide my anxiety over the impending ordeal; I was sure I would fall and disgrace myself. I didn't fall, but I skied so slowly it was a disgrace!

Cornell album

The interior of one of the cabins, the Alpine Fir, ready for skiers — a fire roared in the fireplace. Accommodations were rustic but comfortable. The big window looked out on Vasquez Creek. Each year the cabin's floor sagged a bit more, slanting it toward the creek.

Millers Idlewild Inn publicity photo

The large saunas were the site of relaxation, merriment and occasionally of communal Wesson Oil rubdowns. We had one for men and one for women (shown here). The men's sauna was heated to 200 degrees Fahrenheit, the women's to a mere 160. The timer kept guests from roasting themselves. After dinner coeducational bathing was permitted — even encouraged. The heat was an effective way to soothe aches and pains after a cold day on the slopes.

Guests in the dining room sat around long tables to enjoy hearty meals. Informality was the rule. We didn't have a bar; most guests kept a bottle of something in their room and occasionally brought wine to the dinner table.

Miller family collection

When I first went to the Inn seven tiki torches blazed forth each evening — at the front, side and back of the building. My father had so much fun at a luau on Maui that he decided the Inn needed a Polynesian touch.

Miller family collection

A couple of guest children helped to make home-made ice cream. The electric machine was huge, noisy as a cement mixer and churned out three gallons at a time. Favorite flavors were peach and peppermint. Father also introduced what he called "nectars of the South Pacific" including guava, passion fruit and papaya — another inspiration from his Hawaiian trip.

Millers Idlewild Inn publicity photo

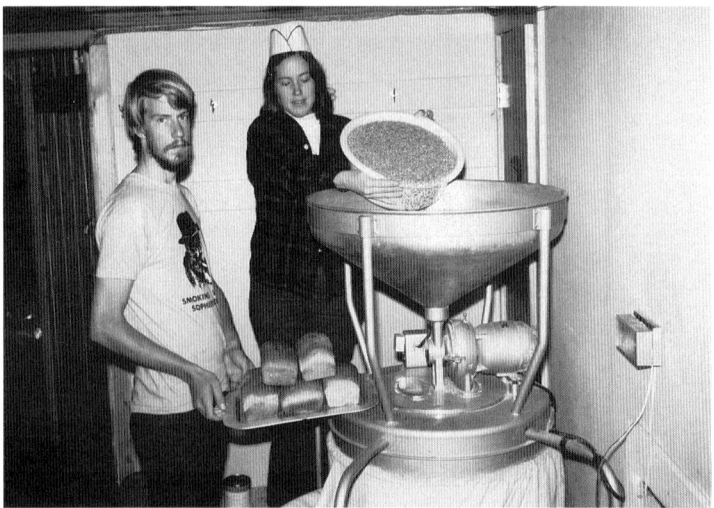

J.B. Brandenburg shows off loaves of bread while Kitty Miller pours grain into the hopper of the flour mill. This picture was taken the summer of 1974 after my nephew Steve was discharged from the army. He and Kitty came to help me manage the Inn.

Millers Idlewild Inn publicity photo

A guest helps herself to our Scandinavian breakfast. The elaborate smorgasbord, set out every Sunday morning, was my mother's pride. Guests could choose from three kinds of meat (ham, summer sausage and swedish meatballs), three kinds of fish (sardines, kippers and marinated herring), three kinds of cheese (cheddar, havarta and goat), three kinds of bread (limpa, flatbread and coffee cake). We also served lingonberries, fresh fruit, chopped boiled eggs, hot cracked-wheat cereal and cucumbers marinated in vinegar.
Millers Idlewild Inn publicity photo

It seemed the staff was forever finding an excuse to dress up. Here, the destination was a fifties party at a local bar. Set to go are my nephew Andy Miller, Heather Wendelken, Bridget Collins, Steve Smith and Tonto.
photo courtesy Sally Jane Ludlow

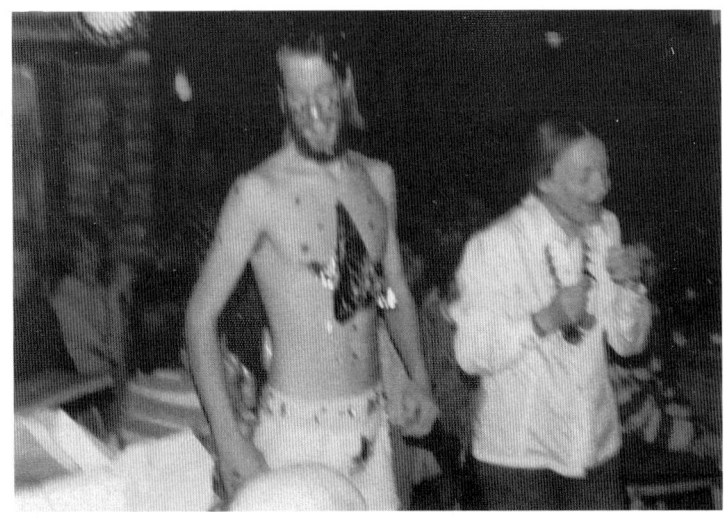

There was a big surprise inside my birthday cake! J.B. was decked out as the birthday elf, clad in the silver stars and glitter. Just after emerging from an enormous tissue paper cake he gave me a big hug.

photos courtesy Sally Jane Ludlow

Chapter 21

Double Trouble

"A guy called for you a while ago," Tonto looked up from his typewriter. "Said he owns Skiville Ranch (NRN). Wouldn't tell me what he wanted, just asked if you had a policy on couples."

"What kind of couples? Guys? Girls? Gays? What does he want to know about 'em?" After nearly a year in the ski lodge business, I had learned the word "couple" could mean almost anything.

"Said he'd call back later." My fellow innkeeper's hotel was smaller than ours but was also referred to as a "family place." Skiville Ranch was, by all accounts, a successful business. The owner and his wife were in their mid-forties, their children about the same age as mine.

Couples? Part of my business was to make people comfortable — right from the start. So when they checked in I tried to pick up cues from guests, clues to their idiosyncracies.

I had certainly encountered many unconventional pairs at the Inn. In some cases I could just about predict their behavior. Married couples, or those who had lived together for a long time, usually unpacked their bags immediately and raced right back to the front desk to ask about ski lessons or sleigh rides.

Then they explored the Inn's public rooms, walked down the path to the creek and strolled to town to stock up on liquor. They were eager to learn who else was registered; obviously they hoped to find pleasant conversation and companionship. Rarely were they disappointed.

When I showed honeymooners or lovers to their rooms, the next sound I heard was water being drawn for a bath or shower. I probably wouldn't see them again until mealtime; just as soon as they finished their pie they vanished.

Ironically, it was always difficult to tell whether two unmarried men traveling together were gay or straight. Both types signed in, got spruced up and hurried downtown to the bars to check out the action.

Single women in pairs were rare. Twenty years ago, they usually came with church or college ski clubs. Skiing was expensive; even if they had the funds many women weren't liberated enough to venture forth on vacations by themselves. Instead, they tried to get a boyfriend or father to foot the bill. But if they paid their own way they viewed the expense more as an investment than a vacation and were determined to maximize their capital. Whereas a man's eyes might rove over a girl's figure, a single girl's glance sped to the ring finger of the man's left hand. After a couple of days, if nothing materialized around the Inn, girls hit the bars, too.

The exception was lesbian couples. They didn't interact with other guests much. Or if they did, they sought the safe companionship of wives. I doubt most women realized they were talking to someone who was "different." More than one man's wife was heard to say, in a wistful tone, "How I envy you your career."

I tried to figure people out, test my observations. I remembered a weekend, the summer before, when I took a phone reservation from a man who requested a cabin for two. The man arrived first in a sporty little MG. Half an hour later another MG purred into the parking lot, its occupant a woman. It didn't take us long to figure out they were married all right — but not to each other.

Absolute privacy was difficult to achieve. Fellows with no companions frequently complained about our thin walls; they coveted the moans of pleasure they could hear, all too plainly, from the next room.

George Armstrong and Errol, the pilot from Atlanta, were fairly typical of a roving multitude of married men on the make. I was always amazed at how many men left their wives at home when they went skiing; or more properly, I was astonished by how many wives sent their husbands off skiing by themselves.

A woman less cynical than I am might have been delighted to discover that, almost overnight, she had emerged from the cocoon of mommydom into a desirable butterfly. Had I suddenly become a fascinating beauty? Hordes of men were pressing their attentions where none had bothered before. But I held no illusions; hanky-panky is ninety percent opportunity.

On the other hand, I was delighted when I realized the same shoe could fit the other foot. It dawned on me that when somebody interesting checked into my life, as the female keeper of an Inn I had an advantage because I had the power to make room assignments. I could move a potential conquest to the chamber of my choice — one with a romantic fireplace or an outsized shower stall. And if I was seen going in and out of somebody's room, what of it? I was an innkeeper, wasn't I? The mere presence of a clean towel over my arm constituted an alibi.

Tonto — who had long since proved himself more reliable as a friend than as a lover — was only too happy to concoct an excuse to move the object of my desire to a more convenient lodging. Convenient to me, that is. Then, too, Roger was at my side, commenting on the charms of new guests. "Alas, not my type," he would sigh. "Better check that one out, Lady. Looks like a winner to me."

In fact I was very interested in one professional man, a frequent guest that winter. He was witty, thoughtful, and an incredibly sensitive lover. On evenings when we shared a late-night sauna and a bottle of wine I could, for a little while, ignore the pressures around me. As much as anything, I enjoyed long, uninterrupted, intellectual discussions; they were blessed relief from mundane gossip around the Inn. He was also discreet. Alas when summer arrived, I realized my charms had faded. Should I have been surprised, the following ski season, to discover the bloom on my cheek had returned?

I was thinking about all of those things when Bridge interrupted my reverie. "Think I finally figured out what's going on out in the duplex," she said, referring to our biggest cabin across the creek. It was divided into two large, identical, side-by-side units.

Since they checked in a couple of days before, its mysterious occupants had generated a buzz of speculation among the staff. A group reservation had been secured for sixteen people. Because their leader was charged with making room assignments, Tonto hadn't given the specifics of sleeping arrangements much thought.

When the guests arrived, I at first took them to be middle-aged couples from some ski club in Minnesota. They were in an ebullient mood, clearly bent on having a sensational holiday. When I led them to their units they were particularly pleased by the presence of refrigerators. "Plenty of room to store beer and mixer," crowed one huge fellow on whose ruddy face was written the map of Ireland.

The next morning when the maids came back from their rounds they were perplexed. "Looks like all the men are sleeping on one side and the women on the other," reported Sandy. "But they seem to get together to party because there's lots of cigarette butts and trash on the men's side. Other side is neat as a pin."

Sandy thought the whole thing very creepy. "Those guys, all their hairbrushes and shaving kits and stuff are so — old-fashioned."

Another male guest, overhearing news of the peculiar sleeping arrangements, asked Tonto if he thought the women were available.

"Could be," Tonto replied. "Heard one of them saying something about a service."

The guest perked up. "Maybe it's a reunion of stewardesses or something. Hubba-hubba!"

Bridget nearly dropped the load of dirty towels she was carrying to the laundry room. "Hate to tell you this, but you better cool your jets." She tossed her blonde mane and snickered.

"What do you know we don't?" asked Sandy.

"One side is priests and the other is nuns."

"Oh God," said the guest, slapping the heel of his hand to his forehead. "Thanks for keeping me out of that one!" He wagged his head in disbelief and headed for the ski storage.

Bridget had an advantage because she had been raised Catholic and attended parochial school. She thought the whole thing a huge joke — far more humorous than other staff members, who were somewhat awestruck at the thought of cleaning up after sanctity. Children of the sixties, they were unable to fathom a concept as arcane as celibacy.

Just then the phone rang. "It's for you," said Tonto, muffling the mouthpiece. "It's the guy from Skiville."

I recognized the gruff voice at the other end of the line, his tone businesslike. "You got any space for the next three nights?"

A glance at the chart revealed we had vacancies. "You filled up?" It was always interesting to know how your competitor was doing.

"No, not filled up. But I need two doubles."

"Sure. I got 'em. Do they have a car?"

"No, they're with a group. I'll bring 'em down after a while if you still want 'em. Virginia, there's something you should know about these people."

"Did they tear your place up?" I asked. I certainly wouldn't want to get stuck with vandals.

"No. Worse. They're not married!"

For a long moment I stood, speechless. "You mean, you kick people out because they're not married?" I glanced at the calendar. Sure enough, it said 1974.

"I have a policy. Won't put up with that kind of thing. They argued with me but I ordered 'em out."

Stunned, I settled the phone back on its hook.

I couldn't believe a not-*totally*-prosperous innkeeper would actually kick people out of his lodge because they were sleeping in the same bed without benefit of clergy. It had never even occurred to me to ask anybody about their marital status. Had it been important to my father, he long ago would have given me very specific instructions on the topic.

Tonto, figuring from my expression something terrible had happened, broke into a huge guffaw when I explained.

An hour later the two young couples struggled in with their luggage. Although visibly annoyed, they also thought the whole episode a huge joke. We welcomed them to Millers, where they blended in very comfortably.

❊ ❊ ❊ ❊ ❊

While Tonto and I were going over the chart, figuring where to put the two couples, I noted a familiar name. "Allison? What's the first name?"

"Wayne. Dr. Wayne Allison and his wife Marsha. Said something funny when he made the reservation. Requested 'anything but Room 5!' Then he chortled up a storm."

"I'm stunned they're coming back at all. I think they had the world's most wretched honeymoon here last spring."

"I put 'em in your writing room in the Balcony House because it's small. There's only two of them, but they wanted a fireplace."

That afternoon I picked up the Allisons when their bus arrived. They hugged me like I was a long-lost relative — a rich one.

Wayne Allison looked about the same. But Marsha was a changed woman! In place of the thin little wisp of yesteryear, Marsha had gained about ten pounds — in all the right places. Her eyes sparkled, she was smiling, her grip was firm. As I stopped the van in the Inn's driveway she practically squirted out its door in her excitement to be back.

When Tonto, who had graduated to a walking cast, hobbled back from showing them to their little apartment, his grin was wide enough to show off his gleaming molar. "Did you say *last year* was their honeymoon?"

"Just about a year ago."

"I barely made it out of their room. She was ready to pounce on him."

As dinner time neared, guests crowded around the dining room door, waiting for the bell to ring. True, all guests had eaten a huge breakfast, then wolfed down a hamburger or a bowl of chili at the ski area. But skiing quickly consumed their fuel, leaving them ravenous. It didn't matter that I had assigned tables so that there would be nothing to be gained by being first in line. I suppose most of our guests shared the experience of having been to camp or living in a college dorm where such pack behavior was encouraged.

While everybody milled about, Marsha Allison perched on a couch in the lounge, sipping a drink she had brought along from their room. Wayne was wrapping up some business at the front desk.

My towering curiosity saw an opportunity; I just had to find out why Marsha was so miserable last year. Since I couldn't figure a subtle way to broach the topic, I just asked her, "You look fantastic. Happy. To be honest, when you two left last spring I wouldn't have given your marriage six weeks. What happened?"

Marsha laughed. "Well, I'll tell you. I was a total fool. I bought a wedding dress a whole size too small for me. I thought the most important thing in the world was for me to look *just so* on my wedding day. Well, I dieted for two whole months — when I saw the wedding pictures I was just stunned to see how awful I looked. I looked like a starving refugee. Then, too, my mother was on our backs the whole time — just making everybody totally miserable. When we got here I was so exhausted — I think I was off my head a little. If I had it to do over again, I'd just elope . . ."

Wayne joined us. "Besides," Marsha whispered confidentially in my ear as she squeezed Wayne's arm with fierce affection, "That virginity stuff just isn't what it's cracked up to be."

Chapter 22

Another Year Older

"There's some old guy cooking his breakfast in the men's sauna." Carolyn's tone of voice said, "Just when I thought I'd seen everything in this business . . ."

On especially busy days Carolyn often helped out. That Saturday changeover, the day the Green Bay group would arrive, promised to be frantic.

Odd things were always happening in the men's sauna — even when it wasn't in use. Once a stray cat took up residence. Another time some freeloaders tried to spend the night. But somebody cooking breakfast?

I stopped folding towels and sprinted across the driveway to the Balcony House. Sure enough, when I yanked open its outer door the delicious smell of frying bacon struck my nose. For once I didn't knock before I jerked open the door to the men's dressing room. A gnome of a fellow, swaddled in an oversized woollen sweater across which marched reindeer, single-file, looked up with an elfin smile. Atop one of the benches a Coleman stove hissed merrily; three eggs were burbling in a skillet. He looked vaguely familiar but for the moment he couldn't speak because his mouth was jammed full of skillet toast.

"May I ask what you are doing here?"

When he managed a swallow he said, "What's it look like? Cooking my breakfast."

"But, but —"

"Remember me from last year? I'm with the Green Bay group; they're checking in later today. Thought you wouldn't mind if I stepped in here and cooked my breakfast. I spent the night in my car in your parking lot."

I was aghast at the thought of an elderly guest spending the night in his car; it probably got down to zero. "Why didn't you ask for a room?"

"No need, no need. Always sleep in my car. Been traveling around, skiing various places. Quite self-sufficient, I assure you."

Perhaps he was the world's oldest ski bum; a retired factory manager, he had hit upon a plan, a scheme, what these days might be called an alternative life style. "My wife got tired of me hanging around the house all winter, so I just take off and go skiing for a couple of months. I sleep in my car. Been on the road six weeks now." He had made himself a comfortable bed across the reclining passenger seat of his battered sedan.

"I pull into a ski lodge and ask if I can use their public restrooms so I can shave, or their sauna shower, and if it's OK to sleep in their parking lot. They usually let me. Hey, how much trouble can an old geek like me make?"

Hanging behind him was a parka; sewed to it were dozens of badges, proof of all the ski areas he had visited. "Lots of places have senior rates. Because I'm over seventy, some of them even let me ski free! Don't you worry. I'll be a registered guest this afternoon."

Perhaps I should have felt honored because this week was to be his exception; so many of his friends were coming from

Wisconsin that he had gone legit and would pay the tariff so he could be with them.

"OK, but at least come into the dining room and have some coffee," I suggested.

We always knew things would be lively when the Green Bay group disgorged from the airport bus, laden with wheels of cheese, home-made sausage, cases of booze. Roger cleared space in the walk-in for their cocktail delicacies. Before they left home, the group organized itself into committees which tried to outdo each other on successive evenings by creating elaborate hors d'oeuvres.

Their return signaled my first anniversary in the ski lodge business. In a few days I, too, would celebrate a birthday. The year had been — eventful.

There was no room in the Inn that week. In addition to the Green Bay skiers, our biggest cabin — so recently hallowed by priests and nuns — was to undergo a reformation. A preacher from Alabama had reserved the duplex for himself and some of his church members. From their correspondence, I got the idea their church was pretty conservative. We were particularly asked whether we had a bar — we didn't — and if we would like for the minister to perform a Sunday service at the Inn — we declined. I wondered how these pious souls would view the Green Bay group's rowdy behavior.

Already my mind was braced for a week of conflict: saints vs. sinners; drinkers vs. teetotalers; Yankees vs. Confederates; Bart Starr vs. Kenny Stabler.

The boatload of pilgrims were the first to land on our shores. "I'm the Reverend Walter Thatcher (NRN). We're checkin' in for two weeks." The preacher was a tall, blond man whose smile seemed to have frozen into a permanent smirk of self-satisfaction. He towered over the twelve people who accompanied him. Although he was rattling off introductions, I was having trouble sorting out his parishioners. I gathered the booming minister had brought along three families from among his flock. As he explained it, "Our ministry is seeking Christ on the ski slopes."

Aside from some out-of-control skier yelling, "Kee-rist!" I hadn't heard many references to religion up there.

The preacher's parka was of the latest style, astronaut silver, which made him look like a side of beef wrapped in aluminum foil. But his most impressive asset was a diamond ring winking from the pinkie finger of his manicured paw; it must have weighed about five carats. It was clear that when it came to the business of doing good, Reverend Thatcher was doing very well.

"I am the founder of the Church of Christ in Action," he paused, as though waiting for me to offer an ecstatic gesture of recognition. I'd never heard of it. He went into swagger mode as he crowed, "We have over three thousand members plus our radio audience. Going into TV in May." Almost offhand he added, "Oh yes, and this is my wife Alva Lee."

Alva Lee was also tall. I wondered if she might be part Cherokee because her exotic good looks were heightened by straight dark hair pulled back into a thick pony tail. From her temple, a single lock of gray threaded backward, heightening her classic features. High cheekbones exuded a sophistication her charismatic husband lacked. Her smile was pleasant, restrained.

I finally decided that besides the minister and his wife, there were two other men with their families plus a woman with two children — no husband. Atop the heads of the other three women perched three almost identical beehives. The only way they differed was by color: red, yellow and blue (well no, platinum, really). Each lady's lengthy fingernails were painted bright red. They wore Priscilla Presley-style eye make-up (lots of eyeshadow and eyeliner), rouge, but no lipstick. I wondered if something about Rev. Thatcher's religious principles dictated this uniformity.

The preacher put his arm around the blond woman, and declared, "We are counseling our sister in her time of need. Belinda is getting a divorce." Belinda assumed a tragic expression, blending herself into Thatcher's hug.

Although I was dreading the necessity of bringing up a delicate matter, I was relieved to be able to change the subject. "Uh, we have a large group checking in this afternoon. From Green Bay, Wisconsin."

"Are they the Packers?" blurted a tall lad.

"No, just people who live in Green Bay. They've been coming here for years. Uh, they usually have a cocktail hour before dinner here in the lounge. You would be welcome to join them."

"Not for us the devil's nectar!" The tall preacher's finger thrust up with such ferocity I feared he might bore a hole in the low ceiling, or else scrape his knuckles. "We plan prayer meetings when we get back from skiing every afternoon."

Maybe things would work out after all.

❄ ❄ ❄ ❄ ❄

I didn't give the preacher and his group much thought because I was worried about Myrtle.

Always, her legs ached — understandable when a person is overweight and forced to be on her feet most of the day. Early in February the doctor had diagnosed a blood clot in her leg and ordered her to stay off it, an almost impossible task for a cook.

We had tried putting her rocking chair in one corner of the kitchen where she could elevate her bad leg on a footstool. In theory, Myrtle could delegate chores to Diane and Sally. Diane had become so proficient she had even mastered the trick of breaking four eggs simultaneously, two in each hand. Even so, it was difficult for Myrtle to impart a lifetime's experience to novices — accustomed as she was to whipping, kneading, stirring and spreading. We couldn't keep her down. When her condition didn't improve the doctor ordered Myrtle to take a week off. I was terrified. Next to Christmas, the week surrounding George Washington's Birthday was the busiest time of the year.

To my relief, Roger volunteered to stay on. "Hey, I like to be with the Green Bay group. They're always a lot of fun."

Early Sunday morning Roger and I were slicing, dicing, setting up the buffet table for what I considered to be the most important meal of the week — Scandinavian Breakfast. My mother had bequeathed responsibility for her very special tradition to me. Back in the summer of 1964, when she and my dad traveled throughout Scandinavia in their camper, she collected ideas and recipes. Although the smorgasbord involved a lot of preparation, its creation every week gave me as much pleasure as it did my mother. I followed her instructions to the letter.

"Lady, what kind of cake do you want for your birthday?" said Roger, as he caught slabs of ham falling from the slicer. I was pleased Roger remembered.

"I don't care. You know me, I'm not much for sweets. Whatever's easiest. What kind won't fall at this altitude?" Cakes were always problematical.

"Chocolate? Banana cream? Carrot?" he suggested.

"Carrot sounds good. I like carrot cake." Just to needle Roger I smirked, "Actually Roger, I'm the same as you. The only kind of cake I ever really wanted was one with a naked man jumping out of it!"

He laughed, while he squeezed icing from a pastry tube on top of the fresh coffee cakes.

"One nice thing about Scandinavian breakfast," I noted, "it isn't forgotten the minute it's eaten. The cucumbers, marinated herring and boiled eggs talk to each other all day. You get to taste them again and again."

"The breakfast's over, but the memory lingers on," sang Diane.

It was always interesting to watch guests choose their delicacies. The least adventurous of them, country boys usually, disgusted us. They merely heaped coffee cake and maybe some eggs and meatballs on their plates. They retreated when I urged them to try kippers or goat cheese.

As people filled their plates their reactions varied: "Marinated cucumbers? Bizarre."

"Oh yum, I love marinated cucumbers."

"Fish for breakfast? Never heard of such a thing." "What's this brown stuff, looks like soap?" (It was goat cheese.)

The Alabama Christians picked a little here and there, but the Wisconsinites came back for seconds and thirds.

❄ ❄ ❄ ❄ ❄

I began to wonder if the holy ghost was playing tricks in our biggest cabin. The week before we couldn't figure out what was happening between the priests and nuns. Probably nothing. But speculation fed staff gossip.

This week, the maids complained. "I hate it when we're trying to make up rooms and somebody tells us to come back later," griped Sandy. "I guess the women aren't too big on skiing. They sit around doing their fingernails all day." Sandy didn't think fingernail polish remover was organic. Besides, my ski bums were always upset when they couldn't make up rooms on schedule. The amount of time they could ski depended on guests' cooperation. These guests seemed to lounge around their cabin all day.

"Which one's the preacher's wife?" Sally asked.

"Why do you ask?"

"I thought it was that tall thin woman but the preacher and the blond are always together."

I was puzzled to see that after skiing each afternoon Alva Lee, the preacher's patrician wife, settled herself into a quiet corner of the lounge to read a book and sip a Pepsi. Absorbed in *The French Lieutenant's Woman*, she seemed oblivious to the boisterous Green Bay cocktail party going on around her. Occasionally, between bites of cheddar, I chatted with the woman. I liked her, couldn't figure out why she had distanced herself from her group.

Finally I ventured a comment, "Your husband said you would be having prayer services after skiing."

"They're over there praying for Belinda's divorce."

"Which one's Belinda? I forgot."

"The blond with the beautiful eyes."

My thoughts flew to Sandy's comment but I said, "I think even a preacher's wife should get to take a little time off from her business, too." She smiled, nodding in appreciation. Then, as though to signal all of this was really none of my business, her eyes went back to her book.

❄ ❄ ❄ ❄ ❄

Tuesday morning, while I was eating breakfast, Roger and Bridget suddenly appeared at each side of me. "Take the day off, Lady, go skiing. It's your birthday."

"Thanks, but I've got a lot to do here today. My day off isn't until Thursday."

"We're giving you an extra day off this week," announced Bridget. "We have everything organized. Just get into your new ski uni and go have a good time. The Green Bay guys have been wanting you to ski with them."

For a fact I had been working very hard and hadn't taken as much advantage of the fantastic ski conditions as I would have liked to.

Why not? It was my birthday. I hustled to get dressed, grabbed my gear and caught the last bus. "Probably see you this afternoon," said Neil. "I want to try out my new skis."

"And I want to try out my new ski outfit," I preened. A local ski shop operator had shamed me into buying a fashionable set of black ski bibs with a matching parka trimmed with yellow and green stripes. She argued that the manager of a successful ski lodge ought not to be seen on the slopes in an old pair of blue jeans. Even with a huge discount the outfit cost me a week's wages, nearly seventy-five dollars.

I sat right behind Neil, chatted with him on the way to the area. "Hey Neil, did your fire phone ring yet?" Neil had been duly elected fire chief; a couple of days earlier a telephone crew had installed an emergency phone in Neil's bedroom. Our new fire chief was on call, especially at night. When there was a fire, Neil would be the first to know.

"Not yet. Who you skiing with, Lady?" asked Neil, as he expertly piloted the lumbering old bus up the road.

"Nobody, if I can help it." I loved to ski alone. It seemed when I tried to ski with somebody else there was always a problem: our skill levels were different; I had to sympathize with somebody's problems while we rode the lift; we disagreed about which runs to take. Life around the Inn was so unrelentingly communal, I relished time to myself.

I was certainly a better skier than the year before. "All you really need is time on the boards," my ski instructor had advised me. She was right. Although I was never to become an expert, I did achieve a level I referred to as "enthusiastic intermediate." I loved to carve huge, swooping turns, as fast as I dared, down forgiving slopes like Allen Phipps or Cranmer. Not for me were tough runs, pocked with tricky moguls, like Upper Hughes or Balch.* On that beautiful February day ski conditions were perfect: bright sunshine, soft snow, no wind, short lift lines.

And I was left alone. I liked to sing out loud to myself as I skied and the song I liked best was a silly thing from *Mary Poppins*: "Let's Go Fly a Kite."

Early in the afternoon, as I was riding up the Looking Glass lift above the trails named Mad Hatter, Cheshire Cat, March Hare, after characters in *Alice in Wonderland*, I spotted Neil. He was with a couple of other employees — by now my staffers all skied elegantly — and some guests, pausing for a breather halfway down the slope. A couple of teen-age girls from the Green Bay group were with him. Even from afar I could hear them giggling; they had a big crush on Neil and seized every opportunity to get his attention. Neil looked so pleased. His red hair, uncovered, shone scarlet in the bright sunshine. When he steered his new Rossignols down the mountain his movements were graceful, expert. I remember thinking — what a great kid Neil is. What would I do without him?

But what was the rascal up to? For a couple of days, Neil had been working on something, after hours, in the garage. I wondered if it had anything to do with fire department business, but I was too busy to pay attention. Several times he had tinkered, in private, on some improvement in one of my father's klunky systems before he showed it to me. In due time he would let me in on whatever it was.

---

* The huge expansion which nearly doubled the trail capacity at Winter Park, known as the Mary Jane Area, was not opened until a couple of ski seasons later.

When I boarded the homebound bus, Neil handed me a note in Bridget's handwriting. It said, "Go straight to your apartment by the outside stairway, take a leisurely bath, relax, and if you go near the garage all of us will quit!"

I sensed a plot.

Awaiting me in my apartment were my own three kids, very excited. "Look in the refrigerator, Mom," said Drew.

Inside rested a cold bottle of champagne with a ribbon tied around it. Keith said Bridget put it there.

Usually, when I returned from skiing, I took only enough time to peel off my longjohns and slip into my jeans before heading to the front desk and kitchen to discover what problems had arisen during my absence. That afternoon I got to do what my guests always did, relax after skiing. No wonder they liked staying at the Inn.

"Want some of my bubble bath?" asked Drew. After a day skiing my hands, feet and rump were always cold. Gratefully, I sank all my cold parts into the hot tub and soaked for a long time, sipping champagne.

Afterwards, it was a treat to be up in my apartment alone with my kids — who by no means saw enough of their mother. I shared my champagne with them. "Don't look out the window at the garage," the kids would warn any time I wandered in that direction.

"Do you guys know what's going on?"

"No Mom, we don't have any idea." They were lying — good lies.

We listened to our favorite Moody Blues and Crosby, Stills, Nash and Young records — until we were summoned to dinner at six o'clock.

"Don't go in the lounge," warned Bridget as she steered us to the dining room.

My kids and I were actually going to sit down to dinner together — a rare treat. The children usually ate early, with the staff; I dined with the guests as part of my "gracious hostess" role. Dinner with the guests wasn't very relaxing. I tried to eat at least one meal with every guest during their week — the good, the bad, and the boring.

Whatever the staff was up to wasn't in plain sight. Surrounding me was a dining room full of tipsy guests plus some sober, sunburned Christians whose bright red noses made them look loaded, too. For some reason every time I took a sip or two from my wine glass it was refilled to the brim.

Toward the end of the meal I was instructed to look straight ahead and not turn around — like a horse wearing blinders. Over the raucous voices of the Green Bay group I heard something scraping along the floor, as though a heavy piece of furniture were being moved.

The overhead lights were turned off. A hush fell over the room; people craned their heads to get a better view. At last, as everybody broke into the strains of "Happy Birthday," I was allowed to turn around.

Before me stood a four-foot high birthday cake which had been framed of wood, then covered with tissue paper and spray painted. Sparklers blazed from its tiers. As the last line of the song droned down, somebody threw firecrackers into the fireplace.

Up through the top layer of tissue popped the head of John Brandenburg — his beard spangled with glitter. Over J.B.'s nipples were glued silver stars.

There it was! My cake with a naked man popping out of it! I got what I wanted for my birthday, for once in my life I really did!

It must have been a tight fold inside that frame for tall, skinny J.B. Like a chick breaking out of an egg, he didn't burst forth all at once. For a split second I was horrified that what might follow his naked torso would be the real thing.

Fortunately someone, probably Bridget, pointed out this was a family place. So his lower half was clad in longjohns over which he had drawn a jock strap — also decorated with silver stars. No matter, the effect was the same.

Over near the phone booth, I noticed that Neil stood grinning happily. So this was what he had been up to out in the garage! Well, his creation had certainly achieved its desired effect.

I doubled over with glee at the sight of J.B., a lanky, unlikely sex symbol. I laughed so hard I dropped to the floor, unable to withstand the huge convulsions of laughter racking my body. For the first, and only, time in my entire life I laughed so hard I wet my pants.

Every woman in the world, just once, should have a birthday like that one.*

---

* We managed to pay J.B. back. On May 24, when he returned for work the next summer, Flossie (who had returned to the mountains) had a big surprise for his birthday. Instead of baking a him a cake or jumping out of one, Flossie Was The Cake. A couple of fellows carried her into the dining room on a litter; she was slathered with whipped Ivory soap flakes and sported lighted candles at strategic spots across her anatomy!

Chapter 23

Bad Chapter

Feted and sated, for the first time in many weeks I slept soundly. My blue eyes were practically rested when I greeted Tonto the next morning.

But he looked absolutely awful. My first thought was that my birthday party had continued on for hours — without me.

"Tough night?" I asked.

"Terrible. Something happened you should know about."

Just then Neil stumbled out of his room, rubbing his eyes behind his thick glasses. It wasn't like him to oversleep.

"What happened to you two?"

Neil nodded toward Tonto, indicating he should fill me in.

"I came back to the Inn about 10:30," Tonto began. "Left my checkbook in my desk and wanted to pay some bills. That preacher, from out in the duplex, was stumbling around the lobby. I asked if I could help. He said he thought he had a problem and pointed to that crisis line number on the bulletin board. Said he dialed it on the pay phone but the line was busy.

"He finally told me his wife took a lot of pills and he couldn't wake her up. So I asked him what kind of pills and he said sleeping pills and Valium. I asked him how many. He said she had a bottle full of sleeping pills, might have been thirty or forty."

It flashed through my mind that if Walter Thatcher wanted to know something about drugs he had certainly asked the right person.

"I told him, 'Sir, you don't need a crisis line, you need a doctor. Fast!'

"So I woke up Neil and we decided it would take too long for the ambulance to come fifty miles from Kremmling. We ran over to the cabin and tried to get her on her feet. The preacher didn't have a car, so we drove them in the van to the clinic in Granby where they pumped her stomach. I think she'll be all right, but they kept her overnight. We had to wait, bring her husband back."

"Why didn't you wake me up?" I was amazed I had slept through so much commotion.

"We tried to keep quiet," put in Neil. "Didn't want the whole Inn in an uproar. Besides, what could you do?"

He had a point.

What could have driven the shy Alva Lee to this? When had I seen her last? I didn't remember her from dinner the night before, during my party.

"Suicide, do you think?"

"Must have been."

"Did you call the police?"

"Didn't see any reason to," said Neil.

So much for my wonderful mood.

The preacher's cocky swagger had slowed to a slink when he and his followers dragged into breakfast at the last minute, although that eerie smirk remained plastered to his face. The two other men, who normally sent their waitress back to the kitchen two or three times for extra pancakes, didn't eat much. The women had obviously been weeping — to the extent they hadn't bothered to apply their eye make-up. Even their beehives sagged. I noted that the red-rimmed eyes of Belinda the blond stared stonily into space. Usually she sat at Walter Thatcher's side and hung onto his every word.

I crouched down next to the minister so I could speak confidentially and said, "You will be needing to get to Granby. I'll loan you my car. I'll come over to your cabin after breakfast and bring you the keys."

When I returned to the office Tonto reminded me, "Did you forget that today is Neil's day off? I really think he needs to get out of here; he's about had it."

Neil had been wanting to go to Denver, to see friends and to order custom-made leather trousers to wear on the motorcycle trips he planned the next summer. With all the time he spent working on my "cake" plus his regular chores, and now this, he certainly needed a relaxing day off.

My immediate problem was vehicles. Neil had long since mothballed his Jeep for the winter. I had planned to let Neil drive my car, but now I needed it so the preacher could go to his wife's bedside. The van had to be held in reserve to meet the airport bus. How would Neil get to Denver?

At the moment, Heather was my only employee with her own wheels. "Heather, I know you have a policy of not loaning your car to anybody, but Neil really needs to get away."

She bristled. I explained about the situation with the preacher's wife. Behind her granny glasses, Heather's eyes grew wider than her lenses. Still, she was reluctant. "I don't know, Virginia. The only person, besides myself, who ever drove my V-dub was my dad. Eighty thousand miles, and they're all mine. Clyde's coming tomorrow and I wouldn't want him to think . . ." Heather often referred to her father by his first name.

"Neil will be back in the morning. Your dad will never know. Besides, you know how reliable Neil is. He has an occasional beer but never does any drugs. Weather looks clear. Roads will be clean."

It was unfair of me to take advantage of my position as her boss. Compounding it, I resorted to bribery. "If you do, I'm pretty sure I can get you some extra time off while your dad's here this weekend. I know you want him to meet Steve." Heather had met a young law student in Denver. She was more than a little interested, all of us could tell.

Grudgingly, she agreed.

I hastened to the duplex and knocked on the door. It appeared as though no one intended to ski. While I talked to Walter Thatcher, Belinda sat by herself in a corner with the back of her beehive toward us, drumming her fingers on the arm of her chair. "Here are the keys. It's the green Maverick in the garage. I sincerely hope Alva Lee will be all right."

"Well, we're prayin' for her. Soon as I get back I'm gonna see about rentin' a car. Hate to bother you."

I assured him we were more concerned about his wife than we were about cars.

But I had no time to linger. My chores that day included driving Bertha, the wallowing old red schoolbus — one of my least favorite duties. I never felt I had her quite under control. My brother Dwight argued I should apply for a chauffeur's license, said I'd probably need it. (Don't let the bus get you by the balls.) I was almost sorry when I passed the test. Wasn't there any little corner where I was allowed to be incompetent?

As soon as I finished shuttling guests, I pitched in to help swab the johns and make the beds. However, when it came time to clean the preacher's cabin, Belinda cracked the door and told us to come back later. I said, "Some of us were up very late trying to help you. If we can't clean now I won't be able to send anybody later." I doubt my father would have approved of my abrupt treatment of a guest.

Belinda said not to bother.

❄ ❄ ❄ ❄ ❄

First thing the next morning Tonto said, "Uh, Virginia, it looks like you'll need to drive the bus again today. Neil didn't get back from Denver last night."

The evening before, the Green Bay group had fired up the sauna for their annual nocturnal romp in the snow. As usual, they screamed with pain and pleasure as their hot bodies hit the snowbank. I didn't get to sleep until late.

Neil's defection was all I needed. My most dependable employee acting undependably. "Maybe Neil just decided to sleep over with a friend. He'll probably call before long," I suggested.

"Probably," answered Tonto.

I tried to avoid Heather, but she had already heard about Neil's absence. "What if he doesn't get back before Clyde?"

"Don't worry, you know Neil wouldn't do anything foolish."

Resignedly, I climbed back into Bertha. How did Neil manage to make driving a bus look so easy?

When I returned J.B. — whose arms and back sagged beneath a load of wood he was carrying to the preacher's cabin — complained, "Maybe those Christians are goin' to heaven, but they're keepin' their cabin hotter 'n hell. I never saw anybody use this much wood. By the way, Lady, you better take a look at the dining room roof from the top side of the bridge."

I crossed the creek, climbed up the steps and looked back at the Inn. What I saw alarmed me. The load of snow, which my father repeatedly said would not need to be shoveled, was probably five feet high. Its base had become a thick slab of blue ice, as wide as the roof itself. And it was sliding glacially downhill. Already its lower edge jutted past the eaves about a foot, like an ice cornice. The roof over the dining room wing sagged visibly. Six or eight feet of bare black roofing showed at the apex of the roof where the ice mass had receded. I would need to keep a close eye on the roof.

❄ ❄ ❄ ❄ ❄

Lunch time arrived, but Neil hadn't. Now I was worried. How dare he quit without notice? And what about Heather's car? Had he lost his mind to be so rude?

There was nothing to be gained by sitting around the Inn, fretting. Carolyn Taylor was helping Tonto get tax records together in the office. I told them, "I'm going to have to drive the guests back from the ski area. Think I'll get in a run or two while I'm at it."

A couple of long, swooping spins down the mountain helped to clear my mind. Snow conditions were magnificent; the wind from my own speed braced my face.

I cheerfully greeted the happy, tired skiers as they trooped onto the bus. "Best day of skiing I ever saw. Just perfect," they glowed.

"Did Neil come back yet?" asked one of the two teen-age girls who had a crush on him.

"Not yet, that rascal. Will I tell him a thing or two when he does!"

Tired, the guests were quiet on the trip home; the only noise was the bus's resonant motor and marginal muffler.

When I pulled up in front of the Inn there were two highway patrol cars parked out front. My thoughts flew to the preacher's wife. Had she tried suicide again?

Carolyn and Tonto met me at the office door; they looked worried as they pointed toward the dining room. "They want to talk to you."

The officers, who remembered me from the policeman's banquet the year before, were standing, sipping coffee. The taller of the two was balding. He held his hat against his chest respectfully, didn't waste words. "Do you know a Neil Brubaker?"

"Yes, he's one of my employees but he hasn't returned from his day off in Denver yesterday."

"I'm sorry to tell you this, ma'am, but he's dead."

A great weight walloped me right below the heart, just above the solar plexus. I slumped into a chair.

The officer continued. "We found his body on the Stanley Slide, east side of Berthoud, early this afternoon. Must have gone over the edge sometime in the night."

"No. My God, no." The man just had to be wrong. But I soon recognized that uniformed policemen don't come to see you without reason.

"Was it an avalanche?" I asked. The Stanley Slide portion of Berthoud Pass was frequently closed due to avalanches.

"No ma'am, no sign of it. One of our officers, patrolling the pass, noticed tire marks that broke through the snowbank. When he looked down he spotted the car."

"He had been working very hard, too hard I guess."

Heather had plopped down in the chair next to me. "I knew I shouldn't have loaned him my car."

Vaguely, I was starting to realize that Heather felt as guilty about Neil's accident as I did. She spoke up, "It was my car," she said — simply, helpfully. The lawyer's daughter, realizing the importance of paperwork, described her car in detail. "But it was only a car," she added as she reached for my hand.

The patrolmen couldn't tell us much. They figured the accident must have happened between two and four in the morning.

"Was it — instant? Did he try to get help?" The thought of an injured Neil, clawing up snowbanks, across rocks, trying to get to the highway for help was horrible.

The patrolman assured me, "No, ma'am. It appeared he died instantly — did not suffer.

"Car's totalled. The wrecker from the garage over at Berthoud Falls winched it up to the highway. Evidently Mr. Brubaker had not fastened his seat belt; he was thrown clear of the wreckage. That stretch of the pass is steep. Going uphill in a Volkswagen, full moon, he must have been awake or he couldn't shift gears. Hard to believe he went to sleep. There'll be an autopsy."

Oh God, I just wanted to disappear, to allow grief to swallow me. But I couldn't let myself run to my room because, when I looked around, I saw that most of the staff members had gathered and were weeping. They were so young, so sure nothing terrible like this could happen to them. Old people died, *they* didn't. Their cheeks, normally plump with grins, were gaunt with shock. If I fell apart, all of them would, too.

I turned to the younger officer, the one with the neat moustache who was scribbling furiously. "Last summer, Neil had a bad accident. He was driving a road maintainer and rolled it off the side of the mountain. He was badly injured. He said he thought he blacked out." The officer jotted that down.

"Do his folks live around here?" asked the older patrolman.

"No. In Arizona. Oh dear, who'll tell them?"

"Do you know them?"

"Yes, I've met them."

"There's two things can happen. We can communicate with the Arizona patrol and they will send a uniformed officer to their house. Or you can call them." He paused for a moment. "Speaking from experience, I can tell you that it would be a lot better if you called yourself."

Tell them? How do you tell people that their beautiful son, the one they raised to be just perfect, was dead? I took a deep breath, wished I could open the floodgates and let the barricade of tears behind my eyes go coursing down my cheeks. But I agreed to make the call.

Maybe I signed some papers, I really don't remember. The officer gave me the name of the people who should be contacted by Neil's parents to claim the body.

I headed for my room to make the phone call. Carolyn stood up and followed, determined to stay at my side. Everybody else sat, stunned. We would have to go into Neil's room first, I told Carolyn, to look for his address book.

Neil Brubaker's room smelled of wood smoke, damp woollen sweaters, Dial soap. It smelled like — Neil. To think he would never walk back into that room, pull on the patched jacket he wore when carrying firewood. In one corner the red fire phone — the one Neil would never get to hear ring — sat silently.

"Carolyn, it doesn't feel right, going through someone else's things."

"You have to, Virginia."

I located his parents' phone number in an address book in his top drawer. It was like Neil to be well organized.

The old Inn's stairs were never so steep; the hall never so long. As I stepped across the mismatched carpet I wondered, what were his parents doing just then? Maybe his father was working in his wood shop or his mother was starting to fix dinner. They had no idea that the worst thing that could possibly happen — had already happened.

"Oh, Carolyn, how can I do this terrible thing? What if that phone were ringing for me, what if it were my son?" I took a deep breath, sat in my father's chair, reached for the phone. Halfway through dialing, my fingers floundered, jiggling the rotary so the sequence was ruined. Flustered, I worked to get my voice under control, to restrain the storm of emotions that thundered through my body — at least until the phone call was made. I knew the longer I waited the more difficult it would be to stick my fingers into the number holes of that black round dial.

"This time for sure," I stood up, determined.

As I dialed, Carolyn leaned against my back and twined her arms around my waist, very tightly. Her small body braced mine — giving me courage, holding me up. I will always be grateful to her.

It was his father who answered the phone. Almost twenty years later now, I can't remember exactly what I said to the man. It still hurts too much. But I managed to stay nearly composed. His stunned father accepted the news and thanked me. Thanked me! How is it possible for two people — sharing anguish — to be so civilized at such a moment?

What happened next is pretty much a blur. People did what they thought might help. Drew remembers that Bridget met her when she got off the school bus. From the look on Bridget's face, Drew's first fear was that something had happened to Pepper, our dog. But Bridget knew Drew was especially close to Neil, didn't want her to hear the news from someone in town.

Drew, Keith and Gordon and I wrapped arms around each other. They needed my strength, too.

When Heather walked into our apartment she wasn't so composed as earlier. "What about Clyde?"

"You weren't planning to meet him in Denver, were you?"

"No, he's renting a car. Where is my car now? What if my dad sees my car when he drives by it? There aren't many light blue VW bugs with sun roofs in this world. What if he looks at the license plate? He will be frantic if he thinks something has happened to me."

Keith spoke up. "Mom, they always park the wrecks right out in front of the garage in Berthoud Falls. I'm pretty sure there's too much snow to hide it anywhere. It'd be where he could see it from the highway." The filling station had only two gas pumps and enough garage space to work on one car at a time.

"You're right. Things are bad enough we can't make them worse," I said. Heather hadn't known Neil for as long as the rest of us. Her concern was for the devastating shock that seeing his daughter's car, totalled and hanging on a wrecker's hook, would be to Clyde Wendelken. Attempting to forestall that calamity provided a welcome diversion.

Tonto tried to call the garage in Berthoud Falls, to find out where and how the car was displayed, maybe ask them to move it out of view. But the owner must have closed the garage for the day, or else the wrecking crew was out on another call. Nobody answered. We tried getting through to the highway patrol, but they couldn't find the garage owner either. I forbade anybody from attempting to intercept Clyde. Nobody was in any shape to drive; besides, how could we know what his rental car would look like? Heather went about her job, alternating between setting places at the tables and pacing to the front door to look for her father.

Mercifully, out of respect, the Green Bay group canceled their nightly cocktail party. The staff staggered through their chores, stopping occasionally to comfort each other in some private corner, to blow noses, to stanch tears.

Privacy is difficult in a hotel; I invited the doubly crushed Green Bay teen-agers up to my apartment, told them to help themselves to my Beatles records. They sprawled on my carpeted couches, their arms twined around each other in salty grief.

Still, no Clyde. Heather kept poking her head out the front door. Night fell — no Clyde. I was closing up the office at nine when someone threw open the front door. Neither tall nor especially imposing, Clyde Wendelken nonetheless had a flair for entering a room and immediately brightening it. Even after a long day spent traveling, his pleasure at being at the Inn, at seeing Heather, was obvious. "I had to take a later plane," he explained, his high spirits fading at the sight of our stricken faces. "Sorry I'm late. Did I worry you?"

"Did you see my car?" asked Heather.

"No. Something wrong with it?"

Heather threw her arms around her father and led him into the lounge to explain. Well, I thought, with our suspense relieved perhaps I would have time to tend to my own sorrow.

What I really wanted was my mother — to sob on her amply padded shoulder, to feel her protective arms around me. To have her tell me everything would be all right. But her health was the reason I was at the Inn and she wasn't. Instead of searching for sympathy, I had to call my parents, inform them of the tragedy and try to sound as if I had everything under control.

I didn't want to be what I had become — the person in charge. The boss. The person who took care of everybody else. The person everybody could look to for strength and courage. Inadequate me. It was awful.

Chapter 24

Walter's Pigeon

On a gray, cold, windy hillside we watched as they lowered Neil Brubaker's casket into a grave in an old cemetery outside Rock Springs, Wyoming. His father told me that after his accident the summer before, Neil had said, "Dad, if anything ever happens to me I want to be here, next to my grandfather." Neil's father thought the request odd at the time, coming from such a young man.

At the graveside, his father asked if I would mind going through his son's things, packing them up, cleaning out his room and probating his small estate. Although I wanted to take a little time for myself, to grieve, it was necessary to postpone sorrow; I needed to keep up my courage. Perhaps I could have delegated the chore to Bridget or Tonto, but I felt obligated to do it personally. Still, I hated riffling through Neil's underwear, sorting his papers, making a list so I could probate the few belongings the government referred to as his "estate." It was a terrible chore — handling his photographs, reading far enough into giggly letters from girls to find addresses of friends who might want to be informed of his death. What should I do with half-worn clothing? A well-worn deck of cards? Should I pack everything or get rid of stuff? "The good die young, the good die young." I couldn't get it out of my head.

The autopsy revealed nothing — no drugs, no alcohol in Neil's blood. No clues to a brain malfunction, either. We concluded he must have suffered another seizure. It wasn't much comfort when people kept saying, "At least he wasn't driving the van or Bertha when it happened. A lot of people could have been hurt."

I wished I could just lock Neil's door and deal with this problem after the ski season was over, but we needed the room for J.B. He volunteered to greet late-arriving guests.

Occasionally, I glanced at that bright red phone that might have summoned Neil to a fire. What a shame he never had the pleasure of responding to even one good emergency. When the phone company man came to remove it, there wasn't space in the tiny room for both of us. I welcomed the excuse to leave Neil's musty little lair and do something else for a while. Even the pesky chore of going over weekly grocery invoices promised relief. Every week, I attempted to figure ways to keep skyrocketing prices in line.

I looked up from my spread of lists to see our former patient, Alva Lee Thatcher, standing before me. Her body, which before had looked slender and graceful, now appeared ethereally transparent. Waiters in the dining room reported she hadn't eaten much.

She wore an expensive green loden wool jacket. Another woman, after experiencing such an ordeal, might have looked haggard. Alva Lee looked tragic; I immediately thought of the sufferings of Camille. She bent over a little. "Uh, I really feel I owe you an explanation and an apology. Could we go out to lunch together?"

Because getting away from grocery bills and Neil's worldly goods sounded like a good idea, I agreed to go, but almost immediately regretted my decision. I'd had my fill of other people's problems.

We walked down the road toward the highway, talking about inconsequential things, such as the difference between the Siberian huskies and elkhounds barking at us as we passed. Tall and elegant, she walked gracefully even in her heavy seal boots.

We were headed for a dingy old saloon called the Winterhof; there's a shopping mall there now. Owner after owner had bankrupted himself trying to make a go of the booze business in its sprawling expanse. Each had the same idea: just one more building addition would allow him to sell more beer, have a bigger band, expand the dance floor, get rich. Even the odor of frying hamburgers couldn't overcome the fetid remnants of cigarette butts and beer, ground into the floors. At our window table we gazed past dripping icicles toward trucks slushing by on the highway.

"I'm really sorry about your employee."

My lips remained tightly pursed — although I wanted to scream at her, tell her if he hadn't been up all night trying to save her life he might not have lost his. Not for the first time I wished I had been raised in a family of Italian screamers instead of one where suffering in silence was a virtue.

She continued. "And I really appreciate all you've done for us — taking me to the clinic in the van, loaning us your own car." When Alva Lee ordered ve-ge-tab-le soup in her soft southern accent, her lips gave service to every single vowel.

"Forget it, part of the job, I'll have a burger. Oh, and a draw."

When she heard me order a beer, she said, "Maybe that's what I need, too. Miss! Would you bring me a cuba libre, please? Be sure it's light Bacardi. Coke, not Pepsi. Don't forget the lime." Maybe she didn't drink, but she sure knew how to order.

She turned to face me. "Guess things finally came to a head. With Walter and Belinda, I mean."

"Walter and Belinda? Belinda the blond?"

"Yes, Walter is in love with Belinda. She left her husband and now Walter wants to divorce me."

OK, so that accounted for the coy Belinda and the attentive Walter.

"You have children?"

"Yes, we have two. They go to a private Bible school."

Slowly, it was sinking in. "You mean, your husband brought his wife *and* his mistress on vacation, at the same time to the same place, even to the same cabin?"

"Mistress isn't a very nice word."

"Do you like *adulteress* better? I think that's the word Jesus used in the Bible."

She ignored my sarcasm. "Walter said maybe if we all got away together we could pray over it. Probably resolve something. He said maybe if he accused me of having an affair the people at the church would take it better."

I couldn't believe my ears. Was she just going to swallow Walter's garbage? "Pardon me, but why the hell do you even want such a jerk? I mean, you're head and shoulders above that guy."

Almost immediately, I was sorry I'd asked. When she sighed, I could see she was going to tell me everything, no matter how long it took.

"My daddy owned a lot of land in Choctaw County. I was the apple of his eye, he used to call me his 'little pigeon.' But when he found out I was drinkin' beer and sneakin' around to meet boys, he punished me by sending me away to a Bible college. I always wanted to go to the university, you know, to 'Bama. Be a Pi Phi.

"After two years of prayin' and singin' in the choir, I was gettin' set to lose my mind when Walter came along. Just a freshman, he was a big hero on our campus, played basketball, was heavy into his religious studies. Told me he had figured out how to make it work."

Alva Lee ignored my rising eyebrow.

"I didn't know what he saw in me but I was nuts about him. Daddy was thrilled, introduced Walter to the governor, Rotary Club president, all that. Walter and my daddy were really thick. Maybe Walter married me for my daddy's connections. Anyhow, Walter finished college and went to seminary. Daddy got him a job as youth minister at our church, and at the age of twenty-eight, he became pastor. Everything was fine until the schism."

I had heard about the carnage caused by schisms in fundamentalist churches; they almost always resulted in appalling feuds.

"Lots of our church members went with Walter. He founded the Church of God in Action. But Daddy wouldn't budge."

"What was the split about?"

"Oh, you know. Virgin birth, creationism, which bank to put church deposits in, the usual thing."

I didn't know, but dismissed it as outside my realm of expertise.

"Those two men with us, they handle Walter's business deals. They're tryin' to work this thing out so it'll cause the least damage. I've been a big disappointment to Walter in his work."

"You mean, the church?"

"Yes, he's always wanted somebody like Belinda. Somebody pretty. Somebody who can sing and look sincere in public. I've never been able to get up on the stage."

"Do you think of religion as a business?"

"Got to. There's so much competition."

I sucked in my breath so abruptly I nearly inhaled a chunk of dill pickle. I had to admire her candor.

"What about you? Do you think you'll try suicide again? I mean, that's what it was, wasn't it?"

"Yes, no. I mean, I don't know. It would have been a lot better if your boys didn't interfere. I mean, Walter would have been free to do what he wants. Now I don't know what I'll do."

I thought I'd offer a little amateur psychology. "Don't you think Walter's just suffering from male menopause? Maybe he'll come to his senses. I mean, wouldn't a divorce be pretty scandalous for your church?"

"Walter's got a way with him. Every time he gets in trouble he gets up in front of the congregation and repents. Sometimes cries real tears. It impresses people, when somebody who seems so strong falls to his knees crying. Some people forgive just about anything he does."

"Are you going to leave him?"

"I just don't know, I don't know." It was becoming apparent that with the elegant Alva Lee, what you saw was what you got. "When Daddy died he left all his money to my children and the other church. I have nothing of my own."

When tears of self-pity teemed, I changed the subject. "Are Walter and Belinda out skiing today?"

"Didn't you know? Walter packed up the rental car and left for Vail this morning — by himself. Said he just couldn't cope with this situation any more. He needed to get away."

My hands shook with such vehement indignation that my meat patty squirted out of its bun and flopped onto the dirty floor. Frantically, I tried to wipe sticky catsup from my hands with a flimsy paper napkin. "I'm trying to get this straight. Your husband, who is fooling around with another woman, leaves her with his wife, who just attempted suicide, because *he* can't cope?"

Our waitress scooped up the offending patty from the floor. I turned down her offer of another sandwich, scraped my chair backwards and bummed a cigarette from a man at the next table. I felt the sudden need for an overt sign of sin, vice and dissipation.

"I just wanted you to know I'll be financially responsible for our bills. But Walter took the check book with him so I'll have to send you a check after we get home."

"Please ask someone else in your party to take care of the bill. You shouldn't have to worry about it." I didn't add that I shouldn't have to, either. "I thank you for explaining all of this." I didn't want to appear rude, but I realized that the story of Alva Lee's life would probably last all afternoon if I stayed. Alva Lee had just ordered another rum and coke. At that moment, even sorting through Neil's things sounded like a better deal.

Chapter 25

Body of Evidence

"Lady, Lady! Come quick! There's a body in Room 22." Sandy was shaking; beneath her stringy, overgrown bangs her eyes were wide with fright.

"A body? Are you quite sure?"

"There's a leg sticking out from under the bed. I almost — stepped on *it*!" Her shoulders writhed in disgust.

The last thing my life needed was another dose of tragedy. A body? Wasn't a dead employee enough? Wasn't a suicidal guest too much? How much was I supposed to take?

I scanned the reservation chart, trying to find the name of whoever had checked into Room 22 in the Balcony House. Carolyn, who had stepped into Tonto's job when he took over Neil's responsibilities as maintenance man, pointed out that it was rented to Frank Putnam (NRN). Clean cut, with the ramrod posture of a military officer, he was a tall, eager fellow in his late twenties. When he arrived the night before he appeared to be in a holiday mood, without a care in the world. He walked with a slight limp, which I hoped wouldn't interfere with his skiing because he said something about being in town for the races. But I didn't pay much attention; every week somebody was having a race at the ski area.

Fighting for control, I attempted to calm myself by taking a deep breath, but it stopped abruptly at mid-chest. Now what? Like J.B. kept saying, There's Always More.

As I led Carolyn and Sandy down the Balcony House hall I was annoyed when grit crunched beneath my feet on the linoleum floor, tracked in from the driveway. My impulse was to grab a broom, sweep furiously. Silly thought, given I was on my way to view a dead man.

Light showed through the open door of Room 22. I glanced inside. The fellow's room was untidy, but not abnormally so. Had there been a fight or a burglary things would have been in a greater state of disarray. The double bed was rumpled — nothing unusual about that.

Averting her head, a squeamish expression on her face, Sandy pointed around the corner — toward the bottom of the bed.

Sticking out from beneath the drape of the bedspread was a Vibram-soled suede hiking boot, askew at an angle. Its upper laces were covered by a blue denim pantleg.

I pressed the palm of my hand to my mouth in horror. My mind was racing, trying to remember all of those detective stories that advised not to disturb the scene of the crime.

But what if the body was alive? What if I failed to offer first aid?

My impulse was to run out of there, to throw myself into a snowbank, to beg the gods for mercy. My second was to simply close the door behind me, call the sheriff and let him deal with the whole mess.

Instead, Sandy, Carolyn and I just stared at that — thing. I felt sick at my stomach, squeamish. As I gawked at it, something occurred to me.

"Wait a minute. I don't think there's room enough under the bed for an entire body. Maybe if you two lift the bed I can pull on — it."

Gingerly, I gripped the boot. It felt kind of stiff. "Ready? One, two . . ."

I braced myself to pull what I calculated would be heavy, concentrating all my energy to yank the entire weight of an adult male body from beneath the bed. With great force I tugged — only to catapult myself backward and smack myself up against the wall and fall to the floor in a heap.

Without comprehension, I gazed at a boot and an empty pair of Levis draped across my chest. There was no body. But inside the jeans was something hard. Boot? Jeans? A hard thing? Nothing made sense.

As I struggled to my feet Tonto appeared at the door. Just returned from driving Bertha on shuttle duty, he heard the ruckus in the Balcony House and hastened to our aid. His obscenely wide grin gave me to understand he was miles ahead of me — as usual.

"Tonto. Did Frank Putnum get on the bus this morning?"

"Sure did."

"How did he look?"

"Fine, for a guy on crutches."

"Crutches? Did he hurt his leg."

Tonto took my reluctant hand, forced it down inside of the waistband of the Levis. "That's his leg, Virginia. Didn't he tell you? He's competing in the Handicapped Ski Races. Viet Nam vet. Told me it's easier to take off his pants and leg at the same time. When he got on the bus he said something about leaving a little surprise for the maids."

Although I had been at the Inn for over a year, that was my first experience with a handicapped guest. The training program for amputees at Winter Park was in its infancy. It came about because a ski instructor named Hal O'Leary wrecked his knee. Reluctant to give up his favorite sport, let alone his livelihood, the fun-loving Irishman invented a method of three-track skiing. A skier stood on his one good leg, balancing himself by means of ski poles fitted at their tips with little hinged skis. O'Leary called them "outriggers." Because the motive power for skiing is simple gravity, amputees could ski very well, sometimes better than "normies," as the amputees called people like myself. But then, one-legged skiers had a couple of things going for them. They never had to worry about keeping their weight on the downhill ski and it was impossible to cross their tips.

O'Leary had the right idea at the right time. He worked with physicians from Denver's Fitzsimmons Army Hospital to design equipment, teaching methods and psychological strategies to turn handicapped patients into skiers. The maiming fields of Viet Nam provided plenty of casualties for them to experiment with.

It was only a short step — hop might be a more appropriate word — from skiing to racing. Because so many amputees were young people who lost their limbs in the course of hazardous professions — such as war — or dangerous pastimes — such as riding motorcycles or driving fast cars — they tended to be a competitive lot. They loved speed; they loved winning.

Every handicapped skier I ever knew came equipped with a horror story so profound, the telling of it evoked pity even as it churned the stomach. Even so, they never presented themselves as victims. I quickly learned that handicapped skiers were every bit as rowdy as college students. When not racing, they were apt to be found in the vicinity of a keg, swilling beer from each other's prostheses!

Pranks involving their artificial limbs, like the one Frank Putnam played on us, were standard. During the course of their races, with the express purpose of startling other skiers, amputees frequently shucked their artificial limbs on their way to the lift — leaving a grisly pile of arms and legs near the warming house for "normies" to contemplate.

To raise beer money, they sold T-shirts. One design showed two bare feet sticking up opposite one foot between them sticking down. The legend read **"Gimps on Top."**

"You created quite a stir this morning," I commented to Frank when he picked up his key. My tone was a shade more severe than I had intended.

He gave me an all-American grin. "Life's never as bad as it seems, is it?" He winked, aimed a crutch in the direction of his room, and swung out of sight.

Frank Putnam had a very good time during his week at Millers. The girls adored him, the men respected him. He even picked up a ski medal or two.

Chapter 26

The Making of a Mellow Fellow

"Mom, that kid is driving me crazy!" Strong words, coming from my thirteen-year-old daughter Drew, an ace baby-sitter normally very patient with young children. Our season at the Inn had turned my shy blond pixie into an emergingly confident teen-ager.

I looked up to see a chubby little boy scamper around the corner into the lounge. It was Tony LoBianco (NRN), the child of one of our guests. Drew was holding down the front desk, a consequence of the attrition that kept claiming employees. The most recent was Sally, who was forced to return home to Lincoln, Nebraska, to seek treatment for an intestinal parasite. Drew had volunteered to help out by taking over the desk during the evening shift. Initially, I was reluctant to allow anyone so young to represent the business.

"Sure you can handle it? It won't be like the napkins, will it?" She shook her head in an emphatic NO.

She had disposed of another chore, folding napkins, by skillfully maneuvering various of my employees into betting on games of gin rummy. When they decided to "humor the kid" by playing with her, they discovered two things: she was very good at gin rummy, and ruthless when it came to collecting a bet. Several times, passing the laundry room, I noticed disgruntled losers in the act of folding Drew's napkins.

When Heather and Diane promised to keep an eye on Drew while she learned her duties, I gave my permission. She learned to answer phone calls with a professional tone that belied her years, to take messages, summon guests to the phone and make change for the vending machines.

I couldn't blame her for griping about Tony LoBianco and his father Vic (NRN). They would have challenged a saint's patience, and this close to the end of the ski season our composure was nowhere near saintly.

The first time I saw Vic, whose divorced wife was elsewhere, he was standing in the lobby, looking at himself in a mirror. I wondered if the fellow's last stop before the airplane had been at a beauty shop. His thinning locks were combed into fold-over strands; as though to compensate, his sideburns were profuse, almost teased. Unfortunately, the hairs on his upper lip weren't any more eager to grow than those on the top of his head; his moustache was pencil thin.

Behind him, in the lounge, a five- or six-year-old child bounced up and down — shoes and all — on the couch in front of the fireplace. His chubby cheeks were smudged with dried, caked chocolate.

Now that Carolyn had taken over the daytime front desk duties, I was grateful for her ability to size up new guests quickly. Her overly bright smile alerted me to trouble.

"Good girl you've got here," LoBianco told me. "You should let her handle all the phone calls instead of that Tonto fellow. Got a way with her." It was clear he had taken a shine to Carolyn — and that she would resist his advances.

I wasn't in the mood to explain to Vic LoBianco why we had been forced to change front-desk personnel.

"Do you have down pillows? Tony is allergic to feathers."

"Rest assured we don't," I told him. I didn't add that they were too expensive for a place like Millers Idlewild Inn.

"Here's a list of our allergies for your cook."

I glanced at the typed column: lobster, shrimp, crab, blueberries, brie cheese, marinated artichoke hearts, fresh tomatoes and strawberries. Boy was this guy in luck!

"Why is there no TV in my room? Tony wants to watch *McHale's Navy*."

"Only TVs we have are in the cabins, black and white. All we get are two channels — sometimes," I explained.

"Do you have room service in case we don't want to get up early in the morning?"

Carolyn suppressed a snicker. "Believe me, you won't sleep in," she said.

Later that afternoon, Vic LoBianco introduced an ominous new appliance into my life. When he turned on his blow dryer it fried all the fuses in the Balcony House. By the next year, blow-dried hair became the fashion; some afternoons I had to troop door to door, pleading with people not to turn driers on at the same time; more and more of my time would be spent flipping circuit breakers back to life.

Nothing ever suited Vic LoBianco. "My food is cold, take it back," he would demand of his waiter. It was probably true. One of my hardest tasks was getting high-altitude food to the tables hot; even so, most people were too hungry to complain.*

"That bed is too soft. I need a bed board."

"The bus left without me."

One of Vic's more annoying habits was his constant interruption of other people's conversations. "I couldn't help over-

---

* My life at the Inn might have been much happier if the microwave oven and the telephone answering machine had been invented sooner.

hearing," he would preface his remarks as he stepped so close to another person's face they could inspect the pores in his nose. He would then proceed to find some excuse to turn the topic to himself — *his* travels, *his* job in the wholesale hardware business, *his* tennis prowess. When Vic entered the sacred precincts of Myrtle's domain and tried to bend her ear, I had to order him, sharply, to stay out of the kitchen.

The only person he seemed completely oblivious to was Tony. The child pitched a vigorous tantrum during his first ski lesson and refused to try again. Vic attempted to palm Tony off on Diane; I forbade him to leave the child at the Inn during the day; I told him he would just have to put Tony in the day care center at the ski area and pay for him, like everybody else.

However, little Tony zeroed in on Drew as the soft underbelly of resistance. At first, she was sympathetic to the child's situation because she had seen it several times before. A divorced father, when the court decreed it was time to exercise his parental rights, planned an elaborate ski vacation "for my kid." But dad's heart was in doing bachelor things — roaming the bars, trying to pick up women. During the evening, a lonely child like Tony haunted the lounge, pestered guests to play ping-pong with him, tried to capture the attention his father was squandering elsewhere. Tony was forever demanding something from Drew — change for the Pepsi machine, games from the cabinet, that we show our black and white 16mm copy of *Mickey Mouse Saves the Airmail.**

---

* We had one of the world's worst selections of movies. Highlights? Try the 1948 Winter Olympics featuring "Canada's beauteous figure skater Barbara Ann Scott" or Lowell Thomas narrating a version of the Hollmenkollen cross-country and ski-jumping event in Oslo, Norway, circa 1950. Worst of all was a medley of cowboy songs climaxed by "Paddlin' Madelin' Home" with Ukelele Ike. The latter was not only the corniest movie ever made, all the fiddle players and banjo pluckers came out left-handed because the film was printed backwards!

Drew issued crayons, even read stories to him. But my daughter's annoyance grew as Tony sucked her in to what had become his favorite game. "Dr-e-w, I locked myself out of my room!" he would plead. "Let me in, let me in, let me in," he demanded as he danced up and down in the lobby. Each room had two keys, but Tony managed to lock both in his room. Time after time, Drew was obliged to trudge across the drive to the Balcony House with a master key to let her tormentor in. Eventually, she tied a string around his neck and attached the key — log and all. The thick log made chubby Tony look like a St. Bernard puppy with a cask beneath his chin.

"Roger," Drew muttered in desperation, "I think little Tony would enjoy a hair race!"

Several of the staff, likewise brattiness-victims, chimed in, "A hair race for Tony. What a good idea!"

"Wouldn't little Tony just love a hair race!" echoed Roger, a devious gleam in his eye.

Intrigued, a couple of other children — ones who were a little older and had been avoiding Tony — followed Roger to the dining room where he removed everything from a formica-topped table. As they knelt on our big pine chairs, the children's corduroy-clad rear ends were higher than their heads. They watched with anticipation as Roger spilled a puddle of water onto the mirror-slick surface. Then, with great ceremony, Roger stood up straight and plucked a hair from the top of his head. He dropped it into the puddle. "Ready?"

The kids, on various sides of the table, puckered up. "Now blow on it! See if you can make it stay on the other guy's side of the table," he ordered. The kids started blowing on the hair, which sailed back and forth in response to the latest or strongest blow. Knowledgeable staff members retreated from the table.

For a few minutes, Roger and the other staffers cheered, egging the kids on as they puffed up their little cheeks and blew with all their might. About the time the kids began to turn purple, Roger stepped up to the table. He lifted his arm, held it suspended for a few seconds, then slammed his flattened palm splat into the center of the puddle. Water flew up into the faces of the panting children.

Startled, the kids jerked their faces upward in surprise. One by one they got the joke and laughed, except Tony, who squalled at the top of his lungs.

Vic LoBianco burst through the door. I hadn't even been aware that he was in the building. I said to Roger, "Oh boy, we've had it now." But rather than stopping to listen to his son's legitimate beef about our shabby treatment of him, Vic scooped up Tony, tucked him under his arm and hauled the flailing kid off to their room — with an eye, I suppose, to disciplining him. As we saw them vanish, Roger, Drew and I exhaled in relief.

My staff weren't the only people annoyed with the LoBiancos. Some guests had problems with Vic but positively hated the kid; some even requested that Vic and Tony be seated at any table but theirs. One night I assigned father and son to sit next to the waterfall; I figured watching the fish might provide the ever-wiggling Tony with some diversion.

When Heather was setting out the soup tureens she warned Tony, "Don't stand up on your chair. You'll fall in the fish pond."

Drew, too, passing fried chicken, admonished the boy, "If you keep tipping your chair backwards, you'll fall into the fish pond."

Vic, bending the ear of the woman next to him, remained oblivious to the child's antics.

I was seated nearby, chatting with guests, when I heard a terrible crash and a wail. I jumped to my feet to see Tony floundering away in the shallow pond where he had fallen. A strand of moss draped itself over one ear and pond water soaked his jeans. Drew was extending a hand to fish the thoroughly soaked child back to land.

Immediately I was at her side. I'm not proud of the fact that my first thought was, "I hope that kid hasn't killed any of my goldfish."

After a long moment's silence the rest of the guests realized what had happened. Without exception, they stood up, applauded and cheered.

❅ ❅ ❅ ❅ ❅

Vic LoBianco's week wasn't going very well either. He hadn't scored, and his kid was making him miserable.

About the only thing that did seem to be working for him were his skis. By the end of the week his face and nose had turned a toasty Mediterranean brown; because it was protected by his stocking cap, his stark white dome beneath his fold-over looked like someone had tacked fringe on a volleyball.*

On his final evening Vic was sitting in the lounge awaiting the dinner bell, sipping a whiskey, a grousing expression beneath his silly moustache. When I walked by him he grabbed the tail of my sweater, pulled me down next to him and said, "Hey, I want to tell you something."

"Sure," I said as I plopped.

"Lemme give you a word of advice. You don't look like you are having a very good time around here. There's not a person on earth wouldn't trade jobs with you; everybody wants to run a ski lodge. But you walk around here like a sourpuss. Why don't you smile more, make people feel better? That's your job, you know."

---

* In the spring, sunburn was as dangerous as frostbite had been in January. On warm days I pleaded with guests to wear brimmed hats to protect their faces. Sunscreen lotions had not yet hit the market. Many a guest suffered a peeling nose before their week of spring skiing was over.

His comment literally took my breath from me. Stunned, I just sat there blinking; my first instinct was to run from the room, hide my head in a pile of dirty towels in the laundry room and wallow in *mea culpa* and self-pity. I had to admit that recently, I *had* failed to live up to the stereotype of the apple-cheeked, dirndl-clad, ever-jolly innkeeper.

For just a moment I sat there frozen, not knowing how to respond to a comment which, even if perceptive, was incredibly rude.

I hardly believed it myself when I stood up, affixed my hands to my hips, stared down at the creep and said in a voice far too loud, "You thundering, up-tight clod! One of my employees, a fine young man I loved as dearly as my own children, was killed in a terrible accident last week. And all you want me to do is smile so *you* will feel better? You sir, have the sensitivity of a toilet seat!"

As I stood there hyperventilating I noticed that guests who had overheard my outburst were trying to keep from laughing as they nodded their heads in approval.

What a crazy time to think about Greek tragedy. But I realized my emotions had just taken a roller coaster ride through pity, fear and catharsis. Little people-pleasing me had just purged all over a guest. I had probably hurt his feelings. He might never come back.

And wasn't that a nice feeling?

Oddly enough, after dinner Vic LoBianco apologized profusely. He was embarrassed when he learned about our recent, tragic loss. My chewing out mellowed him; he came back frequently, wasn't half so obnoxious as his first time around. As it turned out he loved being told off occasionally — said it made him feel needed.

I wonder what ever happened to little Tony? I suppose he grew up and got a job at a ski lodge somewhere.

Chapter 27

This Means Business

Carolyn handed me a set of forms. In a firm voice which I knew meant *this can't wait*, she said, "The time has come to set next year's rates."

Her demand jolted me. "Now? You mean for next winter?"

"Absolutely," she ordered.

"But we haven't even finished this season yet."

"I know, but the travel industry sets its deadlines far in advance."

"Nine months ahead? I've had babies in less time. How do I know what to charge? The way prices are going, I can't even predict what might happen by December. Let alone a year from now. What should I do?"

"Raise 'em, of course. You've been griping about paying the bills. Now's your chance to do something about it."

True enough, I had been watching as the inflationary cycle that started with the oil embargo the autumn before literally ate up the winter's profits. Every week our wholesale grocer in Denver tacked on another price increase. "Due to the price of gasoline, we will be forced to raise our rates," said the laundry man as he handed me hand-scrawled notices at least twice that winter. When we filled Bertha I winced because it seemed

Tonto was pumping liquid money straight into its tank. The Pepsi man even adjusted his mechanism to raise the price of soft drinks from thirty-five to fifty cents. Yet I was required to stick to rates my dad had established a full year earlier.

It did not particularly help when Carolyn showed me the results of her calculations for our corporate income taxes. I was relieved to learn we wouldn't owe anything, but that also meant we didn't make any money in 1973. The prospect for profits in 1974 seemed doomed.

I sat down to calculate a hefty raise in rates. Mathematics had always bedeviled me; I had convinced myself I was a dunderhead when it came to figures. But as I pushed the buttons and pulled the crank on the Inn's ancient adding machine, from somewhere deep in my brain my seventh grade lessons in percentages and ratios fell neatly into place. It took me a very long time to come up with a new price structure. Almost every accommodation we offered, from bunk bed to reasonably luxurious cabins, had to be priced separately.

As I recall, I figured on about a twenty percent raise in rates. After long hours my cramped fingers penciled them in, mailed them off to my father and got ready to go skiing. As I ran out the door, anxious to take advantage of a glorious spring day, what wouldn't I have given for one of those expensive new Xerox machines!

I dreaded his response. Three days later, the phone looked particularly agitated as it rang. When I heard my father at the other end — he was hot. "You can't raise rates twenty percent! Nobody will stand for it."

"But Dad, do you know what's happened to the price of everything?" I quoted the price of a case of lettuce, a bundle of clean sheets, a gallon of gasoline.

"Millers Idlewild Inn has always been a place people could *afford* to stay," he shot back.

"I know, Dad, but most of our guests wouldn't bat an eye if we asked them to pay more. Our rates are a lot lower than anybody else's except Skiville Ranch."

"Gotta keep 'em low."

"Besides, Dad. Something is really wrong here."

"What?"

"Carolyn and I have been going over the figures. We didn't make any money this season."

"What do you mean, didn't make any money?"

"I mean we won't have enough cash in the bank from this ski season to get us to next season. By the time I pay myself and other people's salaries and do those remodeling jobs you have planned, there won't be anything left over. We'll almost certainly have to take out another cashflow loan."

"That's not important."

That was an odd thing to say. I had expected my father to be furious with me, to deliver a blistering lecture on fiscal responsibility.

He went on. "That's OK. Trudy and I were happy to make just enough money to take some trips, keep the place up."

Finally, it was dawning on me. My dad's sole reason for being in business was as a retirement hobby. The property was free and clear of mortgage payments. He and Mother lived simply, had all the money they wanted — so why make any more?

"No point in making too much money when you're on Social Security," he added.

Why did it take me over a year to realize this? My father never intended for the Inn to be a money-making proposition; he considered all the hard work he put into it as worthwhile charity for rich people. What he wanted was for guests to go back to Dubuque or Houston or Atlanta and brag about what a great place C.D. Miller ran.

The realization hit me so hard I fell into the office chair with a thud. I'd have to think about that — a lot. So I changed the subject.

"Dad, the ice from the roof is hanging out about three feet now. And it's at least four-feet thick. The back of the building sags like a hammock."

"Get somebody up there and shovel it."

"You don't understand, Dad. It's too late, too dangerous. Let's just hope that the overhang thaws and doesn't drop off in a chunk. Might do some damage."

Father was uncharacteristically quiet at the other end of the line. I looked up to see one of our favorite guests standing at the counter. "Here Dad, say hello to Chuck Shrader."

The tall, blondish fellow grabbed the phone with alacrity, speaking in his gruff but friendly voice, "C.D., how's everything in Texas? Did you go see the Ink Spots like I told you to?"

Chuck sent my folks tickets to see his friend Charlie Owens' Ink Spots when they played in Brownsville. The musicians even announced my parents' names, invited them up to the stage. Father loved being on the stage — anybody's stage. Chuck was a big fan of the Ink Spots; no "Deadhead" ever followed the schedule of the Grateful Dead more closely than Chuck kept track of the Ink Spots.

Chuck had been a guest so often we treated him like "family." His wife and daughter never came skiing with him, but the fortyish Chuck busied himself looking after the various cronies who accompanied him. A non-drinker, he kept his buddies out of trouble at the bars and stayed at their sides until he drove them home to the safety of the Inn.

After a while, Chuck hung up the receiver. "Your folks sound fine. I'm so glad they're down there in Texas, out from under all this pressure."

Because Chuck was in the dairy business we referred to him affectionately as "The Big Butter and Egg Man from Des Moines." My ski bums anticipated his arrival as eagerly as that of Santa Claus because the fun-loving Chuck always arrived loaded with a case of fruit-flavored yoghurt for them.

Unlike most guests, Chuck made it a point to get acquainted with my staff, to talk to the kids about their families and their ambitions. Endlessly curious, always friendly, he had known Neil well, so he understood the depth of our loss.

Chuck had been coming to the Inn several times each winter for many years. Never choosy about his accommodations, wherever we put him he proceeded to drench the room when he turned on the world's most effusive vaporizer. Maybe it kept his sinuses moist in our severely dry air, but maids complained they practically had to wring out the bedspread when they made up his room every morning.

When ninety-five percent of our guests were sweethearts like Chuck, why do I remember the stinkers so vividly?

"So what is inflation doing to *your* business?" I asked him. Many of my guests were excellent business people and were happy to give me advice.

"I've never seen anything like it. I've had to raise prices five times since November. I don't know where all of this will end up."

Chuck gave me a brotherly hug. "You have to put up with a lot around here. I don't know how you've been able to handle it, what with Neil's death and all. So how's it going, this innkeeping venture of yours?"

Thankful to be asked, I offered, "Buy you a cup of coffee?"

I probably told him more than he wanted to know. "I thought I could just step into Dad's footsteps and do everything as well as he did. It turned out there's a lot more to it than I realized."

"So measuring up to your dad is what you're worried about? Doing as well as he did?"

"Yes. Everybody asks about him. They all miss his wake-up call."

"What about your mother?"

"Oh sure, they miss her, too," I conceded with an offhand gesture.

"Don't you realize? You're trying to fit into your father's footsteps, but what about your mother's? Hey, everybody knew how much your dad did — if they didn't notice his latest improvement he pointed it out, he made sure they admired his work. But your mom quietly went about making people comfortable. She did it so well no one ever thought about it. How can you expect to fill both sets of footprints at the same time? Impossible, my dear."

Until that moment, I hadn't credited my quiet, efficient mother sufficiently for the smooth way the Inn once functioned.

"You're going to have to get yourself more help, I mean management help."

"It's on its way, Chuck."

"Good."

"My nephew, Woodie's boy Steve, and his wife Kitty are finishing up their tour of Army duty in Europe. He's being discharged early next summer and they'll join me to help manage the Inn. That should take a lot of pressure off."

"Good." He patted my hand.

At dinner that night I sat with Chuck and his friends. At the same table were a pilot with his wife and two teen-aged children.

"How'd you find out about Millers?" I asked the pilot. I was always curious to know how new guests learned about our Inn.

"I was having a drink with another Pan Am pilot in Lima."

"Lima, Peru?"

"Told him I wanted to take my kids skiing. He said he remembered this place in Colorado from years before. Said it might not be here any more, but I jotted down the name, called up and here we are."

"Are you having a good time? Is it what you expected?"

"Yes, but there's something I'm wondering about. My friend said this was a nice place to stay — good food, good beds and nice atmosphere. Said there was only one thing wrong with it."

"What was that?" I asked.

"He said some old guy always stood up and made a speech and wouldn't let you eat your dinner."

Chuck Shrader laughed so hard he nearly choked on his food. "See?" he said as he jabbed his elbow into my ribs, "Not everybody wants to be entertained."

Chapter 28

One Last Big Splash

Poised halfway up the ski slope, a young man, shirtless, clad only in swimming trunks, crouched in the starting gate. At the sound of the starter's pistol, he began switchbacking his way down the mountain, gaining momentum as he passed through slalom gates and sprang across a couple of bumps of snow designed to get him airborne. Near the end of the course, when he approached the final jump, he tucked his body into a ball and leaped forward, extending arms and legs outward until his trajectory peaked and he fell, like a rock, into a pond filled with — icewater.

A roar of approval arose from people at the base of the slope. Spectators had gathered to watch people more foolish than themselves actually hurl their nearly naked bodies into the frigid pond. They continued to cheer as the jumper — teeth chattering, body racked with uncontrollable shivering — scrambled awkwardly atop his still-attached, submerged skis in an attempt to reach the far bank of the pond to escape its icy chill. There, ski patrolmen awaited him with the comfort of a dry army blanket.

Every year in April the ski area sponsored Spring Splash, a nutty rite of passage, to salute the just completed ski season.

Maintenance men got out a bulldozer, dug a hole in the ground and flooded it with water.

Theoretically, a good skier could gain enough momentum on the hill to catapult his body across the pond, like a golf ball sailing across a water hazard, when he jumped. But very few skiers, only the most expert, ever managed that feat. Everybody else fell short and was dunked into the muddy, iceberg-filled broth.

Those who volunteered to participate in this arcane custom were very young, very drunk and about ninety-eight percent male. It was hoped the last day of ski season would be so warm that scantily clad participants would bask in beach-like warmth. Often as not, the day fell victim to a spring storm when spitting snow tried to refrigerate the festivities.

Fortunately, that year the day was gloriously warm. Transient ski bums and most guests had already left the valley in search of beaches, golf courses, deserts — any place where the soles of their feet didn't skid on ice. So most of the crowd consisted of left-behind locals. Some of them had spent most of their winter working indoors, tending bar at night, so they started out the day with suspiciously white faces. By late afternoon, they had garnered rosy sunburns. It was a standard joke in the community. "You move here so you can ski; trying to make a living, you never get to."

Because the snow had been so good that year, the ski area experimented with extending its closing date until late April. The trial wasn't successful; with only a handful of bookings on the chart, I decided to close the Inn a week before Spring Splash. We handed what few reservations we had to the manager at Skiville Ranch.

So I was sitting on the balcony of the base lodge, sipping red wine and basking in the glorious spring sunshine. At first, I felt only an occasional drip from melting icicles pending from the roof. As the day warmed up the drips thickened to gushes.

Below me, where people crowded around the pond, the ground was a muddy mass of melting snow. Every single car in the lot was caked with mud.

My kids darted in and out of the crowd. Keith, fifteen, begged to be allowed to participate in the race but I strictly forbade it.

Their cousin Andy and J.B. were entrants. Some participants donned outrageous costumes to call attention to themselves. But Andy and J.B. decided to wow the audience by becoming the first-ever entrants to attempt the feat on cross-country skis. We urged Andy on as he attacked the slope, executing showy telemark turns at each gate. Unfortunately, his cross-country skis played their standard tricks on him. His toe-hinged bindings didn't allow him much spring when he tried to negotiate the jumps. As he approached the final pond, his skis just bent and he stopped in his tracks. There he stood on top of the jump, looking down at the water. Determined to see his experience through to the bitter end — and urged by the howling mob — Andy shrugged, fell to his knees and rolled into the pond.

"That crazy guy!" exclaimed my son Keith, perhaps in envy. "He didn't have to go in but he did anyhow."

My brother Woodie, his wife Barbara (Andy's parents) and I couldn't help shivering, too, as we watched a freezing Andy stomp his way out of the pond. Coming down the slope right behind him, J.B. copied Andy's every move — including rolling into the pond. He ended up just as wet and just as cold as his friend.

Woodie pulled on his pipe as we chatted. My brother and sister-in-law hadn't found many occasions to get away from the university and come up from Boulder that winter, but they were there for Spring Splash. It was a great help when they came because Woodie had inherited our father's gift of gab. He could stand in front of the fireplace, tell stories and entertain guests. Announcements at dinner were the extent of my public speaking aspirations.*

"Are you going back to teaching?" Woodie asked.

"Teaching?" I hadn't even considered the possibility, not for a long, long time. Return to a safe, dull world where fortunes fell and rose at the stroke of a professor's pen? Possibly my pen? What kind of a life was that?

I smiled. "No, I doubt it. Guess I've become accustomed to living in the real world. Probably stay here for now. At least until Kitty and Steve get the hang of things."

"What about your dissertation?"

"I'm starting back on it tomorrow. I'd never forgive myself if I don't finish what I started."

My conversation with Woodie was cut short when someone pointed up the slope, excitedly, toward the ski lift. The crowd was abuzz with expectation because we were waiting for "him." Who *him* might be was of no importance. But 1974 was the Year of the Streaker! We were quite certain that sooner or later a totally naked person would emerge from the trees to attempt jumping over the pond.

---

* Woodie told his story of Noah and the Ark particularly well.

It seems that about twenty days out, the ark sprang a leak. Noah, like most husbands, didn't know where his tools were. So he turned to one of his two dogs and said, "Put your muzzle into the hole to plug the leak and I'll be right back."

He hunted for the tool chest but couldn't find it. By then, the leak was much larger. His wife came by and wanted to know what he was doing. "Mrs. Noah. Put your hands in the hole. I've got to find that tool chest." Of course, she was glad to oblige.

After a while, the old man came back again, but still hadn't found his tools. So Mrs. Noah said, "I think I know where that tool chest is. Here, you sit on the hole and I'll be right back."

Mrs. Noah, before long, appeared with his tools in hand. Noah fixed the hole, plugged the leak and the ark sailed on.

And now you know why dogs have cold noses, women have cold hands and men tell stories with their backs to the fireplace!

And there he was! And there he was again! As it happened, three separate streakers chose various times to make their grand entrances. The streakers were chiefly notable in that they scurried out of the pond at almost the same velocity they plunked into it. If truth be known, when a frigid streaker scrambled out of the icy pond, there was virtually nothing left to see.

Red wine and sunshine were having their effect; I wasn't paying much attention to the "race." In reality, after the first few idiots had piled into the pond, the repetitious, needless suffering became boring. I suppose it might have been that way with the Roman crowds at the Coliseum. You've seen one evisceration you've seen 'em all.

I took advantage of the occasion to exchange greetings with neighbors I had barely seen all winter. "Where you off to?" was the most popular subject of conversation. Almost everybody got away during the mud season if they could. There would be no spring vacation for me; my kids had to go to school, I had to write.

❄ ❄ ❄ ❄ ❄

"It would be better not to set that table nearest the window," I told Barbara, my perky sister-in-law. "I don't trust that ice overhanging the window."

She nodded and began setting places on the table at the other end of the dining room.

Tonto and Bridget had left for Arizona earlier that week. I was sorry to see them leave but knew they were suffering acutely from cabin fever — a common spring disease in the Rockies. I couldn't blame them really. They had suffered during the long, tough winter, too. They loved Neil; and they had worked very hard in my behalf. Any turbulent feelings between us had long since vanished.

Just before they took off I said, "Tonto, board up the windows in the dining room. When that ice overhang breaks I don't want it to take those two plate glass windows with it."

Tonto managed to cover one of the windows with sheets of plywood but balked at completing the window between the fireplace and the waterfall. "I can't find enough plywood," he told me. "Besides, that overhang looks so treacherous I'm reluctant to get under it." I could sense his impatience, his anxiety to be out of the snow and to bask in the desert back home. But at my insistence he darted under the overhang, stood a few boards up in front of it.

That evening, after Spring Splash, the chili I made smelled absolutely delicious. It wasn't the sort of a meal I would ever serve to guests — Mexican food was, in those days, suspiciously foreign fare. But the aroma of pork simmering among peppers and onions pervaded the Inn. I heated big flour tortillas on the stove's huge griddle, slathered them with handfuls of longhorn cheese for *quesadillas*.

Woodie built a roaring fire in the fireplace. The dining room, as always, looked warm and inviting. I was glowing too from all the day's red wine. It had been a long day — and an even longer ski season. Still, I could take satisfaction that somehow I had managed to cope through every emergency. I had been given many opportunities to fall apart at the seams, but my threads didn't rip.

We passed bowls of beans, rice and spicy pork chili, washing everything down with beer, teasing Andy and J.B. about their icy dunk. My back was to the wall as I faced the fireplace. My Mexican cooking had improved since the scalding *mole* of autumn before; the green chili caused a delicious slow burn as it tickled down the back of my throat, reminding me of Arizona. It was so comfortable, sitting there among family and close friends. I was freed from chit-chatting with guests, "And what do you do in Minneapolis?" "Where else have you skied?" "Did you have a pleasant flight?" How tired I was of hearing everybody's war stories about their day on the slopes. How tired I was of thinking of everybody but myself.

Then it happened.

Boom, crack! I looked up to see a shower of glass, boards, ice, and snow implode across the dining room and rush right toward us.

Crash, thud, tinkle! The ice cornice had broken like an iceberg from a calving glacier, smashing through the double panes of the window — hurling sword-shaped shards of sharp glass that landed just short of the table where we were eating.

My composure shattered right along with the glass as I broke into tears. All the time it took for that snow to build up on the roof, I had held my tears to myself. As quickly as the ice broke through the window, my pent-up emotions burst.

In less than a minute, smoke started pouring out of the fireplace, back into the dining room. The iceberg had also snapped the roofjack off its chimney and rearranged the masonry beneath it, so severely that it stopped up the flue. Had I not already been weeping, I would have been choking.

"There's always more!" declared J.B. as he scurried off to make himself useful.

The window was destroyed in just a second; yet I was to see that avalanche of snow, ice, boards and glass over and over in the replays that immediately started running in a continuous loop through my brain.

I wish I could record that I calmly organized the efforts of Woodie, J.B. and my nephews as they flew into action — shoveling snow back out of the window, snuffing out the fire in the fireplace, locating sufficient lumber to board up the window — this time from the inside — and securing the Inn against the freezing night air.

But I didn't help at all. Jolted, my body succumbed to a great cramp of grief that racked through my innards over and over again, refusing to relax itself and let me be.

My children, unaccustomed to seeing their mother in a state of emotional shipwreck, tried to comfort me. "It'll be OK, Mom," assured Keith. "They'll get it fixed."

But I couldn't stop weeping. Fleeing from the smoke I sobbed in the kitchen, I howled in the lounge, I wailed in the office and I lamented in the bathroom. As other people scooped shovels of snow, picked up pieces of glass and trundled out vacuum cleaners, I bawled my head off, heaping a wastebasket full of soppy Kleenex.

Each time I blinked, the sight of ice and glass bursting toward me played in my brain; my year's muddles blew back in my face. Jutting through the snow were frozen pipes and broken beds; Heather's ruined VW, with a glimpse of Neil's red hair, came tumbling through that window; the pores on Vic LoBianco's nose thrust up at me. Out came the hairbrush I whopped across Sandy's fanny. Tonto's toes wiggled from the end of his plaster cast. Chub's "almost" baby was in there someplace.

But it wasn't all bad. I smiled when J.B. jumped out of my birthday cake and leapt right at me one more time — this time through shave cream.

Finally, when he got a moment, my brother Woodie — breathless from the effort of repairing the damage — put his comforting big arm around my shoulder and said, "What's the matter, Sis? Have a hard season?"

His honest question made me stop. I swallowed and tried to clear all that horrible gunk sliding down my throat.

"You might say that."

Postscript

After everybody else left, to enjoy the springtime mud season elsewhere, I worked on my dissertation. I was blissfully alone in the big old building which, absent its lodgers, had turned spooky. Each time I heard a crash I lifted my fingers from my typewriter to listen. Sometimes the crash was followed by the sound of tinkling glass as smaller windows fell victims to the ice build-up. I was relieved when, after a couple of weeks, the last of the ice melted off the roof.

One morning I ran into one of the sheriff's deputies down at the post office. Smartly uniformed, from beneath his trim black moustache he said, in a tone that indicated I had been remiss, "We sure missed your father's nice party this year."

Because of everything that happened, I hadn't even *thought* about the annual police banquet. But I shot back, "Guess I'm just not the man my daddy was." He grinned and drove off in his patrol car.

In July, I descended into the inferno of Phoenix to successfully defend my dissertation at Arizona State University. That was to be my last academic endeavor.

Living in the "real world" was far more interesting so I threw myself at its mercy, willing to be battered about by whatever life had in store. The next year my father finished his book. He called it *Leave the Woodpile Higher Than You Found It*. He wrote it, published it and hit the road in his camper to sell two thousand copies.

I was to stay at the Inn for four more years and survive many more "massacrees" and crises. After my nephew Steven Miller and his wife Kitty joined me, life was never so difficult again. Yet living in a public business while raising boisterous teen-agers was always a strain. As my parents aged, it became apparent that the Inn's business complexities would increase. In 1977 my father, mother, brothers and myself — in a decision that was by no means unanimous — decided to sell the Inn. A year later my father died. Mother outlived him by two years.

Nick Teverbaugh and Stewart Heaton, who first became enchanted by the Inn when they were guests, were the buyers. Teverbaugh was the resident manager; Heaton continued his career as an engineer with the Fluor Corporation, based in Irvine, California. Their partnership brought many innovations and improvements to the aging buildings. I used to tease Nick that the ghost of my father had descended into his body because Nick's alterations were so thoroughly in the rustic style my father would have approved.

Unfortunately, in the early morning hours of October 28, 1988, the old Inn burned — between seasons when the building was completely empty. Nick was out of town; the caretaker in charge was sleeping in one of the cabins and knew nothing about the fire until after the firemen arrived. Before anyone noticed, most of the building was destroyed. What was left had to be torn down. The spark was thought to have originated in an ancient fuse box whose origins went back to the early days of the Inn's construction. In 1988 Colorado was in the abyss of economic doldrums. It made little sense to rebuild.

When I look at the lush green lawn where the Inn once stood, it is almost impossible to realize so much could have happened on such a small patch of ground. But the absence of a building cannot erase tender memories branded into the hearts of people who worked and vacationed there.

Millers Idlewild Inn is gone. The skiing industry has become big business; most people stay in condominiums. Very few small lodges survive.

Soon after we sold the Inn I purchased the *Winter Park Manifest*, a weekly newspaper. I published, edited and wrote a good share of it for five years, then sold it to devote my time to writing.

As for the people who suffered through that first memorable year with me? Some of them — Myrtle Ashton, Bridget Collins, Hal Richardson and Russ Stratton — are dead. Most of the ski bums went on to prosper in careers; some became parents and now take their own families skiing. Not all have been as successful as Tonto, who owns his own business and is president of a service organization. He and Bridget never tied the knot. In 1980 Tonto married Flossie, one of the maidens who fell in love with him that summer.

Whoodathunkit?